D1158023

Greenhill Books

BLOOD
ON THE
PAINTED
MOUNTAIN

*'... we stood there in friendly converse,
representatives of the two nations,
civilised and barbarous,
who had fought so fiercely
and poured each other's blood
like water upon the rugged sides
of this very mountain ....'*

Bertram Mitford
Hlobane Mountain, Zululand, 1882

BLOOD

ON THE

PAINTED MOUNTAIN

Zulu Victory and Defeat
Hlobane and Kambula, 1879

RON LOCK

Greenhill Books, London
Stackpole Books, Pennsylvania

Blood on the Painted Mountain
first published 1995 by Greenhill Books,
Lionel Leventhal Limited, Park House, 1 Russell Gardens,
London NW11 9NN
and
Stackpole Books, 5067 Ritter Road, Mechanicsburg, PA 17055, USA

© Ron Lock, 1995

The moral right of the author has been asserted

All rights reserved. No part of this publication may be reproduced,
stored in a retrieval system or transmitted in any form or by any
means, electrical, mechanical or otherwise without first seeking the
written permission of the Publisher.

British Library Cataloguing in Publication Data
Lock, Ron
Blood on the Painted Mountain: Zulu
Victory and Defeat, Hlobane and Kambula,
1879
I. Title
968.4045

ISBN 1–85367–201–7

Library of Congress Cataloging-in-Publication Data available

Typeset by DP Photosetting, Aylesbury, Bucks
Printed and bound in Great Britain by
Biddles Ltd, Guildford and King's Lynn

CONTENTS

LIST OF ILLUSTRATIONS

LIST OF MAPS

ACKNOWLEDGEMENTS

Many individuals and organisations have generously assisted me in the preparation of this book and, in no particular order, I offer them my thanks: to Major Paul Naish, whose knowledge of the historical highways and byways of KwaZulu Natal is unequalled, I owe special thanks for his encouragement, collaboration and for prompting me to write this work: also for fond memories of our hikes over Hlobane Mountain; Fred Duke of Vryheid, the local 'fundi' of Hlobane, accompanied Paul and myself up the mountain on several occasions and shared his knowledge; S.B. Bourquin who with his unique courtesy and generosity made available his library of illustrations and photographs; Karl Steffen who translated German documents whilst I drank his coffee; John Young, whose hospitality I enjoyed during a rainy day in England and who unstintingly made available all his photographs and illustrations; the staff of the Killie Campbell Library, in particular Stacie Gibson, Bobbie Eldridge and Joan Simpson, who were always cheerful and gave me the feeling that nothing was too much trouble for them; Gillian Berning and George Foster of the Local History Museum, Durban, accommodated my search for photographs and provided copies in record time.

Many institutions and individuals in the United Kingdom responded to my enquiries: the Cameronians (descendants of the 90th Foot) Regimental Museum; The Royal Artillery Trust; The National Army Museum; The Public Record Office; The Welch Regimental Museum of the Royal Regiment of Wales; The Somerset Military Museum, and in particular Brigadier Alistair Fyfe; Jeremy Bagwell Purefoy of the Central Chancery of the Orders of Knighthood; The Victorian Military Society and its informative publications; The Anglo-Zulu War Research Society and in particular Andy Cherry, the editor of its journal; W.A. Williams of Wrexham; Rai England, who made his collection of photographs and illustrations available to me; Gordon Everson whose early constructive criticism put me on the right track; my researchers in the UK, Lee Stephenson and John Nicholson, whose enthusiasm and modest charges had me continually knocking at their doors; Collis Kenworthy for his assistance with details of the 13th LI; The Sherwood Foresters Museum; John Gilbert for his excellent editing of the manuscript.

In Southern Africa assistance was equally generous from the staff of the Natal Archives, Pietermaritzburg; Marie Peddle who researched my requests so efficiently at the Cape Archives; Helena Margeot of the Cartographic Unit, University of Natal; The Africana Museum in Johannesburg; Keith Dyer of *Magnum Magazine* for his expert advice on all types of firearms; Godfrey Symons, who generously loaned me a copy of his ancestors' diary; Gordon Button, whose great uncle was George Mossop of the FLH; The South African National Museum of Military History; The Utrecht Museum, Natal; the staff of the National Archives of Zimbabwe; David Rattray of Fugitive's Drift Lodge, for a memorable day on Hlobane with eagles for company and an Irish kettle for comfort; The City Librarian of Port Elizabeth; The Librarian of Rhodes University; Pam MacFadden of the Talana Museum, Dundee, Natal, for her generous help; Bridgette Du Plooy of Mooi River Museum; Dougie McMaster, Proprietor and Curator of the Blockhouse Museum, Ladysmith, for his ever ready hospitality and permission to photograph many of his unique artefacts; The Pinetown Library; The Transvaal Archives Department and the Department of National Education in Pretoria.

Special thanks are due to Daphne Snyders of Joydene Secretarial Services for her cheerful patience and efficiency in typing the manuscript and providing a 'pony express' service to my pick-up point on her way home; Terry Sole, for his advice on casualties; my neighbour, Roy Bevin, who read the draft and offered suggestions; and Andy May for permission to use his excellent drawing of King Cetshwayo. Special thanks are also due to the late Fred Herbert and my other friends who form the membership of the Battlefields of Natal Society – I have fond memories of our many excursions into Zululand. The last thank you has been specially reserved for Brenda, my wife, for her patience in coping with rooms strewn with books, papers and 'Battlefield Buffs'.

FOREWORD

My interest in the Zulu War began when I was a boy in England during the 1930s. My father was secretary of the local Disabled Ex-Servicemen's Association, and a constant stream of ex-soldiers visited our home. They were mostly men who had been wounded in the First World War and, being in their thirties, seemed very old to me. One was clearly even older than the rest: and instead of the usual drab raincoat and flat hat, Mr James, for that was his name, wore a hat with a flaring brim and a bow-tie which was enough to mark him as someone special.

Ex-soldiers in those days often wore their medals; Mr James always wore his, pinned to his cape, and his medals were as distinctive as his bow-tie. He not only had more medals than his companions but they were also very different. I could tell from the exciting colours of the ribbons that he had been to the most dangerous places and had been very brave.

The men liked to yarn about France and a place called Gallipoli. Although they treated Mr James with great respect (I think he had been a sergeant major) they didn't chat much with him as he hadn't been to France and the other place. So he yarned to me; and it was from Mr James that I first heard of the Zulus. The story I remember best was how he had stood on guard and alone in the African night, the other soldiers sleeping in their tents, with only a flickering campfire for company, and how he had heard the Zulus creeping towards the camp. He challenged, and out of the darkness came a rush of warriors. He grappled with one but as the man had covered his entire body with grease he slipped from Mr James's grasp and stuck his assegai into my friend's leg. I still have a vision of Mr James on guard in the dark, his white hair neatly parted down the middle, wearing his bow-tie, cape and medals.

I was also shown and eventually acquired a set of picture cards entitled *Battles for the Flag*. My favourite was a reproduction of C.E. Fripps's painting *The Last Stand of the 24th at Isandlwana*. I convinced myself that I could see Mr James in the background disguised in a red jacket.

There were other Zulu relics, too, scattered around the suburbs of England in the 1930s. It was not uncommon to see a cowhide shield and crossed assegais adorning the walls of many a terraced house. These trophies, however, evidently did not appeal to the womenfolk and every junk shop seemed to have a pile of dusty assegais and knobkerries among its military memorabilia.

At school Mr Foote, our form master, would read extracts from *Prester John*. In a class renowned for its noise and gross behaviour not a sound was heard nor a fidget made, as Mr Foote transported us to Africa. Later I read *King Solomon's Mines* and was similarly enthralled.

There were to be other remote associations with southern Africa: while completing my national service at Aldershot I was stationed close to Buller Barracks and the Evelyn Wood Gymnasium, both named in honour of commanders who had gained renown in Zululand. I also made the acquaintance of Officer Cadet Smith-Dorrien from Sandhurst, whose grandfather had miraculously survived Isandlwana.

By 1954 I was living in East Africa where I read E.A. Ritter's book *Shaka Zulu*. I studied a map of Africa and saw the Zulus were now quite close; 1800 miles south – not such a distance in Africa.

By the mid 1960s I had reached Natal. But I arrived too late. I could see no Zulu equivalent of the pigtailed, spear-carrying Samburu and Masai of Kenya and Tanganyika; the age of T-shirts and transistor radios had preceded me.

One evening in 1967 I was invited aboard a Norwegian cruise liner in Durban harbour. The elderly, wealthy passengers were about to be entertained by some Zulu dancers from a local tea garden. Dinner over, and the passengers seated around the tiny dance floor in the lounge, the dancers arrived. The surgical cleanliness and air-freshened atmosphere of the ship was suddenly assailed by the smell of old Africa: a pungent smell of woodsmoke, cooking, cattle odours and sweat. The dancers were dressed in a travesty of Zulu regalia: tattered shorts half-covered by bits of cowhide. They carried toy shields and in place of assegais they carried sticks. Slowly they began to dance and then the deep bass chorus of unmistakable Zulu voices boomed forth. The pace of the dancing increased and suddenly, as loud as a thunder clap, they each raised a foot, shoulder high, and slammed it down, followed by a crash of silence. Then, with a chest-deep roar, they beat their shields and scuttled forward, crab-like, in a mock charge. The nearest passengers recoiled in fear but with another thunder clap of sticks on shields, the show was over. The dancers – all smiles and laughter – acknowledged the applause and sang their way out of the lounge. If twenty Zulu dancers could inspire such feelings of alarm, how dreadful must have been the apprehensions of the British soldiers at Isandlwana as they heard the roar of 25,000 charging Zulu warriors?

The fascination of the battlefields, which were now on my doorstep, the history of the Zulu people and the tales Mr James told so long ago, led me often to Zululand and finally to the writing of this book.

PREFACE

In Northern Natal, forty miles to the south of the Swaziland border, there is a flat topped mountain called Hlobane, which in the Zulu language means The Painted Mountain. During the Anglo-Zulu War of 1879, it was the scene of ferocious fighting that should be remembered no less for the barbarities of the battle itself than for the spectacular scenery in which it was fought. For the British, it should be remembered especially as the second worst disaster of the Zulu War, the numbers of British dead being exceeded only by those of the slaughter at Isandlwana. It was also the only engagement of the war that the British fought as an entirely mounted force, although supported by Swazi foot auxiliaries.

The mounted men were mainly locally recruited volunteers; out of a total of over 600 horsemen only 125 were imperial soldiers.

The battle of Hlobane, as it was subsequently called, is also notable for the four Victoria Crosses that were awarded – and the disturbing fact that, although it was the colonial volunteers who were subject to the most bitter fighting, all the Victoria Crosses were distributed among a small and favoured circle of imperial soldiers.

Contemplating the memorials and remembrance with which lesser battles are recalled, one is left with the impression that the British preferred Hlobane to be a battle best forgotten; the colonial dead – and there were many – lay in graves unmarked and unrecorded. Unlike other battlefields, there is no scattering of little crosses proclaiming 'Here Lies a Brave British Soldier'; and those organisations whose business it is to tend the graves of British soldiers, wherever they may be throughout the world, have not ventured to this lonely spot. There are two exceptions, memorials erected over a hundred years ago by grieving families.

To forget Hlobane was an easy matter as, within a day, the British commander who had been so soundly routed on the mountain had inflicted a crushing defeat upon the Zulu army, from which it never recovered. Therefore, with the news of defeat and victory being delivered in one breath, there was no desire to dwell upon the dismal details of ill fortune. In any event, defeat at the hands of the Zulus was becoming commonplace, whereas a British victory was news. Also, this would be one butchers' bill that would not produce a cry of anguish from county towns and villages of some English regiment. The dead were, with few exceptions, all colonials or black men – the former mainly rovers and adventurers far from home and the concern of kinsfolk, the latter nameless.

Yet there is evidence that had the British not been defeated at Hlobane, it is doubtful whether the following day, the Zulu army would have lost the battle of Kambula: rampant with confidence and spurred on by the taunts of the horsemen whom they had so resoundingly beaten only hours earlier, the warriors of the leading Zulu regiments disregarded orders and were lured to destruction.

The events that led up to the battles of Hlobane and Kambula were set in motion by the British invasion of Zululand. On a front several hundred miles wide, stretching from the Indian Ocean in the east to the Transvaal and Swazi borders in the west, the British army, commanded by Lieutenant General Lord Chelmsford, entered enemy territory in three separate, self-contained, columns. This story concerns that of the Northern Column led by Colonel Evelyn Wood VC, CB, who enjoyed a completely unfettered command. The early and frequent successes of his column would more than justify the favour and independence that Chelmsford would bestow upon him.

The area of operations of Wood's small army was a large tract of Africa – wild and magnificent: rolling plains strewn with strangely shaped hills and ranges of flat-topped mountains out of which flowed the major rivers of this part of south-eastern Africa. The boundaries of this remote land were the furthermost frontiers of both Zulu and British authority alike. It was known as the Disputed Territories, for both the Boer and Zulu nations claimed ownership. Because of the absence of law, raids and counter raids were frequent; and dominating this vast area was the Zulu stronghold of Hlobane, 'The Painted Mountain',[1] which will also dominate this story of a much disregarded battle of the Anglo-Zulu War.

---

1. The Zulu meaning of 'Hlobane' is variously explained as a 'decorated mountain' – decorated by the new growth of spring grass, or a painted mountain from the effect of sunlight gleaming on rain-washed rocks.

ZULU PRONUNCIATION

Recently there have been considerable changes and revisions in the spelling of Zulu names, especially so in historical works. For instance, the familiar spelling of Tugela, the name of Natal's major river, becomes Thukela or uThukela. Nevertheless, maps, provincial road signs, the press and writings in general still use the familiar Tugela when referring to the river. In this work I have chosen to use the more familiar form of names with revised spellings in brackets.

PRONUNCIATION OF ZULU WORDS	PHONETIC PRONUNCIATION
abaQulusi	Abu-coo-lucy
Assegai	Ass-a-guy
Cetshwayo	Ketsh-why-o
Dingane	Ding-gaan
Hamu	Ha-moo
Hlobane	Shlo-baan
Intombi	In-tom-be
Intyentika	In-ten-tika
Isipezi	Izi-pear-zi
Langalibalele	Langa-li-ba-lele
Makulusini	Ma-kul-sene
Mbelini	Im-be-leni
Mbulazi	Im-boo-larzi
Mehlokazulu	Mesh-law-ka-zulu
Mnyamana	Im-nya-ma-na
Mpande	Im-pan-de
Mtonga	Im-tonga
Ndondakusuka	In-doda-coo-sooka
Nkobamakosi	In-koba-ma-kosi
Ntendeka	In-ten-decka
Nyezane	In-ye-zaan
Seketwayo	Cek-et-why-o
Sekhukhune	Se-gu-kooni
Sihayo	C-hi-o
Somtseu	Somt-sue
Tshingwayo	Ching-way-ho
Tugela	Too-gela
Zunguin	Zung-gwen

1
PREPARE FOR WAR

'The Lieutenant-General ... will take such measures as the forces at his command will permit for compelling the submission of the Zulu King.'

Sir Bartle Frere
4 January 1879

It was a confident British army that, in January of 1879, awaited the order to cross the border of Natal and invade Zululand. And none was more confident than its commander, Lieutenant General Lord Chelmsford who, in June of the previous year, had successfully concluded the Ninth Frontier War in the Eastern Cape. It had been a wretched conflict of hide and seek in a mountainous land of ravines and bush, where the warriors of the Ngqika and Gcaleka nations fought the British in a protracted guerrilla operation; a tedious campaign that held no prospect of fame and glory for a victorious general – only the certainty of a ruined career in the likely event of a prolonged or unsuccessful war. But Chelmsford, with the aid of native and colonial forces, had succeeded, and as his battalions of now Africa hardened infantrymen marched north to Natal, he looked forward to battles of a more conventional nature. His enemy would still be warriors of Bantu stock but, as was generally known, the regiments of the Zulu nation were as well drilled and disciplined as if they had been passed out of Aldershot and could, therefore, be expected to fight in just such a conventional manner.

The local military experts, the old campaigners, and especially the Boer frontiersmen who had fought the Zulu in many a bloody encounter, warned Chelmsford that the qualities, and above all the abilities, of the Zulu army were of a standard unknown elsewhere in Black Africa and they must not be underestimated. Whilst Chelmsford had listened attentively to good advice, his real concern was whether the Zulu army would stand and fight. Chelmsford, at the age of fifty-five, was in his prime, with all the fitness and resilience that a fighting general would require for the arduous campaign ahead. He was a tall, gaunt man, heavily bearded, whose stringy frame belied the fact that he had been an accomplished boxer in his younger days. Although his family had been German immigrants only a century earlier, it had prospered in England; Chelmsford's father had obtained the highest judicial office in the land and had been raised to the peerage.

At the age of sixteen Chelmsford had commenced his military career in the Rifle Brigade and was soon soldiering in cold, far-off, Nova Scotia. Within a year he was back in England to take up a commission, by purchase, in his first choice of regiments, the Grenadier Guards. After ten years' home service he went with the Guards to the war in the Crimea. In that arduous conflict, he served mainly on the staff until hostilities ended eighteen months later. The next ten years were spent in India; he arrived in time to fight in the final phases of the Sepoy Mutiny and thereafter commanded the 95th (Derbyshire) Regiment. At the age of thirty-nine, and still in India, but now on the staff, he married the daughter of an Indian army general. In 1868, he obtained a position on the staff of the Abyssinian Expeditionary Force. For his 'great ability and untiring energy' during that most successful of all armed expeditions, he was awarded Companionship of the Bath.

On returning to England he was further rewarded by his appointment as ADC to Queen Victoria. Additional service in India and at home followed, and by 1878 he had reached the rank of major general and was commanding troops in southern England. He was well connected and well regarded by his superiors who saw him as an efficient officer who had, perhaps, seen a little too much staff work and not enough hard soldiering. He retained the warm regard of Queen Victoria but lacked charisma – in fact one newspaper correspondent was to write unkindly that Chelmsford was 'more distinguished for his social virtues than his social attractions'. Nevertheless, he impressed most of his acquaintances as a thoroughly decent man, resolute and of even temper, supportive of those under his command and one who, having sought advice from subordinates, would give credit where it was due. The fact that under duress, he would not be beyond blaming dead comrades for his own omissions and calamitous misjudgment, was a frailty only to be revealed in the future. In 1878, Chelmsford's superiors at the Horse Guards saw in him the right man to command all British forces in South Africa.

As he made his way from the Cape to Natal, in anticipation of war with the Zulu nation, his nagging concern was that instead of engaging in swift decisive battles – in which it would be ludicrous to contemplate any victor other than his British infantry – he would, once again, be faced with a guerrilla operation in which the outcome would be less certain.

The prospect of war with the Zulus was nothing new. Now that the tribes of the Eastern Cape frontier had been subdued, Sir Bartle Frere, the British High Commissioner at the Cape, aspired to a confederation of all the states and colonies in Southern Africa. Frere was sixty-three years of age and had behind him a most distinguished career in the service of the Empire. He was, in truth, too senior for the post he now held, but were he to achieve his ambition, Lord Carnarvon, the Colonial Secretary, had promised to appoint him Governor General of the confederated territories. But before confederation could become a reality, the future of the colony of Natal had to be secure – and there could be no security while, across the Buffalo (Nyati) River, which formed the northern boundary, there existed a savage kingdom with an army of 40,000 highly trained warriors. It was plain that the fledgling colony, with its meagre 20,000 white inhabitants, only continued to exist at the sufferance of the Zulu king Cetshwayo. That they lived scattered among a black population of some 300,000 was an added cause for grave anxiety. Many black residents of Natal, for one reason or another, had fled the wrath of Cetshwayo and his forefathers and had sought protection in the colony. Whereas these refugees may have hated Cetshwayo they certainly did not love their white protectors. Add to this dilemma the possibility of a change of heart in the Zulu king, or the emergence of a new monarch of less neighbourly disposition, and the Zulu army could be across the Natal border bent on a rampage of death and destruction.

Indeed, there was just reason for Cetshwayo to attack Natal; less than forty years earlier much of the colony had been Zulu territory. And there was another consideration: for many years the Boers of the South African Republic had been in contention with the Zulu kingdom. The quarrel concerned the ownership of a large tract of rich cattle country, which had become known as the Disputed Territories, situated on Natal's north-western border. For almost two years the British had been acting as mediator between Boer and Zulu and, in the role of honest broker, still presided over a commission committed to proclaiming a just decision. All very well until Britain, in April 1877, had annexed the Transvaal – an area the size of France and previously known as the South African Republic. Thus the British effectively replaced the Boers as the nation in dispute with the Zulu kingdom. Consequently, if the young warriors of Cetshwayo's army were to follow established traditions and satisfy a virtually instinctive desire to raid, and 'redden their assegais' in enemy blood, there was now little choice but to attack British possessions – even if it were only to set about the black inhabitants. As far back as 1875 Sir Garnet Wolseley, then in Natal to stall its plan for self government, contemplated a machiavellian scheme of setting the Transvaal Boers and the Zulu at each other's throats, and acquiring for England the Disputed Territories as a dumping ground for the surplus black population of Natal. Wolseley confided to his journal on 4 May 1875: 'He (Cetshwayo) hates the Dutch (Boers) who have always cheated and dealt unfairly with him; a war between these two parties would be very useful to us....' He went on to muse that such an event could, at one stroke, break Cetshwayo's power forever and deprive the Boers of a possible outlet to the sea. 'I have only to give the King (Cetshwayo) the slightest hint and he would pitch into the Transvaal there and then. I wish I could do so without compromising the Government at home, ... it is a glorious opportunity for England, for we ought to try and force the Boers into our arms.'

The possibility, therefore, of a Zulu onslaught was not just alarmist sensa-
tionalism but, as Sir Bartle Frere chose to believe, a very plausible likelihood. How
fortuitous, then, that Frere had at his disposal Lord Chelmsford's army and his
willing co-operation. Zulu power needed to be crushed and its army disbanded. If
Cetshwayo did not accede to the ultimatum that would shortly be presented to
him, there would be no choice but to invade: inevitably a British victory would
follow, with the war quickly concluded, Cetshwayo deposed, and Zululand under
British rule. All this before the news of the conflict could reach the government in
London.

By mid-November 1878, the three diligent men who formed the Disputed
Territories Commission – the Honourable Michael Gallwey, Attorney General of
Natal, the Honourable John Wesley Shepstone, Acting Secretary for Native
Affairs, and Colonel Anthony Durnford, commanding Royal Engineers – had
reached a decision as to the boundary line between the Zulu kingdom and the
Transvaal. Their pronouncement must have caused Sir Bartle at least a snort of
irritation. The commissioners, all men of the highest standing in the colony, had
found in favour of the Zulu and had awarded Cetshwayo 1800 square miles of the
disputed land. It was not the sort of news that Sir Bartle wished to hear and the
findings were temporarily suppressed. Cetshwayo, it was decided, would hear the
good news only when laced with more bitter tidings.

On 11 December 1878, under a large wild fig tree on the banks of the Tugela
(uThukela) River, Cetshwayo's deputies met with the representatives of the Natal
Government who informed the Zulu of their land award. The pronouncement was
received with some satisfaction and, no doubt, an upsurge in the belief of British
justice. But more news was to follow after a short adjournment. When the meeting
reassembled, a bombshell of demands was dropped in the form of an ultimatum,
containing nine conditions that had to be fulfilled by 10 January 1879. The
interval of one month's grace, given to the Zulu in which to confer among
themselves and meet the demands of the ultimatum, was just about the period
needed by Lord Chelmsford for reinforcements to arrive from England, and to
poise his army ready for invasion along the Zulu border. The ultimatum, if not
complied with, amounted to a declaration of war. The first three of the nine
conditions concerned Zulu 'outrages' against the colony of Natal and were, in fact,
the only genuine grievances that the British could claim. Even so, viewing the
'outrages' against the background of the times and the frontier conditions in which
they occurred, it is obvious that Sir Bartle Frere had really dredged deeply for
excuses sufficiently serious to justify his war.

The first condition to require redress concerned two runaway wives of a senior
Zulu chief named Sihayo. Accused of adultery, a capital offence in Zululand, the
two women had fled across the Buffalo seeking refuge in Natal. An armed party
led by two of Sihayo's sons crossed the river, caught the first wife, proceeded about
fifteen miles downstream on the Natal bank, apprehended the other and returned

home into Zululand where it was probable that both women were put to death. A provocative act but hardly serious enough to induce war.

The second 'outrage' detailed in the ultimatum concerned a white surveyor named Smith who was in charge of a work party building a ford across the Tugela River at Middle Drift. Having completed the approach on the Natal side, Smith, without permission from Zululand, crossed to the opposite bank where he was apprehended and manhandled by a group of young warriors. He was, however, unharmed. As retribution the British required that the sons of Sihayo, who had crossed the border, be handed over for trial plus a fine of 500 head of cattle. A further fine of 100 head of cattle was to be paid for molesting the surveyor.

The third condition was that a man named Mbelini (Umbelini) and his associates, who were to be named later, be surrendered for trial. Mbelini was a notorious renegade Swazi who pillaged along the northern borders of the Disputed Territories and received the lukewarm protection of Cetshwayo.

The remaining five conditions were demands that amounted to direct interference in the internal affairs of a foreign state:

Fourth condition.   The Zulu army should be disbanded and only brought together with the permission of the Great Council of the Nation assembled, and with the consent also of the British Government.

Fifth condition.   Every Zulu on arriving at man's estate should be free to marry, the king's permission being no longer required.

Sixth condition.   The administration generally should be reformed and accused persons should have a personal trial.

Seventh condition.   A British resident should be received at the Zulu capital.

Eighth condition.   The missionaries and native converts should be allowed to return to the mission stations.

Ninth condition.   If a missionary or other European should be involved in a dispute, the matter should be heard by the king in the presence of the resident, and that any sentence of expulsion from Zululand should receive the approval of the resident before being carried into effect.

Most of the nine stipulations could have been complied with by Cetshwayo, albeit with loss of face in order to avoid war, but he could no more agree to the fourth condition, the disbanding of his army, than he could agree to burn the national harvest.

It was, therefore, a disillusioned and subdued group of deputies which returned across the Tugela River to take the news to their king. Lord Chelmsford, on the other hand, was pleased with events and even more delighted by a document he received from Sir Bartle on 4 January 1879. The document authorised him to 'take such measures as the force at his command might permit for compelling the submission of the Zulu king, unless an intonation of an unqualified and complete acceptance of the terms previously proposed should be received before the close of the 11 January'. That was plain enough. Chelmsford had permission to invade eight days hence: nor had he wasted the intervening time of truce. Busy with his preparations for weeks past, already in October he had telegraphed for a contingent of mercenaries of German descent to come up from the Cape; with this force he intended to garrison Luneburg, a small German settlement on the far boundary of the Disputed Territories. Moreover, as early as mid-September five companies of the 90th Light Infantry, accompanied by four guns of the Royal Artillery, had marched a distance of over 500 miles from King William's Town in the Eastern Cape to Utrecht, a little frontier town on the south-western border of the disputed land. It was a march that had been viewed as a glum prospect by the British infantry, with one soldier writing to his parents back in England: 'I hope we won't go [to Natal], mind you father, I am no coward, it is not the fighting that I care about but it is such a distance to march.' It was indeed.

Originally Chelmsford had intended to invade in five separate columns, but reduced the number to three. What would have been No. 3 Column, commanded by Colonel Anthony Durnford RE, consisting of three battalions of the Natal Native Contingent (native infantry) who were armed mainly with spears and shields – only one man in ten having a firearm – and a squadron of native cavalry, was retained in Natal at Kranskop, to guard against a possible counter invasion. No. 5 Column, commanded by Colonel Hugh Rowlands, VC, CB, on the Transvaal Border, was likewise set aside from the invasion force.[1] Some of the men who now made up his command, including Rowlands himself, had seen a great deal of rough marching with negative results since leaving the Cape: Rowlands had made a botch of his mission to quell Sekhukhune (Sekukuni), the troublesome chief of the Pedi tribe, and as a result was much out of favour with Chelmsford. Because Rowlands's blunder would have a profound effect on the events in Southern Africa for many years to come, and would immediately affect the fortunes of Wood and No. 5 Column, it is well to establish how the debacle occurred.

Sekhukhune and his people were of Basuto stock and resolutely independent. Over the years many aggressors had tried to dislodge them from their stronghold in the Lulu Mountains of North-eastern Transvaal, but none, including such redoubtable foes as the Matabele and the Boers, had so far succeeded. As recently as 1876, a large force put in the field by the Boer Republic, and supported by Swazi mercenaries, had invaded the Pedi fortress. Time and again the attackers were led on into a labyrinth of stone walls and thorn tree barricades, to be caught in an ambush of Pedi crossfire. The Boers, it was said, hung back, leaving their Swazi allies to do the fighting. Then, growing disgruntled with the task and disputing with their leaders, the Boers began to drift away, back to their farms and families, taking with them many of the cattle that the more daring Swazis had captured from the Pedi. The Swazis, too, departed in disgust, threatening war against their former Boer allies and leaving Sekhukhune, once more unfettered, to raid the ever encroaching border area that the white farmers and the miners were pushing into his territory.

The British, ever alert for reasons, just or otherwise, for the opportunity to pursue their grand design of confederation, used the Boer defeat and the fact that the government of the South African Republic was completely bankrupt – it being unable even to pay the wages of its postmaster – to declare the Republic no longer capable of wielding authority.

Purporting to be aghast and concerned at the possibility of a general uprising, Britain adopted the pose of a good neighbour with plenty of clout, and decided to step in and take over. Consequently, Sir Theophilus Shepstone KCMG, Secretary of Native Affairs in Natal and Zululand for almost forty years, proceeded to Pretoria in December 1876 with an escort of only twenty-four Natal Mounted Police, and in April of the following year raised the Union Jack. In fairness to Britain, one of the conditions of annexation that had been stipulated by Lord Carnarvon, the Colonial Secretary, was that the population of the Transvaal must consent to British rule. Shepstone, speaking only to those from whom he wished to hear, mainly disgruntled civil servants – who now saw a chance of being paid – and English settlers, believed he had a favourable consensus. He did not, however, consult with the real hard trekboers of the hinterland whose scattered numbers exceeded those of their more accessible countrymen and whose spirit of independence portended a future revolt for freedom. Prior to annexation Britain had remonstrated with the Boers for attacking Sekhukhune's tribe, condemning their unjustified aggression against an independent ruler. Now that annexation was a fait accompli, Shepstone chose to claim the territory of the Pedi as part of Britain's own domain. (Even the Intelligence Branch of the War Office seemed startled at the audacity of this turnabout, the author of its official narrative writing '... and Sekhukhune country appears to have been included without question in the territory which was thus added to the British possessions'.)

It was now necessary for Shepstone to show the Boers how to govern. As a priority he must subdue Sekhukhune and the followers of his warlike sister Legolwana (Legolani), who, legend had it, possessed four breasts. But Shepstone had little material to work with. Only a dribble of men came up from Natal and the majority of these, including all three companies of the 1/13th LI, were retained in Pretoria to awe the Boers and guard against white unrest. The bulk of campaigning had to fall on volunteer units variously made up from a mixed bag of locals, serving in such bodies as the Lydenburg Volunteer Corps and Raaff's Transvaal Rangers. There were also imported volunteers, such as the Diamond Fields Horse, from as far away as the Cape. Also imported, but from Natal, was Shepstone's own brainchild, a force of 100 Zulu Police commanded by a young Natalian, Llewellyn Lloyd, whose father was a retired British general.

The rank and file were armed with breech-loading rifles and bayonets, wore uniforms of sorts and, thanks to their ferocity and ill discipline, were feared and detested more by their allies than by the enemy. (Not only did the Transvaalers loathe this unit, they also resented the high salary of £350 per annum that the Natal officers were paid – almost twenty times that of a British soldier.) The local units were also aided by Chief Pokwana whose tribe were traditional enemies of the Pedi.

These irregulars, both black and white, engaged in skirmishing with the enemy for many months with a number of volunteers being killed or wounded, including Lloyd of the Zulu Police, who received two bullets, one in the shoulder and one in the arm. (Lloyd recovered in time to disband his men on whom a cannon was trained after they had mutinied and run amok.) By the beginning of September all the offensive operations of Captain Clarke, the officer in command, had, due to the appalling mismanagement of supplies and men, come to a grinding halt. Summer was approaching and with it would come fever and horse sickness. Meanwhile, undeterred, the Pedi continued to shout challenges from the hills and even attacked farmsteads within sight of Lydenburg itself – while in the hinterland the Boers seethed with hatred and revolt.

Sir Theophilus Shepstone's administration had failed. His campaigns against Sekhukhune had verged on disaster and were, in the words of Lord Chelmsford, 'not of a nature to impress the native mind with an idea of the strength of Britain. Decisive results should be obtained at once,' he declared. Colonel Rowlands, with 1200 tough British infantry and 600 cavalry, mainly of the renowned Frontier Light Horse, which had completed a spectacular forced march of 430 miles from Pietermaritzburg to Lydenburg in twenty-one days, would quickly put paid to Sekhukhune and show the restless Boers what they would be up against if they contemplated fighting his disciplined forces. So in the midst of summer, Rowlands marched north into a fever-ridden land, and perhaps – even more important from a military point of view – a territory which during the coming months would become rampant with horse sickness, a disease that could cripple a cavalry force by wiping out fifty percent of its mounts in forty-eight hours.

Although there were no less than four military posts within a radius of thirty miles of Sekhukhune's stronghold, by the time Rowlands's force arrived most had been abandoned and the miners of the gold rush town of Pilgrims Rest, fifty miles from the Pedi capital, feared for their lives.

Rowlands re-garrisoned some of the deserted forts and with 130 British infantry of the 1/13th LI, and 338 mounted men, mainly of the FLH, advanced toward the Pedi stronghold. A two-year drought had turned the land into a semi-desert.

A combination of heat, drought and Pedi resistance defeated Rowlands's force. Having marched 500 miles and come within sight of the stronghold itself, he withdrew.

Chelmsford was more than disappointed. But although he supported Rowlands by writing to the Secretary of State for War that he believed the force had no option but to retire without attempting an attack, Rowlands was now marked as a man of indecision. Gradually, and rather deviously, Chelmsford would relieve Rowlands of most of his troops, giving them instead to Colonel Evelyn Wood to do with as he wished. A gossiping officer on Chelmsford's staff summed it up: 'Well, Rowlands made an awful mess of his business. He failed utterly and completely and worse still, rather humiliating for our name and fame. He not only did not take Sekhukhune's place, but he did not even try to take it. This has been an awful blow to the General and the Governor for it has upset all the General's plans about invading Zululand.'[2]

The troops of the mighty British Empire had failed to conquer a minor native chief and Britain would find the Zulu a bolder foe because of it. Almost immediately, the Zulu living in and around the Disputed Territories, close to the Transvaal border, became exceedingly truculent, ordering whites to depart and taking over their farms. And the Boers, gloating at Rowlands's retreat, began to consider that the recovery of their independence by force of arms might not be so difficult a proposition after all.

Rowlands had maintained that he had received the full support of 'one and all' of his officers in his decision to withdraw: not so as far as Lieutenant Colonel Redvers Buller CB was concerned. Having got within sight of Sekhukhune's stronghold, Buller had been contemptuous of Rowlands's decision and said so in no uncertain terms to Chelmsford. Buller was one of the six special service officers who had accompanied Chelmsford on his voyage out to the Cape earlier in the year (Rowlands and Wood were also among the group) and had gained an enviable reputation as a leader of irregular cavalry in the recent war. The son of a Devonshire squire, he had, at forty years of age, seen service in India, China, Canada and West Africa and was to be described by one of his young officers as 'a silent, saturnine and bloodthirsty man, as resolute a fighter as ever drew breath – a born leader of men'. He had also been described as 'brave to the point of insanity', not the sort of man to turn back. Buller found great favour with Chelmsford and after the Sekhukhune debacle was appointed to command the mounted troops in Wood's No. 4 Column where he would find many opportunities to get to grips with the enemy.

As Rowlands's dejected troops retreated, leaving Sekhukhune with a further year of freedom before Lieutenant General Sir Garnet Wolseley KCB would destroy his stronghold in November 1879,[3] Chelmsford continued to distribute his troops along the Zululand border. With Durnford's column guarding the Middle Drift over the Tugela and Rowlands's force remaining in the Transvaal, Chelmsford's remaining three columns would be rather strung out.

No. 1 Column, the Coastal Column, under the command of Colonel Charles Knight Pearson, consisted of 300 mounted men, 1500 imperial infantry from the 3rd and 99th Regiments, 2000 armed natives, five pieces of artillery including one

Gatling gun, and two rocket tubes. It would have its base on the south bank of the Tugela River at Fort Pearson, about two miles upstream from the Indian Ocean and sixty-six miles from Durban.

No. 3 Column, in the centre, under the command of Colonel Richard Glyn, comprised 300 mounted men, 1300 imperial infantry of the 24th Regiment, 2500 armed natives, six 7-pounder guns and two rocket tubes. It would be based 155 miles inland, high up on the escarpment at a place called Helpmekaar, where Chelmsford would also establish his headquarters early in January.

No. 4 Column, commanded by Colonel Evelyn Wood VC, CB, had already established a base 260 miles inland from Durban, at Utrecht on the edge of the Disputed Territories. This would be completely self-sufficient as a flying column and, within the broad structure of the invasion, Wood was in a position to plan his own advance. In the 13th and 90th Regiments, he had some of the finest infantry in Africa, and his mounted troops would soon earn the admiration of all.

The terrain of Wood's future operations, the Disputed Territories, was as magnificent a land as a soldier could wish for: a high, healthy plateau of rolling grasslands, criss-crossed by ranges of flat-topped mountains, 5000 feet or more in height – mountains that were the birthplace of numerous rivers that flowed eastward to the Indian Ocean.

To understand the turmoil and the enmities that dogged this fair land and the reason for the Boer hatred of the British, it is necessary to go back forty years to the time when the trekboers, having left the Cape to escape British rule, finally, after years of wandering and privation, reached Natal, 'The Promised Land', to which they believed their God of the Old Testament had led them, and which He intended for them. It was sparsely populated – but populated nevertheless – with Zulu communities owing allegiance to their king, Dingane. There was also another, totally different, group of inhabitants, mainly of English birth, who eked out a wild existence by hunting, trading and practising subsistence farming around the shores of a harbour recently named by them as Durban, after Sir Benjamin D'Urban, then the governor of the Cape. This small settlement, which existed at the sufferance of Dingane, occupied little more than fifty miles of coastline to a depth of five miles inland.

The leader of the immigrant Boers, Piet Retief, and his party visited Durban whilst on their way to meet King Dingane, from whom they hoped to purchase, with cattle, a large portion of Natal. But Dingane treacherously murdered Retief and all his men, and then sent his warriors to fall upon their unsuspecting kin as they slept in their wagons, strewn out among the peaceful valleys of the Drakensberg Mountains. In a frenzy of destruction, hundreds of men, women and children were slaughtered and those who escaped retreated back over the mountains. The British population of Durban, who had sent out a force of seventeen settlers and some 800 Africans to assist the Boers, also incurred Dingane's wrath and his warriors destroyed the fledgling settlement – the inhabitants either escaping by sea or taking to the bush. Nevertheless the Boers had seen their promised land and they would be back. They also wanted revenge.

Within months the Boers had assembled an invasion force. It was not large in number for the task planned, consisting of 471 white men supported by sixty blacks, but its transport, sixty-four stout ox wagons, would also be its bastion of defence. Stripped of everything except bare essentials, the wagons, when lashed in one behind the other, with thorn tree fencing strung between the wheels, became a mobile fortress. On Sunday, 16 December 1838, the commandant general of this force, Andries Pretorius, having selected his position on a loop of the Blood (Ncome) River, brought a vast Zulu impi to battle and utterly defeated it.

Forming an alliance with Dingane's brother, Mpande (Panda), the Boers waged war and finally Dingane fled to Tongaland where he was put to death. Mpande was then installed as king and for assisting him to the throne, the Boers were awarded Natal, comprising that part of the Zulu kingdom bounded by the Blood, Buffalo and Tugela Rivers on the east and the Drakensberg Mountains on the west.

The inhabitants of Durban, who had returned to the harbour after the destruction of their settlement, decided to throw in their lot with the Boers and the Republic of Natalia was proclaimed.

The British, far off in the Cape, became alarmed. Suspicious of independent white states on their borders which might opt for an alliance with a foreign European power, they decided to bring the Boers back into the imperial fold. Marching a force of infantry up from the Cape and with the support of a man-of-war, Britain dissolved the Republic and declared the promised land now to be the British Colony of Natal.

Some Boers remained and settled down, but many, including Andries Pretorius, who had defeated the Zulu at Blood River, hitched up their wagons and set off north and west into an Africa that was still vast and relatively unknown, and where they yet hoped to find independence. Led by Pretorius they trekked away to the distant plains that lay beyond the Drakensberg Mountains; but the British were not far behind and they were eventually chased into the wilds of the Transvaal where they established the settlement of Lydenburg (Town of Sorrows). Other groups of immigrant farmers tried to set up other republics that were laughably impractical, often lacking boundaries, income or means of government, and with only a sprinkling of prospective citizens. Britain soon put a stop to that simply by declaring jurisdiction over all territory below 25 degrees latitude south, which included Lydenburg. Likewise, in Britain's view, all the immigrant Boers still owed allegiance to the Crown.

Relief, however, was not far away. In a complete volte-face, Britain decided that trying to subdue its unwilling subjects was not worth the effort. The proclamation outlawing Pretorius and others was rescinded and by 1854 the Orange River Sovereignty had become the Orange Free State, which Britain acknowledged by royal proclamation as being independent. At the same time Her Majesty's Government approved of the Boers in the Transvaal forming their own government and assured the newly formed South African Republic of non-interference and non-encroachment. The promised land, though not as green as Natal, was theirs at last. They kept it for a quarter of a century before Sir Theophilus Shepstone annexed it to the Crown, and the Boers, like it or not, once again became British subjects. It is not difficult, then, to find reason for Boer hatred of the British.

During the years of independence the Boers of the Transvaal tried to define the boundaries of their land – and the further these went in all directions the better. Below the Pongola River, which was the accepted southern boundary of the Transvaal, there was an area of land in the shape of an inverted pyramid with its point resting at Rorke's Drift. In their trek from Natal many Boers had passed through this area, and by 1847 a number had settled on the north-western side between the Buffalo and Blood Rivers, founding the small town of Utrecht[4] and calling the district by the same name. It was an isolated little community cut off by vast distances from the main Boer centres further to the north and west. Clearly the land did not belong to them but, through a series of ill-defined verbal and written agreements, they came to believe that they had acquired the territory. Mpande, the Zulu king, believed otherwise; his assessment was that he had merely leased the land. Even the Boers' own Volkstaad at Potchefstroom was unwilling to incorporate the Utrecht district into the greater Boer community because of the suspect nature of Utrecht's title.

At about the same time as the Boers had arrived below the Pongola River another set of immigrants were arriving from the east. There had been turmoil in Swaziland and a large clan had fled south. Having sworn allegiance to Mpande, they were allocated a tract of land east of the Blood River which included the Hlobane and Zunguin mountain ranges and the plains that surrounded them. A military kraal was built as a rallying and training base, and from this kraal (then spelt Makulusini or Bakulusini) they adopted a name for themselves, becoming the abaQulusi people. This military kraal was only ten miles from the Utrecht boundary.

Another group of white people followed the trekboers; in 1860 a handful of German Lutheran missionaries settled just north of the Pongola River, at a place they called Luneburg. It was the policy of this order to train its flock, both black and white, in all the manual skills of farming, and when the trainees were sufficiently tutored, to set them up on small farms on either bank of the river. The Disputed Territories were beginning to fill up.

In 1864 Mbelini and his followers also arrived; loosely allied to the abaQulusi, he was the first-born son of the late Swazi king, Mswazi. Although according to Swazi custom, Mbelini, as eldest son, could not succeed his father as king, he nevertheless attempted to seize the throne when his father died. As a boy he had

1. THE DISPUTED TERRITORIES

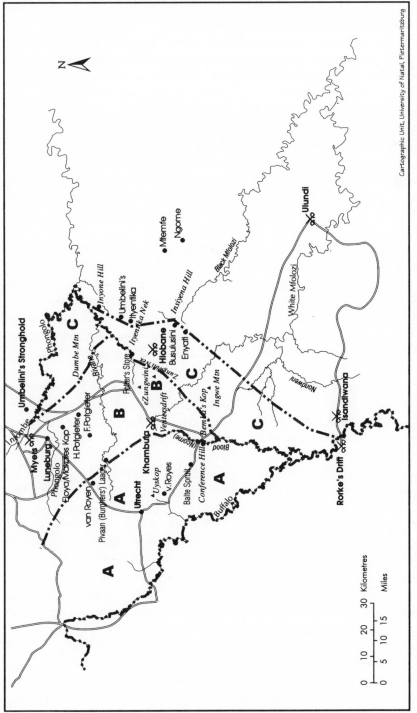

A location map of the disputed territories, based on the Utrecht District map of July 1879, showing present day features. The areas marked 'A', 'B' and 'C' are in respect of land the Boers believed had become theirs at different times through negotiation. The Boundary Commission awarded areas 'B' and 'C' to Zululand in 1879. At the conclusion of the Anglo-Zulu War later that year, Sir Garnet Wolseley reversed the award giving the land to Natal and the Transvaal. (Author's collection)

Cartographic Unit, University of Natal, Pietermaritzburg

been given fearsome cruelties to perform, and did so without hesitation. At the age of twelve, for example, he obediently stabbed to death a captive, bound hand and foot. A wild dog was skinned alive in his presence and the dripping skin sewn around his head – an act, it was believed, that would transfer the vicious nature of the animal into the boy's soul. The usurper, however, lacked the support of the regents, so with a few adherents he fled into the Disputed Territories where he tried to strike a deal with the Boers and obtain their armed support; but his overtures were shunned, the Boers finding him and his cause too risky a proposition. He then turned to Zululand and offered his allegiance and considerable fighting experience to Cetshwayo, who astutely calculated that a man such as Mbelini could help deter white encroachment on his north-west border. Permitted to settle in the Disputed Territories, Mbelini chose as his stronghold the Tafelberg, a mountain fortress formed by nature in the likeness of a medieval castle with a labyrinth of caves to serve as quarters. The flat-top eminence not only provided acres of lush pasture for the many cattle that he seized, but also served as look-out tower from which the country could be surveyed for miles around.

Less than four miles to the west was the stronghold of yet another renegade immigrant, an old-time resident of the area, Manyanyoba, who reputedly had 2000 warriors under his command – men of mixed origins and of decided Hottentot appearance with protruding cheekbones and yellow skin. Manyanyoba's fortress was as impregnable as that of Mbelini and similarly scattered with inaccessible caves.

Between these two ominous strongholds, and 1500 feet below the summit of the Tafelberg, flowed the Intombi (Ntombe) River with Meyer's Drift giving passage to the wagon road north to Derby in the Transvaal. This road would one day be used to transport supplies for the invading British army, and would be the scene of a British disaster.

A further complication for the territory ensued when Cetshwayo sought to establish his succession to the Zulu throne. Although his father, Mpande, was still alive, Cetshwayo had set about removing all opposition to his future kingship. Succession to the Zulu throne was usually a violent business but Cetshwayo's was particularly savage, the climax coming in 1856 in one of the bloodiest battles that Southern Africa would ever witness. Cetshwayo and his Suthu faction of the Zulu nation met with his half-brother, Mbulazi, at the battle of Ndondakusuka on the north bank of the Tugela River. Vastly outnumbered, Mbulazi and his supporters, who included six other of Mpande's sons, were slaughtered, leaving 50,000 corpses to be washed downstream to the Indian Ocean.

There were other claimants to Mpande's throne, one being Mtonga, whose mother wielded great influence and had endeavoured to persuade Mpande to recognise her son as heir apparent. Cetshwayo contrived the woman's murder and when the young Mtonga fled and found shelter in Utrecht, Cetshwayo asked the Boers to give him up. To this they agreed provided Mtonga was not harmed and that Cetshwayo ceded to them an additional tract of land. Cetshwayo is reputed to have assented and honoured his promise, allowing the young Mtonga to live reasonably freely but under surveillance. However, when Mpande eventually died, in October 1872, Mtonga fled once again to Utrecht, causing a disagreeable situation: the Boers had the land but Cetshwayo did not have Mtonga.

By 1878 the territory had become a time bomb of future confrontation, its fuse burning more quickly with the arrival of every additional immigrant family, black or white. Cattle were still the main currency of all races and as people acquired more wealth, so the demand for grazing ever increased. To add to white fears, the abaQulusi, although not subject to group call-up as were most Zulu males, could put a fully equipped regiment into the field at short notice. Mbelini, the renegade, was also a cause of apprehension, making sporadic raids up and down the border area, killing black farm workers, stealing cattle and on several occasions forcing settlers to abandon their farms.

There were incidents which caused particular alarm at Luneburg. Faku, representative of the Zulu king, built a military kraal on the land of a German farmer but assured the local landrost, Adrian Rudolph, that there was no cause for fear and that Cetshwayo had forbidden his people to molest any settlers. Within a few weeks, however, the abaQulusi, disregarding Faku's authority as the king's representative, began a campaign of intimidation, ordering settlers to depart for Natal. By late September Faku himself, his attitude completely changed, ordered both German and Boer settlers to vacate their properties forthwith, while travellers between Utrecht and Luneburg were frequently molested. Those farms that were abandoned as a temporary precaution were quickly occupied by the local Zulu. Thus the whole area was again in a state of fear and uncertainty, with all the local black elements determined to evict the white community – and there was worse to come. As yet Mbelini had played no part in the mounting tension, but now, almost as a sign of his disdain for the shilly-shallying of Faku and the abaQulusi, he set them an example of applied terror tactics. On the night of 9 October 1878 he led his raiders down into the Pongola Valley, plundering and killing. The kraals he attacked belonged to natives mainly of Swazi descent, British subjects nevertheless. At dawn he retired to his stronghold, driving before him a large number of cattle. It was for this raid that the third condition of the ultimatum demanded Mbelini's apprehension.

Such was the state of affairs that confronted Wood when his column marched into Utrecht a few days after Mbelini's raid. Wood also received a message from Sir Bartle Frere, urging him to use his troops to prevent further outrages around the Luneburg area and by their presence dissuade an exodus of German and Boer settlers. Luneburg was not a place Wood had intended to garrison and could only do so by weakening his strength at Newcastle and Utrecht. Nevertheless, he immediately ordered Major Cornelius Francis Clery (the same Clery who was to become, at different times, staff officer to Nos 3 and 4 Columns), with two companies of the 90th Light Infantry, to footslog another forty miles to Luneburg where they built a fort.

The deployment of this detachment without his knowledge was a cause of consternation to Chelmsford who saw it as a further weakening of his invasion plans. However, he need not have concerned himself: in Wood he was to find his ablest commander. At the age of forty, Wood was still young for his rank and responsibility – and a number of years junior to Rowlands, whose authority he would shortly usurp. Wood had started his career not as a soldier but as a midshipman in the Royal Navy and, in 1854, with the Naval Landing Brigade, had experienced some of the fiercest fighting of the Crimean War. He was badly wounded, evacuated back to England and invalided out of the navy. He had been recommended for the Victoria Cross but the award was not confirmed. Nevertheless, he proudly returned home with the French Legion of Honour, the Turkish Order of Medjidie and two campaign medals – an exceptional number of awards for one so young. Recovering at last from his wounds, he sought an army career, obtaining a commission in the 13th Light Dragoons. The war still raged in the Crimea and, with his regiment, he returned to the fighting. On this tour of duty he contracted typhoid fever and pneumonia which came closer to killing him than his earlier wounds. Lying near to death in the dreaded Scutari Hospital, his life was undoubtedly saved only by the arrival from England of his mother, Lady Emma Wood, who hardly left his side until he was fit enough to be taken aboard a British ship bound for home. During this illness he had become so emaciated that his hipbones protruded through his flesh. His mother, an accomplished artist, sketched him as he lay at Scutari, and her portrait reveals the wasted features of a man close to death: it also shows, even at so early an age, the beginnings of a receding hairline.

Hardly had he recovered his health when, in order to get to India and the Sepoy Mutiny, he transferred to the 17th Lancers. Constantly in the thick of the fighting, he was again recommended for the Victoria Cross for leading an attack against a large band of mutineers and, on this occasion, he was awarded that most coveted of all decorations.

Service at home followed with a long spell at Aldershot, as brigade major, where he took every opportunity to hunt – a sport that he would enjoy for another half century. As one of Sir Garnet Wolseley's special officers, and one of the 'Wolseley Ring', he fought in the Ashanti War in West Africa, and was again severely wounded. By 1878, under the command of Lieutenant General Sir Frederick Augustus Thesiger (who would assume the title of Lord Chelmsford within the year on the death of his father), he was fighting in the Ninth Frontier war leading a force of 1700 men made up of a mixture of imperial infantry, mounted volunteers and native scouts.

His military career, nevertheless, was dogged by constant illness and afflictions which he resisted with the same determination as when fighting the enemy. He was also prone to accidents. By the time he was twenty years old he had suffered from typhoid fever, chronic indigestion, faceache, toothache, pneumonia, sun-stroke and ingrown toenails. He had also been clawed by a tiger and, of all unlikely things, a giraffe had sat on his face, 'making a mash' of his nose. Now at the age of forty he was beginning to suffer from deafness and was still accident prone. Out of uniform, with his round bald dome and untidy beard, Wood, for all his soldierly attributes, looked like a melancholy schoolmaster.

Wood also developed into an accomplished diplomat as he set about trying to enlist British support from among the local inhabitants, both black and white, particularly that of the Boers who had been born and bred in the territory. Their local knowledge of frontier matters was unrivalled and Wood wanted these hard men as his allies. Enlisting their support would not be an easy task, as he had already discovered. In his autobiography, which he wrote many years later, *From Midshipman to Field Marshal*, published in 1906, Wood described a meeting that he had with 'Andries Pretorius' and twenty of his kindred at a farmhouse just inside the Transvaal border. In this Wood was mistaken, for Andries Pretorius had been dead for twenty-five years. The error, however, is understandable as the meeting was conducted in Dutch, the language of the Boers, with a Mr Meek interpreting into English for Wood. In fact, the man whom Wood met that day was almost certainly Marthinus Pretorius, the son of Andries, who had much in common with his father. Both had held the rank of commandant general, both had been born at Graaff Reinet in the Cape, both had been on the Great Trek, both had fought against the Zulus, both had striven to bring about the birth of the Boer Republic and, above all, both hated the British vehemently.

Marthinus Pretorius was a very powerful and influential man, for apart from his military accomplishments he had drafted the first constitution of the South African Republic, and had enjoyed the unique honour of being president both of the Republic and the Orange Free State. It is obvious that Wood did not realise the stature of the man he was meeting. Nor would he have known that Marthinus had been imprisoned by the British after the recent annexation of the Transvaal and had not long been released. Even so, half a century later, Wood could still recall that he had a 'remarkable face, resolute and unyielding'.

It is not surprising, therefore, that when Wood arrived cold and wet at that lonely farmhouse, his reception yielded nothing in the way of support: indeed, it is a wonder that the deputation had agreed to meet Wood at all. To show their disdain for the British, the assembled Boers broke the entrenched rules of frontier hospitality which required a host and his family to assist any guest in unharnessing horse and vehicle. The 'surly Boers' offered no help, as Wood put it, except Pretorius, who apologised for his kindred but explained that they 'detested the sight of Englishmen' and went on to affirm frankly that he would have been equally discourteous had Wood not been his guest.

Wood tried to talk the assembly into joining the British against the Zulu, arguing that the farms along the border, many of which belonged to those present, were now deserted because of the turmoil, but would soar in value once tranquillity was established – presumably tranquillity under British rule!

Not only were the Boers indifferent to Wood's appeal, but Pretorius made it plain that he predicted a Zulu victory, pointing out Rowlands's debacle as an example of British military incompetence. He was adamant that the British would get no help until the Transvaal was returned to the Boers.

Another reason why Wood may have assumed he had met Andries Pretorius was that Chelmsford, during those weeks prior to the invasion of Zululand, was somewhat obsessed with the victorious campaign that Andries Pretorius had led against Dingane forty years earlier. Judging from several of his letters, Chelmsford not only believed he could emulate Pretorius's success, but felt, that with his British infantry, he would do even better, as he wrote to Wood in late 1878:

> I have been reading in Chase's History of Natal, that in 1838 Andries Pretorius, with a commando of 460 men, took only six days to march from Rorke's Drift to the hill where Retief and his party were massacred ... Pretorius, when he invaded Zululand to avenge Retief's massacre had only 430 men with him and with these he seems to have easily beat off 10,000 warriors who attacked him. The Zulus in those days were warriors flushed with repeated victories. I doubt the present Zulu making a more determined fight.

Such then was Chelmsford's misplaced confidence a few days before the invasion: not only would he find the Zulu army equally as determined as ever, he would also see it, once again, flushed with victory.

Wood was not wholly discouraged by his encounter with Marthinus Pretorius and next arranged a meeting with the Boers nearer to his base at Utrecht. Many of these men resided, or had property, in the Disputed Territories and lived in the hopes that it would be awarded to the Transvaal. As the award had still to be proclaimed, they may well have thought that their support for the British cause could influence a decision in their favour.

On 4 December 1878, a week before the findings of the Boundary Commission were made public, Wood arrived at the courthouse in Utrecht and addressed a gathering of local Boers. Among those present were the landrost of Wakkerstroom in the Transvaal and the landrost of Utrecht, Mr Rudolph (who, it will be remembered, had met with Faku over the construction of a royal kraal near Luneburg). Rudolph interpreted Wood's address and, after some questioning, the two of them retired so that 'a free discussion could take place amongst the gathering'. By 3.00 pm a committee had been elected comprising seven members: J.C.C. Mol (chairman), H.J. Buhrmann (representing Middelburg district of the Transvaal), E.L. van Rooyen, P.W. Jordaan, P.L. Uys, F. Johnstone and J.L. van Reenen. The committee pledged the co-operation of the assembly and proposed conditions under which 'they would probably serve against the Zulus'. A brief outline of these conditions was:

> That all burghers were to be invited to fight the Zulu in case of war. Pay would be at five shillings a day; that the colonial government pay for all provisions and supply arms and ammunition; that booty must be shared equally; that all burghers remain in the field to the conclusion of operations and that they serve under their own officers.

Wood and Rudolph rejoined the meeting and listened to the proposals which Wood accepted, subject to a few minor amendments. With what could have been a thorny issue safely passed, Wood concluded that he 'rejoiced to find that there is practically accord between us'.

The chairman, also on a jubilant note, replied that he 'trusted all experienced burghers will co-operate to bring the common foe to obedience and civilisation'.

Within a few days all the proposals were agreed in writing and the 'Burgher Force', as the unit was to be named, awaited the call to arms. Wood had won himself the most experienced body of scouts in Southern Africa: unfortunately, they were yet to be appraised of the boundary award.

When Chelmsford heard of Wood's successful meeting he was sceptical, and the day before the boundary award was to be made public, he wrote to Wood suggesting that 'it might be as well to prepare your Dutchmen for a decision on the boundary question adverse to their claims, although, as far as individuals are concerned it will make no difference, as they will be allowed to occupy the farms they have deserted on the same terms as before, only "quit rent" will be paid to the Zulus instead of the Transvaal government' – which showed how little Chelmsford knew about the Boers. They wanted a republic not a Zulu landlord.

It is difficult to estimate the number of Boers who would have joined Wood, had it not been for the award of the Disputed Territories. Certainly some important burghers had attended his meeting and had offered 'their warm co-operation', among them H.J. Buhrmann, representing the Middelburg district, 140 miles away in the Transvaal.[5] Piet Uys had also given his support and had proposed an entirely new strategy for beating the Zulu nation: instead of vast numbers of infantry, guns, transport and all the problems that went with supplying a British army in the field, Uys suggested a body of 2000 local volunteers, all well mounted and provisioned with a good supply of ammunition and little else – except for a few pounds of coffee and sugar per man. They would live off the enemy's cattle and his mealie harvest and destroy every beast and vestige of food that they could not consume themselves. They would avoid large bodies of the enemy, never letting him know where they would strike next, and burn every kraal they came upon. Uys believed that such tactics would bring the Zulu nation to the brink of starvation and defeat within two months.

Such tactics of total war would have been, initially, totally unacceptable to men like Frere and Chelmsford – but after the first British defeat they might well have changed their minds. Most of the older burghers had fought against the Zulu or Matabele in their time; some had survived the Great Trek and had fought at Blood River. But now, a week after their pledge of support, they were 'wrathfully indignant'. Instead of having a burgher force of perhaps 300–400 men – or even as many as 2000, as Piet Uys had hinted – the truculent burghers would shortly plot revolt. Piet Uys was the one exception; he and his small band, many of whom were related in one way or another, remained true to their pledge, believing that the Boers and British still had a common cause in defeating the Zulu nation. Uys had every reason to hate the Zulu for his father, also Piet, and his fifteen-year-old brother, Dirk, had both been killed in battle with the Zulus and the need for vengeance remained unsatisfied. To justify his allegiance with the British, Uys wrote to a relative in the Cape, 'I fight in good faith, and a righteous cause. I must avenge the death of my father and brother, although in doing so I am almost sure to lose my life: Yet I cannot restrain myself when I remember how they were slain.' Brave Piet Uys: within a few weeks he would himself be killed by the Zulu in virtually a repetition of his father's and brother's fate.

During the weeks preceding the expiry of the ultimatum, Wood's invasion force began to assemble around Utrecht while Wood himself made a reconnaissance of much of the disputed land. He travelled light, taking with him only a staff officer and a few men of his personal escort. He was, in fact, foolhardy in riding this volatile area unarmed and vulnerable. On one occasion he sought out the notorious Manyanyoba in his mountain stronghold. Accompanied by his native interpreter, Paliso, he eventually found Manyanyoba, who had with him 100 armed warriors. Wood, carrying only his riding whip, brazened out the meeting for twenty minutes. When he prepared to depart, Manyanyoba had to restrain several of his young men as they raised their assegais in a threatening manner.

Having visited Luneburg, that most vulnerable of white outposts, Wood returned to Utrecht along the Old Hunting Road where he hoped to meet a Mr Charles Potter, who stoutly flew the Union Jack above his store where he traded with the abaQulusi; but Potter, who had been the last white man left in the district, had deemed it prudent to depart – as did Wood when he found the Zulu warriors at the abandoned store excited, aggressive and intent on stealing the belongings from his cart. Whipping up his mules, he and his small escort were wise enough to push on even though it meant a ride of seventy miles to get through the Disputed Territories before nightfall. During the journey they travelled across a country of vandalised farmsteads where immigrant Zulus had taken over the gardens and the fields.

Many of the displaced farmers had gone into laager with their families at Utrecht, while others had trekked off to the comparative safety of the Orange Free State. Luneburg, and its small German community, remained the most likely target for attack, isolated as it was by a two-day march from Utrecht. Mr Ritter, the pastor in charge of the mission, had recently received a visit from Sobelela, the chief of the abaQulusi military kraal, who stated that on Cetshwayo's orders he was to inspect the Luneburg laager and Fort Clery to count the number of soldiers there. The officer commanding the garrison was summoned, and informed by Sobelela that the troops must leave forthwith and return to Utrecht, as his king would not allow English soldiers into his country. Sobelela was pacified with the explanation that the troops were there merely to protect the Great Queen's subjects and would not interfere with the Zulu.

Only recently Chelmsford had criticised Wood for garrisoning Luneburg but, by early December, he was worried that his forces there were not strong enough despite the arrival of Commandant Schermbrucker and his 100 Kaffrarian Riflemen from the Eastern Cape.

Chelmsford and Wood knew Schermbrucker of old from the Ninth Frontier war; a fiery and independent German, fiercely prepared to take offence at any provocation real or imaginary, he had nevertheless given Chelmsford good service in the Cape. He and his men were remnants of the German Legion that Britain had raised for the Crimean War, and on the declaration of peace, the men were given the opportunity to emigrate as military settlers to the Cape. During the recent frontier war, Schermbrucker had upstaged Chelmsford himself when, with a small commando, he had captured a large herd of cattle and killed fifty-five of the enemy, whilst Chelmsford's force had little to show for the same period, except the deaths of three colonial officers. Schermbrucker had, in fact, presided over the funeral of Sandile, the paramount chief of the Xhosa, whose death in 1878 effectively ended the Ninth Frontier war; Schermbrucker had added a macabre touch to the funeral by having Sandile buried between the graves of two British soldiers – the implication being that even in death Sandile was in British custody! Now Chelmsford wrote rather sarcastically to Wood, '... the Pongola Valley ought to be better guarded than by the Luneburg garrison, even though such a redoubtable hero as Schermbrucker keeps watch and ward there'.

The hard-drinking soldiers of the Kaffrarian Rifles and the sober Calvinist missionaries were both German – but that is all they had in common. Schermbrucker found it necessary to issue a proclamation to his men that anyone, black or white, found in possession of hard liquor would be flogged.

Detachments of the 13th and 90th Light Infantry were still stationed at Luneburg, but by early January they would be withdrawn to form up, with the remainder of their regiments, in No. 4 Column. Both detachments would be replaced by men of the 80th Foot, drawn from Rowlands's forces at Derby in the Eastern Transvaal.

On 3 January 1879, Luneburg District received a visit from the warriors of Sihayo, who said that Cetshwayo had not only appointed their chief as commander of Zulu forces in the area of Blood River and Rorke's Drift, but had also given him jurisdiction over the Disputed Territories. Having been awarded the land, despite the consequent ultimatum that had another week to run, Cetshwayo intended to rule it. Sihayo had given his warriors orders that all Zulu workers living in the territory should immediately move their goods and cattle into Zululand; one man refused to obey and his cattle were immediately confiscated and driven to Manyanyoba's stronghold. The incident happened within four miles of Luneburg, but Schermbrucker and his men, being an infantry force, were incapable of overtaking Sihayo's fleet foot warriors. The need for horsemen would become more urgent with every day that passed.

Twenty-five miles to the south at Utrecht, the FLH, under the command of Buller, had arrived after its unsuccessful march with Rowlands. Almost half of the men were shortly to depart when their contracts expired. That they would sign up for another term of service was the hope of everyone, but the recent abortive action against Sekhukhune had left many of these fine horsemen disgruntled; they would think about a further term, but as yet they had not made up their minds.

Four days before the ultimatum expired, Wood's column prematurely crossed the Blood River into Zululand – that part of the Disputed Territories that had formerly been awarded to Cetshwayo. The crossing point was a short distance from a prominent flat-topped hill called Bemba's Kop, after the Zulu induna who, with his small clan, lived at its base.

Chelmsford's invasion plan was for all three columns to converge on Cetshwayo's capital at Ondini, driving resistance before them like beaters driving game.

No. 1 Column, on the coast, commanded by Colonel Pearson, had the longest distance to travel from its departure point on the Tugela River. The central, or No. 3 Column, from its crossing point at Rorke's Drift, had a trek of about eighty-five miles to Ondini while No. 4 Column, commanded by Wood, had the shortest route of about seventy-five miles. Wood had orders to progress slowly in order for the coastal column to catch up. At this stage he had under his command eight companies of the 13th and 90th Light Infantry, totalling approximately 1500 men, four guns of the 11/7 RA, about 200 cavalry, mainly of the FLH, supported by Piet Uys and his burghers, and about 300 native infantry who Chelmsford had named, as a tribute to the column commander, 'Wood's Irregulars'. This would be the second force in Africa to bear the same name; six years earlier during the Ashanti campaign, Wood had raised and trained a regiment of local natives which had been officially designated 'Wood's Irregulars' – so it was flattery for Wood to have another regiment on the other side of Africa, marching under his personal title.

The transport required to move a column of this size, with all its guns, tentage, provisions, ammunition, fodder, kitchens, hospital and the hundred and one other bits of equipment which made up this self-sufficient army, was considerable. It was literally a tented town on the march. The ox-wagon was the main form of transport: a stout, heavy vehicle averaging just under 20 feet long, the height of its rear wheels being almost level with a man's chin. Its usual load was anything from one and a half to three and a half tons and was drawn by a team of between ten to eighteen beasts, yoked in pairs to a long chain called a 'trek tow'. It was 'driven' by a crew of two – a 'voorloper', who walked in front to find the best route for the lead oxen, and the driver who brought up the rear, cracking a long whip and applying the brakes when necessary. The average length of road taken up by each wagon when in convoy was fifty yards. At night, or in times of threat, the wagons could be drawn up as an enclosure and chained together. The effectiveness of such a mobile bastion against attack had been eminently displayed by the Boers at the battle of Blood River forty years earlier and on a number of occasions since.

As an ox subsisted on whatever fodder it could find, much of its day was spent grazing: add to this its ponderous gait and the load that it pulled and it is not surprising that the average distance covered per day was only some ten miles. There was little else in the way of transport except mule wagons which took eight beasts to pull a load of nigh on three-quarters of a ton. Wood's transport consisted of ninety-seven ox-wagons, drawn by about 1700 oxen, which in convoy would span a distance of three miles, one behind the other. At times, when the terrain permitted, the wagons could travel four and five abreast, but this was seldom and any drift or cutting would require them to mark time and to funnel into single file.[6]

The six 7-pounder cannons of No. 4 Column, with their ammunition limbers, were drawn by horses each requiring a ration of grain and hay per day. In addition there were 200 cavalry, 2000 marching infantry, plus all the servants and hangers-on – an impressive sight and an extremely vulnerable target for a swiftly moving enemy. When the weather was dry, the columns moved in clouds of choking dust, but when it rained the wagons had to be manhandled by the infantry, panting and straining in knee-deep mud. Marching in convoy in any kind of weather was a very unpleasant business – the worst aspect being the noise: creaking wagons, cracking whips, shouting drivers, cursing soldiers and bellowing animals made an infernal racket in which the foot-slogging infantry prayed for a moment of silence.

Having crossed the Blood River, No. 4 Column pushed on for ten miles and settled at Bemba's Kop for a few days. Wood's intended route was east into Zululand, toward Ulundi, leaving the whole of the Disputed Territories behind him to be policed by Colonel Rowlands whose headquarters were in far-off Pretoria. Rowlands's troops consisted of the 80th Foot and a few units of volunteer cavalry (Wood having already acquired the 1/13th LI) and were spread out over almost 200 miles of territory from Lydenburg down to Luneburg. Utrecht was virtually abandoned with Wood leaving the 'halt and maimed' to guard his stores and the good citizens to man their own town laager, promising them only a decent burial if the worst came to the worst! Presumably there was an element of chaff and humour in Wood's remarks which may well have been lost on the dour burghers.

The two-year drought had broken; almost every day torrential rain fell accompanied by thunderstorms so violent as to make a brave man flinch. The FLH and the Burgher Force patrolled whatever the weather and in all directions. Shortly after crossing the Blood River, Piet Uys and his men encountered a great number of Zulu in groups of ten to twenty-five warriors. As the ultimatum had a few days to run, the burghers and warriors conversed, both sides pretending to be busy hunting, and each aware of being the vanguard of a greater army in the rear. Wood had wanted the forced removal of all Zulu within the Disputed Territories, but Chelmsford was not too sure – had not they become British subjects? 'I do not think Sir Bartle Frere will approve of your turning out Zulus from your neighbourhood until war is actually declared,' he wrote. 'Sir Bartle's idea is to allow them to remain where they are, but as British subjects...' To Wood this was a lot of diplomatic twaddle; he had enough complications to handle without having to enquire into the nationality of every Zulu across his path. In a note so brief as to be rude, Wood wrote to the Military Secretary and within a few days had the High Commissioner's approval to deal with the matter as he thought best.

For weeks past Chelmsford had been hoping that the Swazis – that warrior race whose savagery made its name a byword for terror – could be persuaded to become British allies. A Swazi army stood ready to sweep down from its mountain kingdom and, with No. 4 Column, strike into the heart of Zululand – or at least that is what Captain Norman McLeod, the British Agent to the Swazis, fondly believed. With Swazi support Chelmsford was confident that he could safely leave Rowlands's force to deal with any uprising or incursions into the Disputed Territories, while Wood advanced into Zululand. But although the Swazis were full of boasts and promises, they were not yet committing themselves; they first wanted to see how the British were going to perform. They had heard much about the might and prowess of the Great Queen's army, but having only Rowlands's performance to judge at first hand, they were sceptical. Had not they themselves, two years earlier, fared better than Rowlands against Sekhukhune? They, at least, had captured a great number of cattle – even if the cattle, in turn, had been immediately stolen by the Boers! If the British wanted their help they would have to buy it and it would cost more than cattle: they had in mind 1000 square miles of territory along the Pongola River – a proposition taken seriously enough for Chelmsford to write to Wood, 'The Swazi, I believe, are to be given the land down to the Pongola River, but on this point I will consult the High Commissioner.'

Frere, with his lofty pleas for confederation, was certainly not giving any land away; in any event, the Swazis could well be the next on his 'hit list'. Nevertheless, the High Commissioner was prepared to consider lower stakes in order to secure the warriors that his Commander-in-Chief so anxiously required. 'Money or arms' was Chelmsford's next suggestion – roughriding the law which forbade the selling of arms to natives. But Frere was not giving away cash or guns either. With a thrift that was commendable, but with no grasp of reality, he suggested a one-off payment of 500 cows and fifty horses (with saddles) in order to induce the Swazis down to the Pongola.

A Swazi move through the Transvaal to the Zulu border would undoubtedly have resulted in much bloodshed, but it was a complication that did not arise, for the Swazis were not ready to proceed – certainly not merely for some horses and cows which they could steal at a fraction of the risk. They were astute enough, however, to keep Britain's hopes high: so much so that Wood was assured in January that Rowlands was ready to march down with the Swazis; while Captain McLeod, at the same time, grandly assured Wood that 'I go tomorrow to the King's kraal to call out the Swazis'. But they never did come – except for those individuals who joined Wood's Irregulars at a shilling a day plus booty. The Swazis would sit on the fence for a long time yet. Six months later, at the end of July, McLeod still believed the Swazi army would cross the Pongola into Zululand and spoke hopefully of them taking Cetshwayo. In fact they did not ally themselves with Britain until the Zulu War was over when they joined with Sir Garnet Wolseley in the annihilation of Sekhukhune and his tribe.

By early January there was no doubt in Chelmsford's mind that he would invade Zululand on the 11th. He further believed that Colonel Glyn's No. 3 Column, which he intended to lead, would be attacked as it crossed the Buffalo River at Rorke's Drift. This prospect, far from causing Chelmsford any apprehension, put him in a jaunty mood of expectation: 'It is said that Sihayo has about 8000 men ready to oppose the crossing,' he wrote. 'I hope it may be true.' But to ensure as successful a crossing as possible, it would be important to distract Sihayo and give him plenty to think about. A diversion by No. 4. Column would fit the bill. On 8 January Chelmsford requested Wood to advance south-east from Bemba's Kop in the direction of Rorke's Drift.

With enthusiasm, Wood set about creating a diversion that would have every Zulu within twenty miles aware of No. 4. Column – and what better way of advertising its presence than the regimental band of the 90th Light Infantry? The twenty bandsmen and their conductor led the way playing for all they were worth, sending the stirring notes of their regimental march ('Blue Bonnets Over the Border') echoing back and forth across the hills of Zululand. The significance of the tune would have been lost on the waiting warriors but the distant martial sound, so strange and dread to the enemy's alien ear, would have caused uneasy ripples of apprehension.

While the infantry built a 'fort' (little more than a parapet of rocks, sods and laagered wagons) at Bemba's Kop, Buller and the FLH, supported by Uys and his Burgher Force, set out on distant cattle-raiding sorties. The fort complete, Wood left one-third of his force safely within its confines guarding his supplies; then, travelling as light as possible, he marched south-east towards Rorke's Drift with the rest of the infantry and native soldiers.

As the column plodded through the night, torrential rain fell incessantly and the Blood River rose to three times its normal height. The lightly loaded wagons, up to their axles in mud, required a full team of oxen, plus fifty straining soldiers, to get them over the smallest watercourse. By nine o'clock the following morning, Wood, riding out ahead, met Chelmsford as arranged at Nkonjane Hill. It was 11 January, the ultimatum had expired and No. 3 Column, nine miles away at Rorke's Drift, was crossing the Buffalo River. Whether or not due to Wood's diversion, the column crossed unopposed. Far away to the south, a few miles upstream from the mouth of the Tugela River, Colonel Pearson and No. 1 Column also crossed without opposition. The invasion of Zululand was under way.

*   *   *

And what of Cetshwayo while all this activity was taking place along his border? With Natal and Zululand separated for the most part by a river that a shout could carry across, and with 300,000 former Zulu living in Natal, there is little doubt that had he wished, Cetshwayo could have known, within twenty-four hours, the number of times the sentries had saluted outside Chelmsford's tent. He and his indunas were well aware of what was going on along the border, but could not fathom what Britain really had in mind.

For months Cetshwayo had been living in expectation of a final decision on the boundary dispute and, with Britain adjudicating, had hoped that the vexing matter would soon be settled once and for all. Yet despite all formalities and the gathering of evidence by the Commission, Cetshwayo was deeply uneasy. For one thing, there was too much Shepstone family involvement for his liking. Neither Sir Theophilus (known by the Zulu name of 'Somtseu') nor his brother, John Wesley Shepstone ('Misjan'), both of whom had been intimately concerned with the fortunes of the Zulu nation – Cetshwayo's in particular – for nigh on forty years, were any longer trusted.

Sir Theophilus, recently knighted, had come to Natal in 1838, as a young interpreter with Major Samuel Charters's mission and had remained there, more or less, ever since. He was a large impressive man who despite the searing summer heat and humidity of Natal never failed to dress complete with wing collar, waistcoat, tie and tails. While Secretary for Native Affairs, he and the post he occupied had grown in status and importance over the years. He was held in great awe by the Zulu whose national affairs he had manipulated to a significant degree. He had been shrewd enough, when Cetshwayo was involved in the deadly business of establishing his succession, to give the young prince his backing; and when Cetshwayo had finally become king in 1873, Shepstone, 'on behalf of Queen Victoria', had recognised him as such by means of a 'coronation'.

This pantomime-like ceremony, devised and directed by the impresario himself, did in fact have all the trappings of a stage production. There was a tinsel crown, a royal robe, a brass band and a full set of extras supplied by the Natal volunteer regiments, clad in their uniforms which were aflow with enough braid and frogging to have come from a theatre wardrobe. The performance, though, was not without its dangers. First Cetshwayo's faction, the Usuthu, had to face down the regiments of other hostile contenders: miraculously, this had gone off without bloodshed or incident. Then, as Shepstone's cavalcade drew near to the royal capital with its thousands of warriors drawn up in their regiments, a rumour, as threatening as a fire in the orchestra pit, raced ahead. Years before, at the battle of Ndondakusuka on the north bank of the Tugela where Cetshwayo had vanquished and slaughtered all opposition, he had not only killed his rival Mbulazi, but had skinned and crucified him on an antheap. Now, word had it, Mbulazi had risen and at that very moment was being borne by 'Somtseu' and his horse soldiers to usurp Cetshwayo and be crowned king in his stead.

Cetshwayo delayed his meeting with Shepstone for days, moving from one place to another while Shepstone and his troupe daily lost prestige and dignity. Finally, the rumour fortunately having run itself to death, Shepstone sourly strode on to centre stage where, in front of a vast gathering of the Zulu nation, he placed the tin crown upon Cetshwayo's head.

It may have been one of life's moments that Cetshwayo could have done without, but it at least underlined for any potential rivals consideration that Cetshwayo was backed by the Great White Queen – and Cetshwayo was not blind to the value of such formidable support. In later years Shepstone had displayed genuine empathy for the Zulu people by whom he was regarded as a friend, albeit a somewhat pompous and interfering one. Furthermore, in dealing with the Boer and their claims to land, Shepstone had consistently aligned himself with the interests of Zululand. When Shepstone had annexed the Transvaal, Cetshwayo had perceived him in the role of a conqueror of the Boers. In this he was deceived. The Transvaal, whether or not inhabited by Boers, had become a British domain and consequently a land henceforth to be favoured by Shepstone in preference to Zulu claims and aspirations. This policy reversal was not entirely evident to Cetshwayo who began to visualise Shepstone, in his office as Administrator of the Transvaal, as a patron of the Boers and an enemy of the Zulu. Indeed, it must be so, for did not Henrique, the son of Shepstone, who as a youngster had accompanied his father to Cetshwayo's coronation, now sit with the two Boers, Uys and Rudolph, as the Transvaal delegation opposing his own three indunas on the Boundary Commission?

For a number of reasons, therefore, Cetshwayo now concluded that Shepstone was about to lead an invasion of Zululand from the Transvaal via the Disputed Territories. Over the Christmas period of 1878, Shepstone had stayed with Wood at Utrecht for a few days, but merely as a guest. The truth was that, far from being the brains behind an invasion, Shepstone was on his way out, having been replaced as Administrator of the Transvaal. But Cetshwayo was not to know this; 'Somtseu's' presence with No. 4 Column (whose mounted men, the Burgher Force and the FLH, were either Boers or had the appearance of being Boers) was enough to convince him that Wood's was a Boer army commanded by Shepstone – so much so that No. 4. Column was known to the Zulu as 'Somtseu's Impi'.

To cap the Shepstone family involvement, John, as Acting Secretary for Native Affairs, was one of the three commissioners forming the British panel. Although almost as knowledgeable as his brother in Zulu affairs, and with an equal command of the language, John did not possess the senatorial appearance of his elder brother (in fact, in an era where men contrived to grow the most grotesque styles of facial hair, his moustache must have been one of the strangest: it neither swept nor bristled, but hung, walrus-like, from under his nose to the bottom of his chin). It was for good reason that John Shepstone was not entirely trusted by the Zulu. Twenty years earlier, when in pursuit of a Zulu chief named Matyana, John had arranged a parley at which it was agreed both sides would attend unarmed. This stipulation was honoured by Matyana and his clan, but John and his men concealed their weapons about them. The parley had hardly started when John drew a hidden pistol and fired at Matyana. In the mêlée that followed, some thirty unarmed Zulu were killed, but Matyana lived to tell the tale of John's treachery that would forever blight his name in the eyes of the Zulu people. John's present choice as a member of the Commission was perhaps a mistake, but to make matters worse it was he who had accepted the task of verbally delivering the ultimatum, which he duly did, in lengthy sententious style, to Cetshwayo's deputation on the banks of the Tugela River.

It is unlikely that Cetshwayo himself was immediately made aware of the full requirements of the ultimatum, his indunas delivering the bad news in gradual doses. Certainly the written copy, which had been entrusted to John Dunn, Cetshwayo's white adviser, never reached the Zulu king and was never read to him. Consequently, Cetshwayo was very perplexed; he had been awarded a good slice of the Disputed Territories but was being ordered to comply with the most outrageous demands that he could not understand and that would be quite impossible to fulfil. He had no argument with Natal or the British, and had initially found it difficult to take the ultimatum seriously. But as his requests for clarification and more time were rejected out of hand by the British (who more often than not bound and imprisoned his emissaries), he began to grow alarmed as the deadline rapidly drew closer. He summoned his council and whereas a number of chiefs, including his royal brother Hamu (Oham), were in favour of handing over Sihayo's sons and paying the fine of 600 head of cattle, the majority, including Cetshwayo himself, would only agree to parting with the cattle, in the mistaken belief that the British would be pacified if they did so.

Hoping to persuade his people that the fine was a national responsibility, Cetshwayo appealed to the chiefs to help assemble a herd, but his appeal went unheeded – Zulus were in the business of acquiring cattle, not giving them away. If the king wanted them to fight, that was a different matter, but if he wanted to give away cattle, he had better get them from Sihayo as it was his sons who were the cause of the trouble. (There is evidence that a portion of the required herd had been gathered together but were lifted by Buller, close to Sihayo's kraal, on the day the ultimatum expired.)

Having had no success in cajoling his people to contribute towards the fine, Cetshwayo issued a royal command for his regiments to assemble. Within a few days close on 35,000 warriors had responded and stood under orders at Ondini. Any chance of a negotiated peace passed and Cetshwayo, reluctantly, was ready for war.

*   *   *

Once he had assisted his commander safely across the border, Wood retraced the wet and rutted track back to Bemba's Kop. He was not to advance further for a few days yet; Pearson, with No. 1 Column at the coast, needed to make up some distance before all three columns could obtain the cohesion that Chelmsford's invasion plan required. But Wood could find plenty to occupy his troops. Cattle raiding was not only effective but lucrative. During the last few days, the mounted men under Buller had scooped up hundreds of beasts to add to the large herd already captured. To the enemy it was devastating; cattle were, at one and the same time, the common currency and the means of reckoning wealth. Without cattle it was impossible to live a normal daily life, to buy a wife or to earn respect. Without this self-replenishing wealth, a man was impoverished and stripped of pride and status. Each beast was named and its unique coloration memorised so that in a herd of hundreds, any single animal could be recognised and called by name. The ultimate indulgence of the rich and of the king himself was the breeding of single-colour herds. The greatest pleasure of Cetshwayo and of his predecessors was to have the white cattle of the monarch, numbered in their thousands, driven past the admiring royal gaze.

By the time Wood and the infantry had returned to the base at Bemba's Kop, Buller and his men had assembled a gigantic herd of over 2500 captured beasts and had illustrated to the enemy how easy it was for horsemen to raid and steal their cattle.

To the north, on Wood's left flank, and between twenty to forty miles from Bemba's Kop, there still remained the strongholds of Manyanyoba, Mbelini and, even more formidable, the mountain fortress of Hlobane with its abaQulusi warrior clan, commanded by Chief Seketwayo, all unsubdued and fiercely belligerent. Of the 2500 cattle in Wood's possession, about 2000 had been lifted from the abaQulusi, and of those a great number were royal beasts belonging to Cetshwayo – it being common practice for the king to farm out his herds to where the grazing was plentiful. Wood had a strategy of blackmail in mind: he had Seketwayo's cattle which he would give back if Seketwayo, in return, surrendered and entered into a pact of non-hostility. The same offer was made to Manyanyoba. Messages had been sent proposing these terms and Wood demanded an urgent answer. But Seketwayo was faced with a fearful dilemma: he had lost the royal cattle, which could bring fearful consequences upon his head; he could, however, get them back simply by defecting to the British, which could result in even more dreadful repercussions. It was a dilemma to which he could find no answer – but it was an answer for which Wood was prepared to wait no longer, as the captured cattle were consuming grazing required by his transport oxen. Abruptly, Wood made up his mind and the great herd was set in motion for the Orange Free State where it was sold to the contractors. With it went any possibility of further negotiations with the abaQulusi. On the summit of Hlobane, the Painted Mountain, the abaQulusi sat and waited; they had a score to settle with 'Somtseu's Impi' and they would shortly have the opportunity of doing so.

Aware of the danger that now existed to his left flank, Wood determined, while he had time in hand, to clear the strongholds of Hlobane and its two allied fortresses – a task so formidable that had he attempted it his force would never have recovered to take an effective part in the invasion. He was, however, spared the attempt for the time being by the disaster which befell Chelmsford's column three days later.

Instead Wood marched purposefully north to get to grips with the abaQulusi, and to establish another camp on the banks of the White Umfolosi River at a crossing called Tinta's Kop.

As stealing cattle seemed to guarantee a reaction from the enemy, Wood again sent Buller and his men raiding, this time deep into the hills at the western end of Hlobane. They climbed the Zunguin range, lifting cattle all the way until they encountered a large force of abaQulusi several hundred strong. Close to being surrounded, Buller, excelling in leadership, managed to extract his small force and retreat. It was also the infantry's turn for an outing: led by Wood, a contingent of the 90th Light Infantry following in Buller's tracks set out to join forces with the horsemen. Marching most of the night they began to ascend the Zunguin in the early morning, pushing hundreds of warriors before them and taking cattle as they went. At last they reached a ridge from which they could overlook the plain at the western end of Hlobane, and there they saw a sight that none would ever forget – the enemy below treating them to a spectacular display of precision drill. Until this time there was hardly a British soldier who had seen more of the enemy than distant skirmishers. Every one of them had, of course, heard of the supposed discipline of the Zulu army but it was assumed to be all a bit of a myth. They would now appreciate that, far from being a myth, Zulu discipline had been understated.

Below, drawn up in companies that were distinguished by the colours and patterns of their cowhide shields, were 4000 warriors who, to the intrigued and astounded gaze of the British audience, marched and counter-marched, per-forming manoeuvres that would have done credit to a passing-out parade at Aldershot. Having witnessed much to ponder, Wood and his men withdrew from the mountain, taking their booty of cattle with them.

Within the last week or so, including the 2500 already sent to the Orange Free State, the raiding had netted almost 7000 beasts – a feat that would earn the FLH the dubious sobriquet of 'The Cattle Catchers'. There was an element of envy in the nickname, which had been coined by the men of No. 3 Column, for Buller and Wood had acquired the reputation of sharp dealers when disposing of their booty to the contractors. They would argue and haggle until they got the best price going – unlike some of the officers of No. 3 Column who were inept when it came to bargaining; their men complained that the captured cattle were sold to the butchers at thirty shillings a head and bought back by the column contractors at £18 a head, and that the men who made the captures 'did not get a sovereign as their share [of the booty] at the end of the campaign'.

Later that day, sitting around a campfire below Hlobane, Wood and his officers heard the ominous sound of distant cannon fire. The noise had travelled through the quiet and immensity of the African night from Isandlwana fifty miles away. Everyone cocked their heads and listened. Then the brief gunfire abruptly ceased. There was an immediate discussion and Wood was questioned as to the possible meaning of the barrage. He replied, simply, that guns fired after dark indicated an unfavourable situation – a realistic assessment, though immensely understated. At the moment when the guns were fired, Chelmsford, and what remained of No. 3 Column, stood horrified in the darkness amidst the death and destruction of what had been their camp. Only days earlier Chelmsford, in his over-confidence, had written '. . . by this plan we shall oblige Cetshwayo to keep his forces together . . . and . . . we shall oblige him to attack us which shall save us the trouble of going to find him'. Cetshwayo had indeed obliged and in little more than an hour had slaughtered more than 1300 men of Chelmsford's column.

1. Rowlands had won his Victoria Cross twenty years earlier at the battle of Inkerman, when he had led 100 men of the 41st Regiment in a charge against 1000 Russian soldiers.
2. A letter from Major Cornelius Francis Clery to his friend Major General Sir Archibald Alison, Chief of British Army Intelligence at the War Office.
3. Wolseley succeeded where Rowlands failed; the forces at his command, however, 1400 British infantry, 400 colonial horse and 10,000 Swazi warriors, far exceeded the number of Rowlands's troops.
4. Named after the town in Holland.
5. Other prominent burghers who had attended the meeting and supported its proposals were A.H. Labuschagne, P. Kempt, L. Meyer, N. Smuts, R.J. van Rooyen, C. Maritz, L. Viljoen, J.W. Ferreira, P. van Reenen and Cornelius van Rooyen.
6. In order to be as independent as possible and avoid being held to ransom by unscrupulous owners, Wood had advocated the purchase rather than hire of transport. It is interesting to note that only 20 percent of the wagons and oxen in his column were hired whereas Rowlands hired over 80 percent of his transport.

2

ISANDLWANA

'It was the most horrid sight that was ever seen by a soldier.'
Pte Patrick Farrell, 2/24th Regiment

The battle of Isandlwana has been described in great detail in a number of works. For several reasons it is necessary to outline it once again. Without a description of the battle it is not possible to understand its crushing impact on British morale, which in turn may explain the adverse behaviour of certain officers two months later at the battle of Hlobane. There is also new evidence on the battle itself to offer. Among the 'Sir Evelyn Wood Papers' at the Killie Campbell Afrikaner Library, Durban, there are copies of two letters written by Inspector George Mansel, who commanded the Natal Mounted Police at Isandlwana, which throw new light on events and on the conduct of Lord Chelmsford and his staff. In addition there are two maps of the battlefield which show the intended route of the Zulu attack (to have been delivered the morning after the actual battle) as being around the rear of the Isandlwana Hill, and not the frontal assault which actually took place. The maps also show that on the night preceding the battle, the Zulu army was not camped *en masse* in a gorge on the northern side of the Nqutu Plateau, but was bivouacked, in regiments, over a distance of about four miles, all along the Nqutu Hills and that the regiments attacked in the same strung-out line as that in which they were bivouacked. This would explain how the Zulu army appeared with such speed, already fanned out four miles wide, to encircle the camp.

The papers contained in the Wood File are a lifetime's collection of letters, documents, drawings and photographs of people, places and events that were of especial interest to their owner – in some respects it was a 'For My Eyes Only' file. From its contents dealing with the Zulu War, it becomes plain that although Wood was a friend and a protégé of Chelmsford's, he doubted his commander's ability. Also, Wood did not believe the blame for the disaster of Isandlwana lay with Colonel Anthony Durnford whom Chelmsford had elected as principal scapegoat. Wood, in fact, supplied Colonel Edward Durnford, Anthony's father, with information that would enable him to put together the true sequence of events and assist in clearing his son's name. Arthur Durnford, Anthony's brother, in turn, gave copies of Inspector Mansel's letters to Wood.

* * *

The dawn at Rorke's Drift on 11 January 1879 was dull and the countryside damp with heavy mist. The bugles had sounded at 2.00 am and Lord Chelmsford, with No. 3 Column, was ready to cross the swollen Buffalo River; a formidable task for almost 5000 men, as many oxen, and all the equipment of an army. The six 7-pounder cannons of the Royal Artillery unlimbered on a rise on the Natal bank, which on a clear day commanded the opposite shore, and the gunners peered into the enveloping gloom.

The volunteer horsemen were first into the water, led by the Natal Mounted Police closely followed by the Natal Carbineers, the Buffalo Border Guard and the Newcastle Mounted Rifles. As they waded over on to the Zulu bank, they formed up and scouted forward into the mist. The men of the Royal Engineers had been busy throughout the night working on the pontoons with their complexities of cables, ropes and pulleys. Now close behind the horsemen, the first of the infantry, the 24th Regiment, stepped ashore with dry boots and in double time were drawn up in squares – formations designed to receive charging enemy cavalry – the very same formations that Wellington's soldiers had taken up when engaging Napoleon's horsemen at Waterloo.

There was too much congestion at the drift itself; and the officers of the 2500-strong Natal Native Contingent led their men upstream to another, but narrower drift. There the men linked arms, forming two human chains from bank to bank, through which their comrades waded, neck deep in places, making an indescribable din of high-pitched, bee-like buzzing, to keep away the crocodiles.

Before 7.00 am the last of the NNC were ashore. They joined the cavalry in forming a protective line along the ridge above the crossing place, while the men of the 24th set up camp below them. Long before it was light, Chelmsford, with a strong cavalry escort, had set off to rendezvous with Wood. By mid-afternoon he had returned, the camp was taking shape and there was no sign of any opposition.

Not far away, lying adjacent to the route that Chelmsford intended to take to Ulundi, was the stronghold of none other than Chief Sihayo. As it could be said that he and his sons were partly responsible for the war, it would be a seemly lesson to inflict punishment upon him. So once again the whole column was awakened in the dead of the night. Leaving a reserve to guard the camp, the remainder marched off to set about Sihayo. Although he and his eldest son, Mehlokazulu, had already left for Ulundi, there were enough of his clan and family remaining to put up a fight. It would be good experience for the troops and an inexpensive introduction to enemy fire.

Sihayo's people had a number of elephant guns that fired all sorts of missiles, including pot-legs, which one soldier contended could do as much damage as a 9-pounder cannon. These frightening missiles kept the infantry at bay for a while, but it was not much of a battle. Eventually, the core of resistance had to be smoked out by choking the entrance to their cave with burning scrub. At the end of the brief engagement, during which the NNC showed a marked reluctance to fight, Sihayo's village was burnt, the goats and cattle confiscated and the inhabitants taken temporary prisoner. A head count of Zulu casualties showed twenty enemy dead, one of whom was Mkumbikazulu, the other of Sihayo's sons named in the ultimatum as a wanted man. It was a satisfactory conclusion to the first skirmish on Zulu soil and as a reward the troops were given the following day off to recuperate and attend to kit repairs.

It was Chelmsford's plan to set up a number of fortified posts along his intended route to Ulundi. After a scouting expedition by the Mounted Infantry led by Lieutenant Colonel John Cecil Russell, it was decided that the first post would be at Isipezi Hill (Siphezi) about twenty miles east of Rorke's Drift. As the track was encumbered with some boggy ground that would take the engineers several days to make passable, orders were given to set up an intermediate camp. The site chosen was at the foot of a strangely shaped hill which looked as though a giant had once carved it into the likeness of a lion, now reduced by the elements and time to nothing more than a crumbling impression of a resting beast. The name of the hill was Isandlwana and its highest end was linked by a shallow neck to a large stone kopje (hill). Half a mile to the north, Isandlwana was dominated by the Nqutu range of hills that stretched away towards Babanango and the track to distant Ulundi.

As an intermediate campsite Isandlwana had the advantages of firm ground, a plentiful supply of drinking water, good grazing and firewood. It also had some serious drawbacks: it was dominated by the Nqutu Plateau and, unless constantly patrolled, the broken ground behind the hill could provide excellent cover for a stealthy enemy.

It was not until 20 January, eight days after the destruction of Sihayo's kraal, that the track to Isandlwana was made passable for the column's advance.

The first to arrive were the scouts of the Natal Mounted Police and the irregular horse who accompanied one of the column's principal staff officers, Major Clery. They were led by Inspector George Mansel of the NMP, an experienced soldier who had been the first officer to be appointed to the force on its foundation five years earlier. He and Clery rode over the nek on to the eastern base of Isandlwana, from where they could see Isipezi Hill in the distance. Clery, who had once been Professor of Tactics at the British Army Staff College, decided that the site where they stood 'would do'. Mansel replied that he did not like it one bit, pointing out how the ground was commanded by the stone kopje and by the shoulder of Isandlwana itself. Clery repeated tetchily that 'it would do' and sent Mansel off to post vedettes. This task took until well into the afternoon with Mansel placing his men, two to a vedette, high up on the summit of the Nqutu Hills from where they would be able to survey an approach from whatever side, and most important, any movement from the direction of Ulundi. With the task almost completed, he was recalled by a fellow officer who said that Clery wanted him back in camp immediately. Having presented himself to Clery, Mansel was asked to indicate the positions of his vedettes, whereupon Clery declared that they were no use three to five miles out and especially the vedette at the rear of Isandlwana. A brief confrontation followed as Mansel pointed to the broken ground behind the hill and the possibility of an attack coming from that direction. But Clery had his way, declaring that the vedettes were useless where they were: 'the rear always protecting itself'.

He then ordered Mansel to draw his vedettes in closer. With reluctance, Mansel rode again to the crest of the Nqutu Hills from where he had a splendid view of the camp spreading across the plain below like a peace-time army preparing for manoeuvres in Hampshire. Mansel was not the only officer who was unhappy at the way sensible precautions were being ignored. Major Dunbar of the 24th, a veteran of the Crimean War and the Indian Mutiny, also expressed his concern about the unguarded rear of the hill, only to be told by another offensive staff officer that if he was nervous his men could be replaced by native pioneers. Sub-Inspector F. L. Phillips, also of the NMP, who was colonial born and an experienced frontiersman, went directly to Chelmsford's private secretary and impressed upon him the danger of the undefended and broken ground behind the hill. Chelmsford's reply was, 'Tell the police officer my troops will do all the attacking but, even if the enemy does venture to attack, the hill he complains about will serve to protect our rear.' Lieutenant Teignmouth Melvill, who would earn the Victoria Cross the following day, bluntly told another member of Chelmsford's staff, 'These Zulu will charge home and with our small numbers we ought to be in laager, or, at any rate, be prepared to stand shoulder to shoulder.' But the staff were satisfied with their own arrangements and were pleased that there was room for the camp to spread out, seeing no fault in it sprawling along the base of the hill for three-quarters of a mile.

Thirty wagons were still stuck down the track toward Rorke's Drift whilst the remaining 190, containing among other things almost 450,000 rounds of Martini Henry ammunition, were mostly parked on the nek over half a mile away from the further end of the camp; and, around and about, grazed upward of 3000 oxen and cattle. As one officer said later, '... the camp was no more defensible than an English village'. There was a standing order, issued by Chelmsford himself a few weeks prior to crossing the Buffalo, that every camp must be laagered; ie the wagons had to be formed into a defensive circle or square. The wisdom of this precaution had been hammered home to Chelmsford by the veteran Boers, whose use of laagered wagons in their encounters with the Zulu army had turned death and defeat into victory on a number of occasions. Only four days earlier Chelmsford had received a visit, at Rorke's Drift, from Mr J.J. Uys, elder brother of Piet Uys, and a member of Andries Pretorius's commando which had fought at

Blood River forty years before. 'Be on your guard and be careful. Place your spies out, and form your wagons into a laager,' he had advised. Similar advice had been given by Willem Landman and Gert De Jager, both experienced men of the frontier. But Chelmsford had ignored both his own instructions and the burghers' advice for he was anxious to move on and laagering took time: he had been in Zululand for almost two weeks and his column had hardly seen a Zulu. However, had Clery left the vedettes where Mansel had placed them, they might already have glimpsed the vanguard of the Zulu army, for it was at that moment, 25,000 strong, not twelve miles away to the north of Isipezi Hill.

Four days earlier, after Cetshwayo had killed 120 head of cattle for it to feast upon, the Zulu army had begun its leisurely march from Ondini. By the same hour on the morrow its commanders, Chiefs Ntshingwayo and Mavumengwana, intended to be poised in the Nqutu Hills directly above the British camp.

Chelmsford had his own plans for the following day. Before dawn on 21 January he dispatched a large reconnaissance force, consisting of 1500 men of the NNC, under the command of Commandant Rupert Lonsdale, and 150 mounted men under the command of Major John Dartnell of the Natal Mounted Police, in two separate columns, east toward the Mangeni Falls. The Zulu army and Dartnell's force passed each other, travelling in opposite directions, and approximately five miles apart. The bulk of the Zulu army, beyond the ridge of hills, went undetected but a flanking force of warriors, about 800 strong, were encountered by Dartnell's men at about 10.00 am, while Lonsdale was five miles distant to the south. The Zulus were 'very anxious to fight' but Dartnell was not going to engage so large a force unsupported and the longer he watched the enemy the more difficult it became to estimate their numbers with any accuracy. Dartnell believed it imperative that he should not mislead Chelmsford with a slipshod calculation of the enemy's strength, but there was little that could be done except watch and wait until reinforced.

By early evening Lonsdale and his men, who had spent a wretched day thrashing around in thick country, arrived tired, hungry and despondent but in sufficient numbers to give Dartnell the support he needed. As the sun was going down, Inspector Mansel was ordered to take forty men and provoke the enemy into revealing its strength.

The Zulu warriors swarmed forward throwing out their flanks to encircle the mounted men, but refrained from firing, seemingly intent on capturing their enemies. Mansel, in his anxiety to see their numbers, almost stayed too long and was nearly caught. As he and his men galloped away, they were hotly pursued by racing warriors who only turned back when they encountered Dartnell and the rest of the mounted men drawn up across their path. A strange engagement – not a shot had been fired.

It was jointly decided by Dartnell and Lonsdale to bivouac where they were so that in the morning they could keep track of the enemy and a message was sent to

Chelmsford asking for two companies of infantry to support a morning attack.

Dartnell's reports were not the only ones to be received by Chelmsford that evening. All indicated Zulu forces in the vicinity of Isipezi Hill, close to Dartnell's bivouac. Chelmsford became convinced that the Zulu army, or at least a large impi, was located there. In fact, a report sent in early in the day by one of Lonsdale's colonial officers (based on information obtained after torturing two young Zulus who were playing truant from their regiment to visit their mother) confirmed that the Zulu army was in the immediate area.

For the mounted men and the NNC, it would be a long night as they tried to settle down to a cold and hungry vigil. They formed a square: the NNC on three sides, the troopers on the other with the horses tethered in the middle. There was no moon and as the darkness intensified so did the imaginings and fears of the men increase. There would be many false alarms before the welcome dawn appeared.

At Isandlwana, the camp stood to in the early hours of the morning and at first light Chelmsford led out along the track toward Isipezi Hill with approximately half his command. Instead of sending just the two companies of infantry that Dartnell had requested, Chelmsford had decided that there was every chance of engaging the main Zulu army if he marched fast. He would meet it with four of his six cannons, his mounted infantry, six companies of infantry and a contingent of native pioneers. The men were in light marching order, carrying one day's rations and seventy rounds of ammunition each. By early morning they had reached Dartnell at his bivouac.

Unlike the British, the Zulu army, on that morning of 22 January, was inactive. The previous day it had completed its march through the hills and was now encamped, in regiments strung out for about four miles, along the Nqutu Plateau above Isandlwana, from where its scouts could survey the camp and the whole route of Chelmsford's march. It was completely concealed by the Nqutu ridge but would have been easily visible to Mansel's vedettes had they not been withdrawn by Clery's order.

Once Chelmsford had left, those of his force who remained at Isandlwana also looked forward to a day of relative inactivity, and the camp seemed quiet and empty. Seventy men of the Royal Artillery, with two guns, had stayed behind, as had thirty of the Mounted Infantry, eighty mounted volunteers (including some men of the NMP), five companies of the 1/24th Regiment, one of the 2/24th, four companies of the NNC and fifty men of the staff such as engineers, hospital orderlies and army service corps: a total of 856 white officers and men and approximately 400 native troops, all under the command of Lieutenant Colonel Henry Pulleine of the 24th Regiment. They had a camp to defend with an all-round perimeter of about two miles, which had neither entrenchments, laager or redoubt. It was cluttered with hundreds of tents, equipment, kitchens, and had several thousand grazing beasts milling around. But there was no feeling of apprehension for if there was going to be any fighting it would fall to the lot of Chelmsford's column which had marched off looking for trouble.

Chelmsford was certainly not perturbed at leaving his vulnerable camp when guarded, as it was, by British infantry. He had formed an opinion, as far back as November, that the Zulu army would cringe at their first experience of British fire power. 'I am inclined to think,' he had written, 'that the first experience of the power of the Martini Henry [rifle] will be such a surprise to the Zulus that they will not be formidable after the first effort.' A contention that would that day be put to test and a bitter lesson learned. Before he rode off toward Isipezi Hill, Chelmsford's military secretary, Colonel Crealock, had sent a note to Colonel Anthony William Durnford, who commanded what remained of a very depleted No. 2 Column, ordering him to march to Isandlwana.[1] Durnford's force was not great in number but, in addition to his 300 native infantry, he had a trump card in 250 men of the crack Natal Native Horse who were, black or white, second to none. He also had a Royal Artillery rocket battery (of dubious effectiveness) carried by mules and operated by one officer and nine gunners. By early morning, with the NNH leading, Durnford was on his way to Isandlwana.

The battle started in a dilatory manner. Soon after Chelmsford had departed, Colonel Pulleine began the daily routine of deploying his troops. 'G' company of the 2/24th, by far the strongest of the rifle companies, comprising about 110 officers and men, was ordered out almost a mile from the camp, in the same direction as taken by Chelmsford, to where a deep donga (dry river gully) formed a natural defensive position. Once there, the men were positioned on the camp side of the donga, in groups of four, ninety yards apart. To their left, 200 men of the NNC continued the defensive line to the base of the Nqutu foothills. Another company of the NNC was posted further up into the Nqutu Hills overlooking the camp, while various mounted vedettes gazed into the distance with little expectation of seeing anything of interest.

Breakfast time arrived but was disrupted by a galloping trooper from one of the vedettes bringing news of a large Zulu force sitting up in the Nqutu Hills. The bugle was sounded and the whole camp fell to arms with the two 7-pounder guns of the Royal Artillery being run out to the centre of the infantry line. It was a thin and ragged defensive screen with spaces to be filled, but there seemed to be no cause for concern. Pulleine sent a brief message to Chelmsford advising him of what had been seen. After a while it appeared to have been a false alarm and as there was no further news from the vedette the troops were stood down and breakfast was resumed.

A little later, several disconcerting incidents occurred; another vedette came in to report the sighting of a large impi moving beyond them to the north-west; then the camp came under observation from a group of Zulus silhouetted against the skyline on the crest of the hills. Thereafter distant firing was heard, but because of the re-echoing, it was difficult to discern the exact direction.

At ten o'clock Durnford and his column arrived, having hurried up from Rorke's Drift. Pulleine, who was junior in service to Durnford, did not hesitate to put himself and his men under Durnford's command. Whilst the two officers sat down to discuss the situation another message arrived, brought in by Lieutenant Adendorff, but his report of Zulu movements was garbled and difficult to understand. Durnford dismissed him and sent the two troops of Sikali's Horse from his own NNH, led by Captain George Shepstone[2] and Lieutenant Charles Raw, to scout the hills above.[3]

What, of course, had been seen by the various vedettes were the tail-enders of the Zulu army and various foraging parties picking up cattle.

Shepstone and Raw had not long departed on their mission when yet another message was brought down from the Nqutu Hills stating that a large impi was heading eastward. It now seemed apparent to Durnford that these Zulu forces were intent on attacking Chelmsford's column in the rear. Firing was again heard from the hills, which was assumed to be the NNH encountering the impi.

Durnford listened for some time but the shooting was not resumed and he decided to seek the enemy and cut him off before he could strike at Chelmsford's rear. Being senior to Pulleine, Durnford could have ordered a couple of companies of the 24th out with him, but although he made the suggestion, he was satisfied when Pulleine told him that his strict orders were to defend the camp and that his whole force was required for that purpose.[4] In fact Pulleine was beginning to wonder if the troops under his command were adequate. A particular worry was the outpost of the NNC which was still isolated up on a shoulder of the hills above the camp, with every indication of there being Zulu in that vicinity. If they should come down in any force it would take more than 100 men of the NNC with ten guns to stop them. Pulleine, therefore, ordered 'A' company of the 1/24th to march almost a mile up into the hills and reinforce the NNC outpost. At the same time Durnford instructed Shepstone and Raw, with their NNH, to pursue the impi along the plateau while he, with the rest of the NNH and the rocket battery, went forward with the intention of heading off the impi and catching it between his force and Shepstone's troopers.

Shepstone was not having much success; there was no sign of the impi and the horsemen split up. Raw and a few troopers went off to the north-east where they began to overtake a herder driving cattle towards a ravine. Raw followed in hot pursuit but frantically reined in at the edge of the drop. There below him, silent and ominous, was the enemy he sought – the Zulu army of 25,000 men. In fact, Raw had almost ridden into the bivouac of the Umcityu (umCijo), a regiment of twenty-eight-year-old warriors, 2500 strong. Chelmsford had been thoroughly duped; led ever further away from the camp by the same skilful decoy of skirmishing warriors who had encountered Dartnell the previous day, they were now engaging Chelmsford's force in will-o'-the-wisp manoeuvres.

Raw and his handful of men bravely fired a volley into the stirring Umcityu,

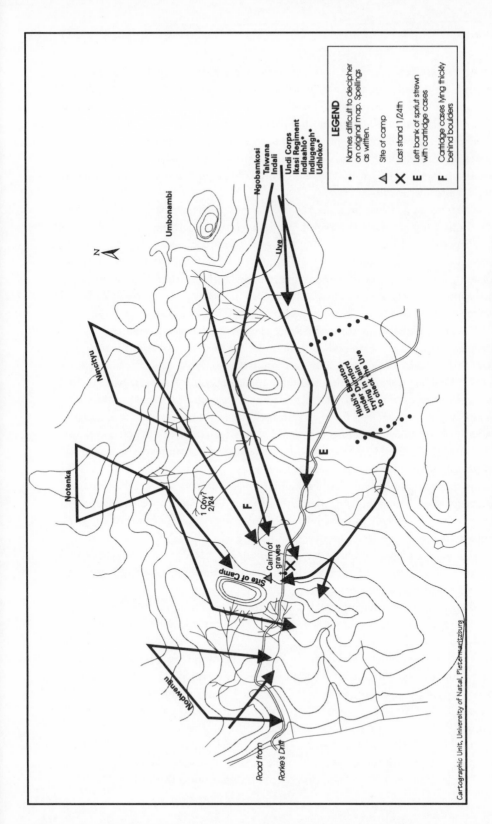

Cartographic Unit, University of Natal, Pietermaritzburg

2. THE ZULU ATTACK AT ISANDLWANA
(Caption on facing page)

who rose up with a roar of anger. The Zulu army had not intended fighting, for their plan was to rest and do battle the next day. Now discovered, however, they were committed to immediate action. All along the plateau the regiments snatched up their arms and trotted forward, getting into order as they went, forming an arc of skirmishing warriors four miles wide above the British camp.

Raw's troopers galloped back, charging down upon Shepstone and the rest of the patrol. For a moment they all paused and gazed at the savage but magnificent sight of the advancing Zulu army. Shepstone's first thought was for Durnford whom he knew to be riding straight into the advancing regiments and was now in great peril. He dispatched three troopers of the Natal Carbineers, who had been on vedette duty, spurring away to find and warn him. Then, ordering Raw and the NNH to do whatever was possible to delay the Zulu advance, he left to take the dread news to the camp. Raw and his men dismounted and fired several volleys into the advancing enemy but to no effect. On his way down from the plateau, Shepstone shouted the alarming news to 'A' Company who had now arrived at the NNC outpost a mile above the camp, and then raced on, arriving at Pulleine's tent shaken and breathless. At Isipezi Hill, Chelmsford, by now tired of trying to come to grips with the elusive enemy, and convinced that the Zulu army was nowhere in the vicinity, had ridden off with his staff to select the next campsite. When this was done, and breakfast taken, he ordered one of his special service officers, Captain Alan Gardner of the 14th Hussars, to ride back to Isandlwana and order Pulleine to dismantle the camp and transport it to the new site above the Mangeni Falls near to Isipezi Hill. Chelmsford also ordered Commandant Hamilton-Browne, with a company of Lonsdale's NNC (who had not eaten for thirty-six hours), to start marching back to Isandlwana to assist in dismantling the camp. When Hamilton-Browne asked what he should do if he encountered the enemy on the way he was told to 'just brush them aside and go on'.

Caption to Map 2 (on facing page): When Colonel Sir Evelyn Wood returned to South Africa in 1880, some months after the conclusion of the Anglo-Zulu War, he investigated, for his own satisfaction and curiosity, a number of controversial issues concerning the course of the recent conflict. One such issue was the blame that had been put upon Colonel Anthony Durnford for the defeat of the British forces at the Battle of Isandlwana. Consequently, Wood interrogated on the battle site a number of Zulu warriors who had fought there, writing various remarks onto maps of the area. His evidence indicated that had the Zulu army attacked the following day as it originally intended, there is little doubt that its main thrust would have been the unguarded route behind Isandlwana Hill and over the nek into the British camp. Wood's information further indicated that, in the event, the Zulu attacked exactly as they bivouacked – all in a line of regiments. Wood forwarded his maps to Durnford's father who was attempting to clear his son's name. The facing map is based on Wood's sketches. (Author's collection)

Captain Gardner and Captain Shepstone arrived at Pulleine's tent together, but how different the tidings they bore.

Shepstone, waving wildly toward the plateau whence heavy firing could now be heard, blurted out his news to the astounded Pulleine who was still holding Chelmsford's order to strike camp. What should he do? Gardner came to his aid by advising him to ignore Chelmsford's order as it was written without any knowledge of the peril that now existed.

The alarm was sounded and once again the men hastened to grab their weapons and equipment. But Pulleine had failed to comprehend that it was not an impi of a couple of thousand men, but the whole Zulu army that was about to descend on the camp, and he diluted whatever strength he had by pushing his companies further out where they were most vulnerable. Worst of all, instead of bringing in 'A' Company and the NNC from their isolated perch he reinforced them by sending the eighty men of 'F' Company doubling away up the hill. Their arrival at the outpost coincided with that of Raw and his troopers who were being closely followed by a surging wall of warriors. At about 600 yards, the infantry and troopers opened fire, whilst the NNC, having fired their fifty rounds, turned and fled back to the camp – and who could blame them? Further away to the left, there was another chilling sight; several Zulu regiments were descending around the back of Isandlwana Hill which would bring them, unobserved, into the rear of the British camp.

Sustained volley fire by the men of 'A' and 'F' companies was now dropping many warriors as they advanced, but it had no effect whatsoever in halting or diverting the enemy. It was clear that within minutes the infantry and troopers, if they did not move, would be overwhelmed by odds of perhaps twenty to one. Firing steadily, the little force began to withdraw toward the camp where no one seemed yet to have grasped that the whole Zulu army was fast approaching – so much so that messages sent to Chelmsford, by both Pulleine and Gardner, merely mentioned heavy firing and fighting a mile away from the camp (Gardner actually reported Shepstone as having remarked that 'the Zulus are falling back'). Therefore, when the messages got through and were taken by one of Chelmsford's staff officers, they were read without any sense of urgency or alarm.

Accompanied by the Hlubi and Edendale troops of the NNH, Durnford had set off at a brisk canter, eager to get to grips with the enemy. He had every faith, as well he might, in the quality and skill of his native horsemen. Each man, armed with a carbine, a bandolier of ammunition, knobkerrie and quiver of throwing spears, made a formidable foe and, unlike the Bantu of the NNC, their courage would never be held to question – indeed their valour would be an example to all. In his haste Durnford had left the rocket battery far behind and unescorted except for a company of NNC who, on foot, were lagging even further back. For some reason the battery had not followed in Durnford's tracks, but instead had turned sharply up into the foothills of the Nqutu Plateau. Being higher up, the battery was first to encounter the advancing Zulu army; there was only time to load and fire one rocket, which had not the slightest effect before the Zulu, in an over-whelming mass, were in their midst stabbing the gunners and mules. Such was the crush and the eagerness of the warriors to pursue the men of the NCC, who had fled at the first sight of the enemy, that three gunners, although trampled upon and left for dead, lived to tell the tale.

Durnford received Shepstone's warning moments before the enemy came in sight and at a glance realised with what he had to contend. Forming a line across the Zulu path, the NNH retired in good order, firing volley after volley into the packed lines of warriors until they reached a deep donga about a mile from the camp. Here they dismounted, and with adequate cover for both men and horses, set up such a withering fire that the left horn of the Zulu army was sent tumbling to cover. The remnants of the other mounted units, which had remained in camp, rode forward to join them. They had found themselves a good position, but it could only be held as long as their ammunition lasted. Being mounted troops, they carried only fifty rounds apiece in their bandoliers.

By this time the main line of British Infantry, still strung out with the men yards apart, were firing steadily and had stopped the centre of the Zulu advance at 400 yards. 'A' and 'F' companies had got safely back from the hills and Shepstone and his horsemen now formed part of the firing line. Next to them the two cannons of the Royal Artillery had taken up a position in the centre of the infantry. When the gunners had first opened fire they had torn gaps through the enemy ranks, but the warriors were quick to notice that a moment before the cannons fired, the gunners stepped back to avoid the recoil. Now the artillery had little effect, for as soon as the gunners moved, so the warriors opened a path in front of the pointing guns and the rounds passed harmlessly through their ranks. The ineffectiveness of the artillery had caused little concern in the British ranks; the men of the 24th had laughed and shouted as they fired one crushing volley after another and stopped the Zulu army in its tracks. Now something was amiss.

Unnoticed, the angry mass of black warriors had crept closer, emitting a strange, ominous humming sound. Yet, still, the soldiers knew that imperial volley fire would win the day and they scrabbled in their pouches to find another round. Up and down the line, with mounting apprehension, men were turning to seek the ammunition carriers or beg a few rounds from a mate. Close on 1000 men had been firing steadily for half an hour, getting away something in the order of three rounds per minute. Some 70,000 rounds had been fired, and if the enemy was to be held, 70,000 rounds would have to be replaced. One unit estimated its rate of fire at much more than three rounds per minute – 'after the first flush of excitement, each man poured in eighteen shots a minute with deadly effect'; at three or eighteen shots per sixty seconds, seventy rounds would not last long and the reserve ammunition, in the wagons, was almost a mile away from the far left of the British line.[5] The officers had long since sent runners to bring back supplies but clearly there was a problem. A recent standing order required the securing screw to the lid of the reserve ammunition boxes to be removed. This had not been done and now the quartermasters were finding great difficulty in getting the boxes open – so much so that men were attempting to smash the lids apart with any implement that came to hand. However, the boxes had been made to withstand the rigours of rough campaigning: constructed of one-inch teak or mahogany planking dovetailed together and bound with copper bands for added strength, there was only one way in, and that was via the tongue and grooved lid secured by a two-inch brass countersunk screw. (There was a theory that the lid could be removed by a heavy kick or blow with a rock, but that was nonsense put out by the War Office following the disaster of Isandlwana and after a new, quick release device had replaced the two-inch screw. Two years later, in 1881, the War Office stated '. . . the sliding lid was secured by a brass screw, which had to be unscrewed before the lid could be opened. It was found that on service this occasioned loss of time and even more serious consequences.')

For present purposes, therefore, the only way to open the lid was either with a screwdriver – and not enough of these were available – or after a succession of blows with a heavy implement. Once opened, it would take two men to lift a box and it was a daunting task to carry it further than a couple of hundred yards. The contents were jealously guarded by the quartermasters and only passed out to members of their own units. A number of soldiers who survived the battle would vividly remember the frantic efforts to get into the ammunition. 'Artillery men were trying to break open the cases on the wagons . . . but it was too late': 'The boxes in which it was packed were all screwed down and we had no tools to open them'; 'I noticed Quartermaster London of the Natal Carbineers, opening one of these boxes and he was killed by a bullet in the head while doing so'. Even the Zulu commented on the failure of the enemy ammunition supply: 'The British became helpless, because they had no ammunition and the Zulus killed them . . . we searched the pouches of the men, some had a few cartridges, most had none at all. . . .'

With 450,000 rounds in the camp, the firing line and the mounted men who had rallied to Durnford ran out of ammunition. The thundering volleys of only minutes ago were reduced to a feeble crackle and the Zulu army that had suffered such fearful punishment rose up with a sound of fury – 'Zu-Zu-Zu-Zu' – and set about the slaughter of the red soldiers.

The companies of the NNC fled as the maddened warriors came charging through the puny line of defenders who, too late, were attempting to reach the camp and make a stand. But no refuge was to be found among the labyrinth of tents, for the right horn of the Zulu army, having covered the three miles round the back of Isandlwana Hill, was already swarming through the undefended back door of the camp, seizing the stony kopje and the base of the hill. The British had been unable to anticipate or comprehend the speed with which the Zulu could

move. Living closer to the earth and sky than their enemy, naked and unen-
cumbered except for their weapons, and taught since infancy to speed over the
roughest going in the pursuit of goats and cattle, the warriors were possessed of an
astounding athletic agility. They had also cut off the road to Rorke's Drift.

Those of the British force who had been more prudent than brave, and had
departed from the camp in the early stage of the attack, would get through but no
more would survive in attempting the road to Natal via Rorke's Drift.

Durnford and his mounted men on the extreme right of the British line had
kept the left horn of the Zulu army at bay as long as their ammunition lasted and
had prevented the full encirclement of the defenders. The right and left horns had
not quite met. There was a gap below the southern slope of the kopje and through
this began to flee the broken line of soldiers. Paul Brickhill, a civilian interpreter,
who had wisely got himself a horse earlier on, describes the awful scene:

> Men were running everywhere but I could see no officer. I saw one of the field pieces
> [cannon] brought into the camp; the men jumped off and took to their heels.
> Simultaneously with this, the only body of soldiers still visible rose from firing their
> last shot and joined in the general flight. Panic was everywhere and no officer to
> guide, no shelter to fall back on.

There were some, especially those from companies that had manned the left of
the British line who, cut off from any chance of flight, rallied and fought back-
to-back with bayonet and clubbed rifle. They died where they stood – for the
most part being shot or brought down by a thrown spear, for the warriors
quickly found that a hand-held spear was no match for a rifle and bayonet.
Another group of the 24th built up a little parapet of ammunition boxes and
eventually died among a heap of empty cartridges. A warrior of one regiment,
late in arriving, remembered:

> When I got in sight of Isandlwana the whole place was a twisting mess of soldiers
> and Zulu fighting, the Mkankempemvu and the Umbonambi were all killing and
> then we attacked. I heard the 'Bye-and-Bye'[6] firing ... I carried no gun, only two
> throwing spears, shield and stabbing assegai ... I prepared to stab a white man, he
> was holding on to an assegai held by a friend of mine with both hands ... and I
> stabbed the white man in the back ... I saw a line of soldiers, shoulder to shoulder
> and I was afraid to attack them ... they were standing like a fence with bayonets ...
> they were killed by the same two regiments ... some white men who had climbed on
> to the top of Isandlwana were followed and thrown off the top of the rock....

Flight was now the only chance of life for there would be no prisoners or mercy
– and, in any event, without a horse there was little hope of survival.

Along the track leading to Isipezi Hill, Commandant Hamilton-Browne and his
company of the NNC who, as mentioned, had been ordered to return to

Isandlwana, were halted, trapped between some late arrivals of the Zulu army and the besieged camp. For over an hour, as he had advanced, Hamilton-Browne had witnessed the progress of the battle through his field glasses. As early as 10 am, after questioning two Zulu prisoners who were reconnoitring for the Zulu army, he had sent a message advising Chelmsford that the enemy was up on the northern plateau. As he rode closer to Isandlwana and the battle for the camp commenced, Hamilton-Browne had sent, by well-mounted officers, two further messages categorically stating that the camp was under attack. Now, close enough to hear the shouting and watch the pandemonium as the Zulu charged, he sent back a last frantic plea. There could be no mistaking its urgency: 'For God's sake come back, the camp is surrounded and must be taken unless helped.'

Under the slopes of Isandlwana, the last pockets of imperial resistance were being overcome. Colonel Durnford had dismissed his native horsemen and had rallied about him what remained of the mounted volunteers; cut off from their horses and with ammunition finished, they were fighting with hunting knives and clubbed rifles.

A similar scene was taking place high up on the shoulder of Isandlwana, where Captain Younghusband's company of the 24th had formed a fighting square. Further out, beyond the tents, the artillery were attempting to save the guns by limbering up and galloping for the nek, but the Zulu warriors pulled the gunners from their seats, stabbing them as they passed until only the drivers were left: they managed to get the guns free but were defeated by an impassable donga; there the drivers were killed and the horses assegaied in their traces.

'The tumult and the firing was wonderful,' recalled a warrior. 'Everyone shouted "Usutu!" as they killed . . . the English fought long and hard, there were so many warriors in front of me that I did not get into the thick of the fight until the end.' But the majority of the British soldiers who were left were fleeing in the wake of the native companies, blindly hoping that the route would take them to safety across the distant Buffalo River which they had crossed only ten days previously, confident of smashing the Zulu army. On all sides raced the fleet foot warriors, as fast if not faster than the mounted fugitives who could make little haste through the broken terrain of deep dongas, swamp and rocks. The stumbling infantry, hampered by their boots and thick uniforms, were assegaied at will. None survived the journey to the Natal bank – except for those fortunate enough to have acquired a horse or a piggy-back ride. Brickhill wrote:

> Our flight I shall never forget. No path, no track, boulders everywhere – on we went borne now into some dry torrent bed, now weaving our way amongst trees of stunted growth, so that unless you made the best of your eyes[7] you were in constant danger of colliding against some tree or finding yourself unhorsed at the bottom of some ravine . . . our way was already strewn with abandoned shields, assegais, hats, clothing, guns, bandoliers and saddles . . . our stampede was composed of mules,

oxen, horses and flying men – all strangely intermingled; man and beast apparently all infested with the danger which surrounded us. . . .

Years later a warrior of the Uve Regiment still remembered how he had killed a soldier who was fleeing to the river '. . . as he raised his right arm that held a "volovol" (revolver) and as he was about to fire, I stabbed him in the armpit, I pushed it in, I did not hear him cry out, I pushed it until he died.' For those who survived the terrible ride across country, there would be no respite on reaching the river; the weeks of constant rain had turned the Buffalo into a deep, swirling torrent. A short distance beyond the drift it plunged into a rock-strewn gorge and became a maelstrom from which no one could emerge alive. At the river's edge there was a crush of fugitives as they queued, one behind the other, and tried to jump their horses down into the rushing water.

One unit that had retained discipline and fought with resolution was the NNH under its senior NCO Simeon Kambule. On gaining the Natal shore they had formed up, firing steadily across the river, keeping the enemy away from the water's edge and giving the fugitives a chance to enter the swirling current unmolested.

Despite the efforts of the NNH, most of those who reached the water were swept away and drowned; some were shot in the river, and others speared on reaching the Natal bank by men of Sihayo's clan whom Chelmsford had released the previous day. Later, a Zulu warrior recalled: 'Only a few crossed the Buffalo; some escaped, some died in the water, for the people of Gamdana, a brother of Sihayo, who had just before submitted to the Government, fell upon the fugitives by the river, and killed many both on the banks and in the water.'

Among those who were killed after reaching the Natal shore was Lieutenant Melvill, who had expressed his grave concern regarding the defenceless state of the camp the previous day. At the height of the battle, Colonel Pulleine had handed to him the cased Queen's Colour of the 1/24th with an order to take it to a place of safety. With a companion, Lieutenant Coghill, of the same regiment, he managed to scramble almost half a mile up into Natal, where both men were overtaken and stabbed to death. There would have been much more killing had not a senior induna called the warriors back, for Cetshwayo's orders were not to cross into Natal.

In all, over 1350 British troops, including colonials and natives, perished at Isandlwana, the majority being slain in flight along the track down to the Buffalo and in the river itself. Henry Francis Fynn, an interpreter and magistrate, who accompanied Chelmsford on his abortive foray to Isipezi Hill, later recalled that beyond the crossing place of the fugitives, where the river plunged into the gorge '. . . more than a wagonload of arms were found at low water . . . there can be little doubt that in attempting to cross those terrible rapids more lives were lost than were actually lost at Isandlwana.'

3. ISANDLWANA BATTLEFIELD

Inspector George Mansel, of the Natal Mounted Police, made this sketch of the Isandlwana battlefield specifically for Colonel Anthony Durnford's father who later passed a copy to Colonel Sir Evelyn Wood.

Mansel's Key:

1. The Hill; 2. Black's Koppie; 3. Camp of the 1/24th Regt; 4. Camp of the 2/24th Regt; 5. Camp of R.A. and Mtd. corps; 6. Camp of Native Contingent; 7. Head Qrs. tents; 8. Signal Hill, Rorkes Drift; 9, 9, 9, 9. Nqutu Range. The figures are put in the places I placed my vedettes on the day we pitched camp. I also had vedettes on the right front about 2 miles away; 10. Stoney Koppie; 11. Where the Zulus came down and attacked Colonel Durnford's Basutos; 12. Where the rocket battery was destroyed, distance from camp 2.1/2 miles; 13. Donga held by the Police and Volunteers, and where Col. Durnford joined them when the Basutos left him, and where they checked the left horn of the Zulus; 14. Where Col. Durnford fell, surrounded by the Police and Volunteers; 15. Where the 2 companies 1/24th went up, and were driven in by the right horn of the Zulus; 16. Where about 50 of the 1/24th were killed; 17. Where the right horn of the Zulus came around the hill and came into the rear of the camp; 18, 18, 18, 18. Donga and small stream in front of camp from which it was supplied with water, about 600 yards from Neck (Nek); 19. Neck; 20. Position of Fugitives Drift; 21. Where the left horn of the Zulus came into camp. (Killie Campbell Africana Library)

By the order of Major Clery, senior staff officer of the 1/24th, the vedettes that Mansel had placed on the summit of the Nqutu Range were withdrawn, thus allowing the Zulu army to advance undetected.

Above left: Sir Bartle Frere, the British High Commissioner at the Cape, aspired to confederate all the states and colonies in Southern Africa. In order to realise his goal, the conquest of the Zulu nation was imperative.

Above: Lieutenant General Lord Chelmsford, Commander of British Forces in South-eastern Africa, planned and led the invasion of Zululand. (John Young collection)

Left: Cetshwayo, King of the Zulu nation, was reluctant to engage the British in war, but it was impossible for him to comply with the British ultimatum which made war inevitable. (Andy May collection)

Above: The three men who comprised the Boundary Commission. They unanimously found in favour of the Zulus but the award was withheld by Sir Bartle Frere, the High Commissioner. *Left:* The Honourable Michael Gallwey, Attorney General of Natal. (S.B. Bourquin collection). *Centre:* The Honourable John Wesley Shepstone ('Misjan') Acting Secretary for Native Affairs (S.B. Bourquin collection). *Right:* Colonel Anthony Durnford RE, Commanding Royal Engineers, Natal.

Left: Mbelini (right) seated on the boom of a transport wagon. Of wiry build and a natural guerrilla fighter, he terrorised the area around Luneburg for a number of years until he was mortally wounded by a young German settler. (S.B. Bourquin collection)

Right: Colonel Hugh Rowlands and some of his advisers as seen by Lieutenant Fairlie. The sketch of Rowlands is a good likeness and the other characters have been identified as (clockwise from bottom left) George Potter whose son was killed on Hlobane; Gert Ferreira; M. Du Pont; and Swart Hos Potgieter. (Courtesy of the Director, National Army Museum, London)

TRANSVAAL

The man who takes care of Oham's cattle!

"Do I look like a liar!"

Col. Rowlands V.C., C.B. and some of his advisers.

The Confidential Adviser of Their Excellencies, the High Commissioner, Lord Chelmsford, Col. Rowlands &c. &c. &c.

Below: Chief Sekhukhune of the Transvaal resisted all attempts to conquer his stronghold, defeating Matabele, Boer and British armies. He was eventually beaten in November 1879 by a British force led by Sir Garnet Wolseley.

Below right: Colonel Evelyn Wood VC, CB, commanded No. 4 Column. Wood is seen here in the uniform that he wore during the Ashanti War of 1873. Note the strange 'barley sugar twist' handle of his sword. By coincidence, this picture was first published in *The Whitehall Review* on the day that Wood was fighting the battle of Kambula 6000 miles away. (John Young collection)

Above: Marthinus Pretorius had the unique honour of having been president of both the South African Republic and the Orange Free State. He hated the British. Wood wrote of him, 'He had a remarkable face, resolute and unyielding.' (Cape Archives)

Above centre: Colonel Redvers Buller, VC, CB. A tough and resilient fighting soldier, much admired by his men and the envy of many of his fellow officers. (John Young collection)

Above right: Sir Theophilus Shepstone, a colossus in the affairs of South-eastern Africa. (S.B. Bourquin collection)

Above: A posed picture: a member of the Uys family, 'Swart Dirk', demonstrates how he fought the Zulus at Vegkop in 1838. The splendidly attired warrior co-operates for the camera. 'Swart Dirk' sold ponies to Evelyn Wood shortly before the battle of Hlobane. (Natal Archives C1234)

Right: A Boer family typical of those who settled in the Disputed Territories. (S.B. Bourquin collection)

Centre right: Piet Uys and his four sons. A picture taken in Wood's camp shortly before the battle of Hlobane during which Uys was killed in going to the assistance of his eldest son. Note, Uys has a British officer's patrol jacket and helmet. (S.B. Bourquin collection)

Bottom right: The Zulu kings from the time of Shaka. Starting at 12 o'clock and going anti-clockwise:
a) Shaka: Born c1788. Founder of the Zulu nation. Killed by his brother on 24 September 1828.
b) Dingaan: Born c1795. Brother of Shaka whom he murdered and succeeded. His might was broken by the Voortrekkers at the battle of Blood River in 1838.
c) Mpande: Also a brother of Shaka: Succeeded to the throne in 1840 and died 1872 after a long and peaceful reign of thirty-two years.
d) Cetshwayo: Son of Mpande: born c1826. Succeeded his father to the Zulu throne. Last king of the Zulu empire. Defeated and banished by the British in 1879. Was eventually allowed to return to Zululand where he died in 1884.
e) Dinuzulu: son of Cetshwayo: born c1868. Succeeded his father to a kingdom much reduced in size. Charged with high treason by the British and banished to St Helena from 1888 to 1898. Again charged with treason in 1906 and banished to the Transvaal where he died in 1913.
f) Solomon: son of Dinuzulu: born in exile on St Helena in 1893. No longer referred to as king by the British but as Paramount Chief of the Zulus. Died in 1933.
g) Cyprian: Son of Solomon: born 1924, died 1968 at Nongome, Zululand.
h) (Mid-centre) Goodwill Zwelitini: Son of Cyprian: born 1948, King of the Zulu nation. (S.B. Bourquin collection)

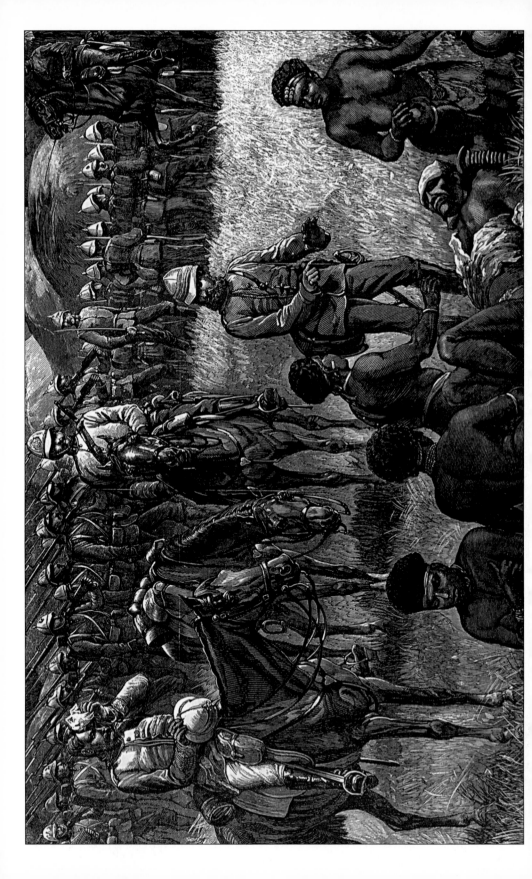

Opposite page: The British army invades Zululand; the troops, in light marching order, are called to a halt as they enter an enemy kraal whilst a medical officer attends to a wounded warrior. Later in the war, especially during the second invasion, the British were not so benign and every Zulu kraal was burnt to the ground as a matter of policy. (John Young collection)

Right: A fearsome-looking Zulu warrior and friend. He wears an elaborate hair style of an unmarried man, as was fashionable at the time of the Anglo-Zulu war, and is dressed for battle. Note the large-bladed stabbing spear. (S.B. Bourquin collection)

Below: Isandlwana: before and after the battle. The top picture conveys how completely defenceless the camp was with the tents strung across the plain as though on manoeuvres at Aldershot. Note the camp extending into the distance at the top right of the picture. Below, the utter devastation after the Zulu attack. (Local History Museum Durban)

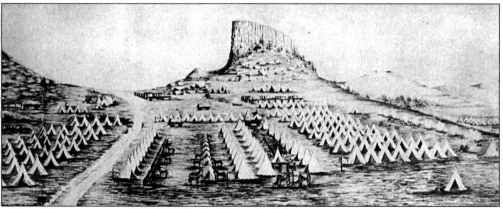

Above: In the dawn after the battle of Isandlwana Lord Chelmsford, and the remnants of No. 3 Column, prepare to depart the devastation of the camp, strewn with the mutilated bodies of their former comrades skewered to the ground with Zulu spears. An eye-witness sketch by Trooper W. Nelson of the Natal Mounted Police. (Natal Archives C637)

Below: Prior to the British annexation, Zululand was policed by a force named 'The Zulu Reserve Territory Carbineers.' It was commanded by George Mansel but little is known of its history. This rare photograph was taken in 1883. (Natal Archives C5055)

Above: George Mansel, sitting on the right next to Colonel Dartnell from whom Mansel eventually took over command of the Natal Mounted Police. (Natal Archives)

Below: After the British disaster at Isandlwana, the white population of Natal panicked in anticipation of a Zulu counter-attack. Here the citizens of Pietermaritzburg set out to fortify the courthouse. (S.B. Bourquin collection)

Top: The British military laager at Utrecht which served as the main supply depot for No. 4 Column. (Local History Museum Durban)

Above: A civilian laager, of which there were many scattered throughout Natal and the Disputed Territories. This picture, judging by the hats of the ladies, is of an English laager. The Dutch or Boer women preferred a large bonnet as headwear, which completely shielded the face from the sun. (Local History Museum Durban)

Left: William London, quartermaster of the Natal Carbineers, whose father owned a bookshop in Pietermaritzburg. Like so many young men of the town, William was killed at Isandlwana; he was shot through the head whilst endeavouring to open an ammunition box. (Natal Archives)

Above: The most vulnerable of the white settlements were the two farming communities located in the Disputed Territories at Luneburg and Utrecht. These contemporary sketches give an idea of the vastness of the countryside and the isolation of the settlers. (John Young collection)

Below: A sketch at Utrecht, showing where the Prince Imperial lived. Sketch by Capt. H.B. Lawrence, 4th Regt. 1. Residence of the late Prince Imperial. 2. Officers' mess-quarters. 3. House of the late Mr. P. Uys. (John Young collection)

Above: Among the many disasters that dogged Chelmsford was the accidental sinking of the *Clyde* off the Cape coast. Fortunately, none of the reinforcements on board lost their lives, but all the ammunition, guns and stores were sunk. (S.B. Bourquin collection)

Below: Hamu, like most princes of the Zulu royal family, was a man of ponderous build. He had a number of white men living among his tribe prior to the war, and European contact is reflected in both he and his son riding horses – and the latter wearing a shirt. (A sketch by Lieutenant Fairlie. By courtesy of the Director, National Army Museum, London)

Right:: Prince Hamu, brother of the Zulu king, defected to the British early in March 1879. Here he is seen discussing his surrender with British officials. (S.B. Bourquin collection)

Centre right: This contemporary sketch of the massacre at Intombi River vividly portrays the fury of the Zulu attack. The artist has the British soldiers fully dressed and armed – however, as they were caught abed many were naked or in their nightshirts.

Below: This present-day photograph, taken close to the spot where Sergeant Booth made his stand, gives an idea of how vulnerable the temporary camp of the 80th, on the banks of the Intombi River, was to a Zulu attack. It also emphasises Captain Moriarty's inexplicable complacency which resulted in the death of almost a hundred men. Key: A) Manyanyoba's stronghold, B) The site of Moriarty's camp on the Intombi River, just beyond the trees, C) Mbelini's stronghold, D) The old road to Derby went through the gap in the distant hills. (Paul Naish collection)

Col. Serg. Anthony Booth, 80th Regt rallying the survivors of th disaster at the Intombi River, Zulu War 1879.

Above: A scene from an early cigarette card series entitled *Heroic Deeds* depicts Sergeant Anthony Booth winning his VC at the Intombi River. (John Young collection)

Left: Captain David Moriarty who commanded the temporary camp of the 80th Regiment on the banks of the Intombi River.

Right: Lieutenant Henry Harward forsook his men and, taking the only horse available, fled to Luneburg. He was subsequently court martialled.

Below: This contemporary illustration from *Pictorial World* may well depict Buller's raid on the Makulusini military kraal on 1 February 1879. (S.B. Bourquin collection)

Bottom: NCOs of the Native Contingent attempting to train their horses to the sight and sound of battle and being thrown in the process. There would have been similar scenes at the battle of Kambula after Buller's volunteers, many of them riding untrained horses, fired a volley at close quarters into the advancing Zulu army. (S.B. Bourquin collection)

Above: In the foreground three volunteer horsemen relax while a comrade prepares to unsaddle. A good example of the rough attire that was worn by many and which was described by an officer as 'fearfully slovenly'. Note the swords which were not issued until after the battle of Kambula. (John Young collection)

Meanwhile at the stricken camp the Zulu army was indulging in a frenzy of mutilation and destruction. The dead were stripped, disembowelled and left like carcasses of bloody meat. Disembowelment was a necessary act of Zulu religious belief; it removed any evil that might follow in the wake of having killed a man. It is not surprising that the British failed to see any religious significance in what they regarded as a bestial and barbaric practice.

The warriors rampaged through the camp dressed in bloody uniforms of the dead soldiers, killing oxen, horses and anything that moved. What they did not want they burnt or smashed. They ate whatever food came to hand and drank anything found in a bottle – many dying in agony from the consumption of paraffin and poisons taken from the medical supplies.

Chelmsford, at last believing that all might not be well at Isandlwana, was on his way to the camp. Numerous messages had reached him and his staff during the course of the day: most had been ignored or treated with flippancy. The staff were, if anything, more infected with over-confidence than their general. 'How very amusing! Actually attacking our camp! Most amusing!' was one staff officer's response. There seems little doubt that Chelmsford's staff had elected not to bother their commander with some of the messages, or had delivered them in a manner which clouded their urgency.[8]

Then Hamilton-Browne's breathless courier, Captain Develin, galloped up to a still largely complacent group of officers. 'For God's sake come back, the camp is surrounded and must be taken unless helped,' he shouted. Greatly alarmed, Lieutenant Colonel Arthur Harness, who commanded the four guns of the Royal Artillery, immediately responded, as did two officers, Major Black and Captain Church, of the 2/24th, and within a few minutes the guns and two companies of infantry were ready to make the best time possible, over the rough terrain, to camp. But the reaction of Captain Matthew Gossett, ADC of Chelmsford's staff, who was also present, was only scorn: 'It's all bosh! I do not hear guns,' he said. A few minutes earlier, Gossett had given Harness and the two companies of the 24th orders to proceed to the site chosen for the new camp at Mangeni Falls. Now, as Harness was about to move off and despite Hamilton-Browne's urgent cry for help, Gossett informed Harness that he had better go to the new campsite as ordered. But neither Harness nor the infantry would be deterred by Gossett and they immediately set off for Isandlwana, being joined *en route* by the Mounted Infantry commanded by Lieutenant Colonel Russell. After covering perhaps two miles, they were overtaken by Gossett who, in the name of Chelmsford, gave them a direct order to turn back. They had no option but to obey. Whether or not Chelmsford had been consulted, or whether Gossett had issued the order off his own bat, is uncertain.

Chelmsford, however, was now uneasy and decided personally to find out if there was anything wrong at the camp. With an escort of the returned Mounted Infantry, he was on his way back to Isandlwana when he came upon Hamilton-Browne who, with his NNC, had not moved since sending off his last dramatic message hours earlier. Chelmsford's immediate reaction on seeing him was astonishment, which seemed to indicate that he had not received Hamilton-Browne's call for help. 'What are you doing here, Captain Browne? You ought to have been in camp hours ago,' Chelmsford remonstrated. When Hamilton-Browne replied that the camp had long since been taken, Chelmsford chose to believe that the commandant was, for some reason, lying. Just at that moment a lone horseman appeared, coming from the direction of Isandlwana. It was Commandant Lonsdale who had just survived one of the most remarkable escapes of the entire war. He had endured, on top of a recent concussion, two exhausting days in the hot sun, and had that morning made his way back to Isandlwana to organise rations for his ravenous NNC. The day was hot and as his pony 'Dot' plodded its way through the hills to the south of the camp, Lonsdale dozed in the saddle. He was more than half asleep as his pony, needing no guiding, made its unerring way through the death and destruction of the camp toward its picket line. Lonsdale suddenly awoke from his half-slumber and found himself in a nightmare. The men dashing about him in red coats were not soldiers but Zulus wearing the bloody trophies of victory. At the same moment the nearest Zulu realised it was not a warrior, but a lone white man who, head down, was quietly riding through the camp. A yell went up and the hunt was on. By a miracle Lonsdale managed to push his reluctant mount into a canter and, dodging spears and knobkerries, escaped with his life. Lonsdale came face to face with Chelmsford and confirmed that the camp was taken. Still hoping that all was not completely lost, Chelmsford ordered Russell to take the Mounted Infantry and as closely as possible reconnoitre. When Russell returned, appalled and shaken at what he had found, all hope was gone. The camp was destroyed.

It was not until evening that Chelmsford and his column stood, in battle formation, three miles from the still-smouldering tents. The British were in a perilous position. Most were exhausted, having marched and countermarched almost thirty-five miles that day at the height of the Zululand summer. Some had not eaten for forty-eight hours. Everything that the column possessed, except what the men carried with them, had been either captured or destroyed. They had no reserve ammunition as none had been taken; much of the seventy rounds that each man had carried had been fired off whilst skirmishing earlier in the day. The NNC was in a highly strung state ready for flight and the only way back to Natal was through the gutted camp.

Young Fred Symons, a trooper in the Natal Carbineers, remembered: 'Before darkness set in we had seen the Nqutu Hills so covered with Zulus that it looked like it would in winter time when the grass had been burnt off freshly. I have never seen such a crowd in my life . . . it seemed to us (that we were marching) right into the jaws of death.'

Astride his horse, Chelmsford addressed the men of the 2/24th: 'The enemy has taken our camp and I mean to retake it this night. There is nothing left for us now but to fight our way through with the bayonet – and mind, we must fight hard, for we will have to fight for our lives. I know you and I know I can depend upon you.' The men cheered and the column advanced and before long were marching through heaps of Zulu dead.

At a little stream, the column halted again. It was still light enough to perceive what appeared to be a line of wagons drawn up across the nek, barring the way back to Rorke's Drift. The guns were unlimbered and opened fire with twenty rounds, blowing the wagons apart.[9]

As the column prepared to advance, Inspector Mansel described how Dartnell besought Chelmsford not to let the NNC go in front, '... as they would most likely bolt immediately they were attacked and move back throwing the rest of the column into confusion'. With the NNC in the rear, the British infantry, with fixed bayonets, led by Major Wilson Black of the 24th, surged forward to take and secure the stony kopje above the camp – but the enemy had gone.

In youthful admiration of Major Black, Trooper Symons found his own officer, 'Offy' Shepstone, wanting as 'he and a few others began shaking hands and saying goodbye to each other for we shall never see the sun rise again'. Symons concluded, 'Major Black's the man for me – "cold steel is our motto".'

A night of dread descended upon the column as men tried to settle down, cold and hungry, among the dead and the chaos. The enemy was no longer in the camp but he had not gone far; his bivouac fires encircled the British camp. Stretching out a hand in the darkness to clear a place to rest, men found their fingers encountering the grisly remains, still sticky with blood, of some former comrade. 'It was a most trying time for young soldiers, indeed for all,' wrote Captain Penn Symonds. 'Every instant we expected to be attacked. As we neared the camp we stumbled constantly over naked gashed and ghastly bodies of our comrades.' A letter from Lieutenant Q. McK. Logan, of 'E' Company 2/24th, was published in his old school magazine: '... sleep was impossible for a time; but we were worn out, and I know I slept a little but on jumping up when some shots were fired, I fell down with cramp and shivering. We could see Zulu signal fires all round us, and I never expected to get out of Cetshwayo's territory alive....'

But it was not only the bivouac fires of the enemy that burned all night; away to the south-west the sky became illuminated by a mighty blaze. Those who were aware of what lay in that direction knew that the post at Rorke's Drift, with all that remained of the column's stores, must be burning and the implications of this conflagration were too dreadful to think about: the Zulu army could already be well into Natal.

The first dim light of dawn revealed the full horror of what had happened and to save the men the sight of their mutilated comrades, Chelmsford got them up and moving – but not soon enough. Inspector Mansel, who would command the rearguard as soon as the column trundled off and would be the last man to leave the camp, wrote:

The sun was about half an hour high when I left the field. The sight was simply awful. In a few places stands had evidently been made and the men died fighting, but I much fear, in fact I am certain, that there was a general stampede and the greater number of men were killed running. In the camp of the 1/24th there was about eighty men lying altogether and in the camp of the 2/24th there were about forty together who had evidently died fighting. . . .

Whether or not they had died fighting, the British dead had been robbed by the enemy of all dignity. Perhaps it was worse for the officers, especially the young ones who had been brought up to believe in the glory of a soldier's death in battle, for there was no glory at Isandlwana; the enemy had reduced their comrades to animal-like carcasses of slaughtered meat. The morale of those who witnessed the battleground that morning, from Lord Chelmsford down to the lowest private soldier, would never be the same again. For some time they would lose all heart in soldiering.

There was anger, but the overriding feeling was shock and a desire to escape, leaving Zululand far behind. Private Henry Moses of the 24th wrote home to his family: 'I wish I was back in England again, for I should never leave . . . you that are at home stay at home.' Lord Chelmsford's feelings were equally emphatic: two weeks after Isandlwana he wrote to his confidante and commander of No. 4 Column, Evelyn Wood: 'I wish I saw my way with honour out of this beastly country and had you as my travelling companion.'

In the grey dawn, leaving Isandlwana and its growing stench of death behind them, and abandoning the strewn corpses where they lay – and where they would continue to lie for many months to come – Chelmsford and his column began the twelve-mile march back to Rorke's Drift, whence firing had been heard for most of the night. Now there was silence. Had the post been overrun as well? After what they had seen, it seemed unlikely that approximately 150 men, a number sick and lame, and a company of NNC could have survived the night against the Zulu army.

The column expected to be attacked at any moment and had not gone far when Mansel was appalled to see about 3000 warriors appearing from a valley just behind him. They were so well concealed that they got within 300 yards before Mansel and the rearguard were aware of their presence. To the right of the road, at a distance of no more than a few yards, there was also an assembly of several hundred warriors who, trance-like, just stood and stared at the passing troops, 'simply gazing at us like sightseers at a review,' as Captain Henry Harford put it '. . . we were absolutely dumbfounded at this extraordinary spectacle'. Mansel raised the alarm and Dartnell arrived at a gallop from the head of the column, ordering the NMP to form up and prepare to prevent the warriors from closing in or cutting off stragglers. The police, however, did not attempt to shoot as they had so little ammunition left. Apart from catching one or two of the NNC, who had lingered to search for plunder, the Zulu force came no closer and eventually turned off. It had been part of the Zulu army retiring from its defeat at Rorke's Drift, for the little garrison, fighting for eleven hours behind a makeshift barricade of mealie bags and biscuit boxes, had miraculously fought off 3000 of the enemy and despite the destruction of the thatched hospital building by fire, had won the battle. Thirty days' rations for the whole column had been saved plus some ammunition – and there was a victory to report. A record number of eleven Victoria Crosses would be awarded for the night's work.

On arrival of the column at Rorke's Drift the exhausted men settled down for a meal of bully beef and biscuits, while Chelmsford and his staff made haste towards Pietermaritzburg, the capital of Natal 110 miles away. It was essential to organise the defence of the colony – and to meet with Sir Bartle Frere as soon as possible.

There was the problem of the invasion of Zululand having been made without the knowledge of the British government – in fact against its clear instructions to avoid a conflict. As far back as October, Sir Michael Hicks Beach, the Colonial Secretary, had expressed to Sir Bartle Frere 'a confident hope that by the exercise of prudence and reasonable compromise, it would be possible to avert the very serious evil of a war with Cetshwayo'. Now he would have to report the most catastrophic defeat that a British force had ever suffered at the hands of a native army. As one perceptive young volunteer had predicted in a letter to his father, 'There will be an awful row at home about this.' Someone would have to carry the blame and there were those who were now conveniently dead to choose from.

Chelmsford sent a dispatch on ahead by a senior staff officer, Major Francis Grenfell (who had missed the events of the previous day having been delayed *en route* to Rorke's Drift), and followed with the rest of his staff, arriving in the capital early in the morning on 26 January. By the next day Chelmsford was being absolved of any blame. Sir Bartle Frere dispatched the following message to London: 'In disregard of Lord Chelmsford's instructions, the troops left to guard the camp were taken away from the defensive position they were in at the camp, with the shelter which the wagons, parked, (laagered) would have afforded....' And a few days later, 'It is only justice to the General to note that his orders were clearly not obeyed on that terrible day at Isandlwana camp.'

A so-called court of inquiry was held at Helpmekaar five days after the battle; it revealed nothing, drew no conclusions and offered no opinions as to the cause of the disaster. Those of the living who knew the most, Lieutenant Colonel Harness, Captain Church and Commandants Lonsdale and Hamilton-Browne, were not called as witnesses. In fact Colonel Harness was made a member of the court, which effectively prevented him from giving evidence. Lord Chelmsford's comments on the inquiry, when forwarding its findings to the Secretary of State for War on 8 February, were that 'the court has very properly abstained from giving an opinion, and I myself refrain also from making any observations or from drawing any conclusions from the evidence therein recorded'.

Not so his senior staff officer Major Grenville who, as mentioned, was nowhere near Isandlwana on the day of the battle, or the day after, and who had formed a very firm opinion on the matter – a conclusion, in fact, that he could only have drawn from Chelmsford or his staff officers. After the court of inquiry, Grenville wrote to his father, 'The loss of the camp was due to officer commanding not Colonel Pulleine, but Colonel Durnford of the Engineers who took command after the action had begun and who disregarded the orders left by the General ... Durnford is dead so this will probably never be known publicly but this is the case....' He continued his letter with what was to become the popular myth of Isandlwana: '... officers and men dying back to back – and at last rallying around the colours, not a man of the regulars attempted to escape till all was lost....' Conversely, Inspector Mansel who was deeply involved in the events of the 22nd and 23rd, wrote in a letter to Colonel Arthur Durnford, the dead Durnford's brother: '... the dispatches have always said that the Imperial Troops died back to back ... quite untrue, nearly two thirds were killed between the nek and Fugitives Drift.' And of Colonel Harness, Mansel wrote:

> I daresay he could tell you a great deal more than I can if he liked .... I am fully convinced that the General thought he knew too much and put him a member of the court in order that he should not give evidence.... I have no hesitation in stating, Lord Chelmsford's description of the camp is utterly false.... I know that a dead set was made against your brother. Lord Chelmsford and staff, especially Colonel Crealock, tried in every way to shift the responsibility of the disaster from their own shoulders on to those of your brother.

There can be little doubt that there was not only a shifting of blame, but also a careful cover-up regarding the actual course of the battle which became more and more apparent to certain officers, including Wood, who for reasons best known to themselves, kept quiet.

Six months after Isandlwana, Major Frank Russell, formerly of the Intelligence Department, writing to his old chief Major-General Sir Archibald Allison, related the visit he made to the battlefield in company with Lieutenant Smith-Dorrien, one of the Special Service officers, and the civilian interpreter, Brickhill, both of whom escaped from Isandlwana:

> ... Mr Brickhill, who was one of the last to leave the camp, gave a most vivid description ... by his account the Natal natives (NNC) bolted three-quarters of an hour before the general flight. I fear, however, that there is no doubt at all that there was a general panic, the position where a very great proportion of the 24th Regiment bodies were found, proved this. Mr Brickhill says the Quartermaster rallied a few as they were breaking and the bodies of these were found where they stood and died, but those of the others were scattered in all directions. This of course, is most private.

In a letter to his father three days after the battle, Smith-Dorrien had this to say: 'Well, to cut the account short, in half an hour they were right up to the camp. The Zulus nearly all had firearms of some kind and lots of ammunition. Before we knew where we were they came right into the camp, assagaing everybody right and left. Everybody then who had a horse turned to fly. . . .'

That many of the fugitives including, perhaps, Melvill and Coghill, were killed by the prisoners released by Chelmsford the previous day, was also kept quiet, but it was a fact well known to Chelmsford's staff. Major Grenvill, who as we have seen, was extremely loyal to Chelmsford, wrote in a tactlessly worded letter to his father, dated 3 February: 'Some of them (fugitives) got right down to the river – six miles off and were killed by a lot of scoundrels whom the General had taken prisoner and had liberated a few days before. . . .'

Immediately following the catastrophe, Chelmsford seemed to fluctuate between confidence and despair. Six days after the battle he was all for engaging the enemy again. 'If we establish ourselves in a good position . . . and make good use of the mounted men for reconnoitring and raids, we ought to be able to bring the Zulus down upon us again when thoroughly prepared to receive them.' Less than a week later, writing privately to Wood, he confided: 'The situation of affairs does not appear to me to improve and I am fairly puzzled when I contemplate our future operations.'

On 16 February, when contemplating a visit to Isandlwana with a strong force to bury the dead (he was coming under pressure to do so), he wrote:

In fact, I am not sure whether it would not be a good plan with such a force, to throw down the gauntlet to the Zulu army and allow them to try what they can do against us when prepared, even though not behind entrenchments. I do not believe that they would have got the better of the force left behind for the protection of the camp (Isandlwana) had it been brought together, with its back to the precipitous sided hill where their flanks could not have been turned, and where they would have had an unlimited supply of ammunition.

But he did not throw down the gauntlet and the dead remained unburied for four months.

Durnford had been a good choice for a scapegoat. He was not popular in Natal due to a debacle which had taken place five years earlier and for which the colonists held him responsible. So when looking for someone to blame for Isandlwana, Durnford seemed to have been made for the part.

But Chelmsford and his staff had misread public reaction – especially so after a brief visit to the battlefield revealed that Durnford had died surrounded by dead carbineers, Natal Mounted Police and other volunteer horsemen, proving conclusively, as reported earlier by a number of survivors, that he had led the colonials in making a gallant stand.

Although initially *The Times of Natal* and *The Natal Mercury* came out in support of Chelmsford, it did not take many days for these papers to change their stance and, along with most others in South Africa, point to Chelmsford as the main culprit. *The Port Elizabeth and Eastern Province Standard*, in a long editorial, blamed Chelmsford and concluded by hoping that 'no consideration for the living will cause obloquy to be attached to the memories of brave men simply because being dead they cannot be heard in their own defence'. It was not long before *The Cape Argus* was able to inform its readers that 'Lord Thurlow, addressing the House of Commons, asked if, in the opinion of Her Majesty's Government, the officers who had sat on the court of inquiry were sufficiently independent of their Commanding Officer to justify the hope that their report will be as unprejudiced, and authoritative, as the magnitude of the disaster renders it desirable'. And, even further afield, in Russia of all places, it was reported that '. . . the Tsar has been so struck by the terrible reverse sustained by the British at Isandlwana, he has ordered the Etat Major to discuss the subject at one of its earlier sittings . . . and a map of Zululand is to be suspended in the library of the Winter Palace for his own special use'.

Yet, although shaken and depressed, Chelmsford appeared unperturbed and maintained that he had not been responsible in any way for the defence of the camp at Isandlwana. He continued to use euphemisms such as 'misfortune' and 'incident' to describe the defeat and, as his greatest critic, Frances Colenso, who had been Durnford's devoted friend, was to write in condemnation of Chelmsford: 'We do not find one word of regret for the untimely fate of gallant men who fell doing their duty.'

Chelmsford, however, had powerful friends: none less than the Great White Queen whom he had once served as aide-de-camp. It must have been with some satisfaction that he was able to pass on her message to the press for publication, below the headlines, 'A Message from the Queen ... Confidence in Lord Chelmsford':

> The Lieutenant-General commanding has the highest satisfaction in publishing the following gracious messages received from Her Majesty the Queen and His Royal Highness Field-Marshal, the Duke of Cambridge: from the Secretary of State for War, London, to Lord Chelmsford, Pietermaritzburg.
>
> The Queen has graciously desired me to say she sympathises most sincerely with you in the dreadful loss which has deprived her of so many gallant officers and men, and that Her Majesty places entire confidence in you and the troops to maintain our honour and good name. . . .'

Chelmsford, however, had no such influential friends among the politicians in the government and those were the men that counted. His replacement was already being discussed. But, with luck, whether he was superseded or not, Chelmsford would have just enough time to conquer the Zulu and redeem his reputation.

* * *

In 1881, two years after the close of the Anglo-Zulu War, Wood, now a brigadier-general, publicly stated his opinion of Durnford and the part that he played in the battle of Isandlwana, and this he did in heroic Victorian prose when addressing a gathering of veteran colonial volunteers at Durban. Wood not only praised Durnford as a hero, but also acclaimed him for giving his life to cover the retreat of the guns – an entirely new view of Durnford's death.

> Yet surely no greater proof of devoted steadiness was ever given than that shown by the Natal Carabineers on 22 January 1879. Imagine a gentle slope up which is storming a resistless surging wave of encircling black bodies, which, though constantly smitten by leaden hail, breaks but to sweep on again with renewed force. Imagine a crowd of terrified non-combatants, and friendly Natives, flying through the already burning camp, and pressing on to the rapidly narrowing outlet over the fatal Nek.
>
> Then there comes on the scene a one-armed man [Durnford] who, having slowly fallen back before the ever-increasing foe, is now determined to die. 'Save yourself, as for me I shall remain.' He thus dismisses the Staff officer, and H'Lubi's black soldiers, who vainly urge the great Chief to retreat with them.
>
> Recognising his commanding courage, around him gather some twenty similar spirits, who, nobly disdaining death, resolve to cover the retreat of the guns, or die with them. He himself was fully worthy of their devotion, and history will narrate how the ring of dead White men that encircled him, formed a halo round his, and their renown.

1. Crealock's precise orders were 'You are to march to this camp at once with all the force you have with you of No. 2 Column – Major Bengough's battalion is to move to Rorke's Drift as ordered yesterday. 2/24th Artillery and mounted men with the General and Colonel Glyn move off at once to attack Zulu force about 10 miles distant. J.N.C.

    P.S. If Bengough's battalion has crossed the river at Elandskraal it is to move up here [Nangwani Valley].'

2. Another of Sir Theophilus's sons.

3. Two troops of the NNH, the Edendale Troop and one troop of Basutos, Hlubi's Troop, were under the immediate command of Durnford; the other two troops of NNH, Sikali's Horse, were under the immediate command of Shepstone.

    As early as October Durnford had received authority from the Natal Government to raise a hundred mounted men from Sikali's tribe of the Upper Tugela Division, and fifty from Hlubi's tribe of the Weenen County, Escort Division.

4. It was Clery, on his own initiative and as Colonel Glyn's chief staff officer, who issued orders to Pulleine for the camp's defence; Chelmsford later took the credit for Clery's initiative.

5. Nineteen years later in 1898, during the battle of Ondurman, the 1st Sudanese Bri-

gade, under the command of Major General Hector Macdonald, kept at bay 30,000 Dervish warriors who got to within ten yards of the Sudanese line. In an engagement that lasted little more than twenty minutes, and firing the same type of Martini Henry rifle as the British used at Isandlwana, the whole brigade was left with but a few rounds when the enemy retired.

6. Zulu name for cannons.

7. Brickhill was shortsighted and had lost his glasses.

8. On two occasions Chelmsford had sent his naval ADC, Lieutenant Archibald Barkeley Milne, to a hilltop to observe the camp, twelve miles away, through his powerful telescope. The distance and the haze were too great for accurate sighting. Milne reported that he had seen a large herd of cattle being driven through the camp, which was nothing to cause alarm. What he had seen was, in fact, the Zulu army.

9. It was the sound of this barrage that Wood heard fifty miles away sitting around the campfire near Hlobane.

3
PANIC IN NATAL

'Everyone was demoralised and ... that worse catching of diseases had entered into the marrow of all ranks.'
Sir Garnet Wolseley

'At this moment the tables are completely turned on us.'
Major Cornelius Clery

Bad as they were, things could have been worse for Lord Chelmsford: had the Zulu army attacked on 23 January, as it had originally intended by dispatching much of its force around the rear of Isandlwana and falling on the column at first light, it would have caught the enemy divided and strung out between the camp and Isipezi Hill. Many of the men with Chelmsford would have been low on ammunition and fresh supplies difficult to acquire until the wagons arrived from camp. The predictable outcome of the Zulu army descending upon this fragmented force would have been the latter's total annihilation.

Other factors of good fortune were that Rowlands's No. 5 Column, being scattered around the Transvaal, was hardly affected and that Wood's No. 4 Column, receiving early warning of the catastrophe, had retired to its fort at Tinta's Kop. Pearson's No.1 Column, marching along the coastal plain, had had a very successful day on the fateful 22nd – albeit a success that was completely overshadowed by the immensity of the disaster at Isandlwana. Pearson and his men had been ambushed by the impi which had left the main Zulu army the day after departing from Ondini. The column had just crossed the Nyezane River when its vanguard, comprising a company of the NNC, encountered a hidden impi and were completely routed. Pearson, drawing up the rest of his command into a fighting formation, repulsed the Zulu with heavy losses in a battle that lasted little more than an hour.

It was at this, the battle of Nyezane, that the Gatling gun was first used in action and was reputed to have 'scythed down the enemy'. British losses were minimal in comparison to the 300 Zulu dead later found on the battlefield.

Pearson pushed on into Zululand and the following day reached the abandoned mission station of Eshowe, which he immediately fortified. It was just as well that he did, for he would remain completely ignorant of the catastrophe that had taken place at Isandlwana, and in consequence, ignorant of the extreme danger he was in. His column at that time was still less than thirty-five miles from the Tugela with an open line of communication all the way back to Durban. That Pearson was not informed of his peril underlines the state of lassitude and indecision that had overwhelmed Chelmsford.

The first indication that all was not well came in a message from Bartle Frere on 27 January which merely told Pearson that 'Colonel Durnford had been defeated'. The following day Pearson received a note from Chelmsford advising him to ignore all previous orders, to act in any way that he thought best for his force and to be prepared to have the whole Zulu army down upon him at any moment; it was the same form of message as received by Wood. Obviously there had been a calamity of some sort, but Pearson had no idea of what had happened. That night he held a conference of war with his commanders and by a small majority it was decided to defend Eshowe with a garrison that the fort could comfortably accommodate. The rest of the men, with all the transport animals, were sent back to the Tugela (losing 600 oxen on the way). It was not until 2 February, ten days after Isandlwana, that Pearson finally received a message from Chelmsford which, to quote the Intelligence Department of the War Office, '... gave tolerably full particulars of the Isandlwana disaster ... and the garrison (Eshowe) for the first time realised the position in which they stood'.

By 11 February the Zulu had begun to gather in large numbers around the fort and messengers could no longer pass through to Natal. The garrison was under siege and would have to hold out for over a month before relief arrived. In the meantime Natal had been seized with panic. Where was the Zulu army?

The first awful rumours of a British defeat started to be whispered across the Buffalo River during the late morning of 22 January, and took substance as the first of the fleeing men of the NCC reached the tiny settlements close to the Zulu border. The bad tidings spread with a speed that seemed to be carried without any human agency: legend has it that by the next day the natives of Cape Town, 1200 miles away, were aware of the catastrophe.

At Umsinga (Msinga) on the Natal Bank, less than twenty miles from Isandlwana as the crow flies, Janet Smith was about to give birth to her first child. Her husband William, who commanded the Buffalo Border Guard, was with Chelmsford somewhere in Zululand. By the time Brickhill, in his headlong flight from the battlefield, arrived she had been delivered of a son. Janet was taken to Mrs Fynn, the wife of Chelmsford's interpreter, who organised the barricading of the local courthouse. The two women spent the night in prayer and fear, listening to the gunfire from Rorke's Drift and watching the night sky redden from the blazing hospital. Mrs Smith's prayers were answered: her husband was safe and survived.

Fifteen miles further north at Helpmekaar, the first of the exhausted fugitives from the battlefield were beginning to arrive at the fort. They brought with them firsthand accounts of the slaughter, shredding their comrades' nerves with apprehension.

As the news spread, the whole of Natal was gripped with panic. No time was lost in the erection of barricades and fortifications, as hourly the victorious Zulu army was expected to descend on every town and hamlet. At Rorke's Drift, the doorstep to Zululand, and the recent scene of a gallant defence, the routed remains of Chelmsford's column were also in the grip of confusion and dread. The men, however, were kept busy improving the fortifications and burying 500 Zulu dead. The latter task took two days, the corpses being flung into pits and burnt with piles of brushwood and thorn trees. It was a grisly business but necessary if an epidemic was to be avoided. Nevertheless, the awful stench of burning flesh did nothing to release tension or improve morale. The troops had only the clothes they wore, and so great was the fear of a sudden attack that Colonel Glyn, who was in command, would allow his men neither to wash nor to remove clothing to sleep.

All along the border the remnants of the NCC, several thousand in number, who had either deserted or had been disbanded, fled homeward, often coming under fire, having been mistaken for an invading impi. At Pietermaritzburg the fine brick courthouse was faced with loopholed boarding and wells were dug inside the walls. Signal guns were set up and stocks of food hoarded. There was also much lamentation as many of its young citizens – 'the flower of Pietermaritzburg' – had been slain: they included George Shepstone, who had galloped down from the Nqutu Hills bringing the news of the Zulu army; Quartermaster William London, son of a local bookseller; Quartermaster Sergeant Bullock, the chemist's son; Trooper Borraine, who had worked on the local newspaper; Trooper Blaikie, a local farmer; Trooper Macleroy, the only son of the bank manager; Trooper Mendenhall, the draper's son; Trooper Whitelaw the blacksmith ... and many more.

At Greytown, twenty-eight miles from the border, the residents were awakened at one o'clock in the morning with great cries of alarm. The Zulu had crossed the Tugela River and were fast descending on the town. Everybody hurried to the laager, and as one immigrant farmer from Hereford described it, '... not a lady fainted or a child run over ... some of the ladies are very brave and will arm themselves' – but it was a false alarm.

A British regiment marching through Natal received news of Isandlwana as it reached Ladysmith. The column commander immediately ordered his men to the shelter of the local laager. A few minutes later his quartermaster, in a high state of excitement, reported that he had brought all the companies into the laager except one which would have to remain outside and be sacrificed!

Colonel Edward Bray, 2/4th Foot, was on his way to Helpmekaar and Rorke's Drift with a large convoy of ammunition when he was passed by fleeing fugitives

going in the opposite direction. He immediately formed a laager and instead of
hurrying on with the badly needed ammunition, buried it. Shortly afterwards
there was a violent rainstorm which obliterated all signs of where the ammunition
lay; some maintain that it was never found again.

At Durban, far from the Zulu border, the panic was equally intense: the
courthouse was loopholed, naval ships promised to bombard any invading impi,
and shipping lines did a roaring trade in evacuating those who could afford the
passage to Cape Town. The good ship *Melrose*, arriving at dusk in thick mist, fired
a warning gun which set all the church bells ringing in general panic. Various
places of importance were allocated permanent guards: the Orient Bank rated five
men of the Town Guard, the Natal Bank ten men of the Royal Durban Rifles,
whilst the local convent rated more protection than both banks put together – one
sergeant and twenty men of the 88th Regiment of Foot.

The people of Pinetown, twelve miles inland from Durban, descended on the
railway yard and, with the assistance of the Railway Department, constructed a
laager using 4000 wooden sleepers and 200 steel rails, around Murray's Hotel.
The barricade was 280 yards long and could accommodate 1500 people. The
mayor pronounced the laager 'a perfect place of refuge'.

Every little town and village had its laager. In the outlying districts, families
abandoned their farms for the safety of the nearest town or began trekking to the
Free State or the Cape. One volunteer, having escaped from Isandlwana, galloped
home to Newcastle but found the town all but deserted; an instant panic had
carried most of the citizens away to the west.

In the Disputed Territories the settlements were particularly vulnerable. Wood,
as mentioned, with misplaced jocularity, told the citizens of Utrecht that the only
thing he could promise was a decent burial. Now, apart from Piet Uys and his
Burgher Force, the male population had been labelled 'funkists'. The correspondent of *The Natal Mercury* reported bitterly: 'The young able-bodied men (of
Utrecht) are sticking to the lee of their wives' skirts under the protection of the
laager walls . . . before the war it was amusing to listen to loungers bombastically
shooting any number of Zulu with their tongues.' A volunteer of Baker's Horse
recorded: 'All the inhabitants were in laager every night and a complete panic
prevailed amongst the townspeople.' A wounded officer, writing from Utrecht
hospital (an abandoned dwelling), described the place as 'hideous and detestable',
where dysentery and diarrhoea were so commonplace they went unnoticed.

Luneburg, seventy miles from Isandlwana in a straight line, received news of the
disaster, brought by native runner, within twenty-four hours. The last British
troops to garrison the village, two companies of the 13th LI, had marched away
three weeks earlier leaving Commandant Schermbrucker in sole command with his
Kaffrarian Riflemen. All the local settlers, 120 men, women and children, were
immediately brought into the laager, where, during the baking hot days that
followed, disease flourished in the cramped conditions that prevailed. Within a few

weeks the number of people who died at Luneburg of typhoid and malaria exceeded the total deaths of the previous three years – and far more than would ever die at the hands of the Zulu. However, as elsewhere in Natal and the Disputed Territories, the overwhelming fear was that of the Zulu army. But where was it?

The answer was that it had temporarily ceased to exist. It had scored a great victory but the price had been high. The true number of Zulu casualties will never be known. They have been variously estimated at between 1000 and 3000, though a midway figure of 2000 dead would seem more likely. In any event, the casualties were devastating to the Zulu people. At the beginning of the war a young Dutch trader, Cornelius Vijn, found himself trapped in Zululand and lived there under Cetshwayo's protection for many months. He described the anguish at the kraal in which he was sheltering when news was brought of Isandlwana and Rorke's Drift: 'They kept on wailing in front of the kraals, rolling themselves on the ground and never quietening down; nay, in the night they wailed so as to cut through the heart of anyone. And this wailing went on day and night for a fortnight; the effect of it was very depressing; I wish I could not hear it.' Cetshwayo summed up the feeling of his people when he declared, 'An assegai has been thrust into the belly of the nation. There are not enough tears to mourn for the dead.'

At its hour of victory the Zulu army quietly disbanded itself and the warriors, some with appalling wounds, dragging their loot with them, disappeared in all directions as they made their way homeward, there to recuperate physically and mentally and to be cleansed. Natal need not have trembled; at what seemed to be its greatest hour of peril it had never been safer. But the fear of invasion would remain real for some time to come. Seven weeks after Isandlwana, on 12 March, the Governor of Natal, Sir Henry Bulwer, declared a Day of Humiliation for the colonists; all shops throughout Natal were closed, business was totally suspended – and the churches were expected to be packed. However, reinforcements were beginning to arrive and the colonists released a pent-up breath as the regiments of British infantry and cavalry marched toward the border. Consequently the colonists did not observe the Day of Humiliation as they might have done a few weeks earlier. As one volunteer officer observed: 'The people of Pietermaritzburg did not look as humiliated as they ought to be, in fact the day was gone by for that; most of them thought it a bore, others took advantage of a holiday and a fine day, and went on picnics.' (Yet, as will be seen, 12 March would indeed be remembered as a true day of humiliation, for at dawn, 150 miles to the north on the banks of the Intombi River, Mbelini and his followers had inflicted another defeat upon the British army.)

By this time Lord Chelmsford had also recovered himself and although he had neglected to warn Colonel Pearson of his perilous position, he had been in almost daily correspondence with Wood to whom he bemoaned Pearson's loss of 600 head of oxen, but expressed no word of praise for his victory at the Nyezane River.

Wood, as we have read, was one of the first to hear the news of Isandlwana –
but not from Chelmsford. It was brought by Captain Alan Gardner, the same
officer who had taken Chelmsford's message to Pulleine and had been one of the
five imperial officers to escape. With the rest of the fugitives he made his way to
Helpmekaar and on arrival decided, quite rightly, that Rorke's Drift and No. 4
Column should be warned. Wood and the majority of his command were
skirmishing on Zunguin Mountain at this time. Being fifteen miles from their
fortified position at Tinta's Kop, and less than fifty miles from the victorious Zulu
army at Isandlwana, they were extremely vulnerable. Gardner had had a long day
for by the time he reached Helpmekaar he had survived the battle, escaped across
the flooded Buffalo River and ridden at least fifty miles since dawn. He wrote a
brief message, describing the fall of the camp, and tried to find someone willing to
ride with his warning to Wood. As there were no takers and no one prepared to
accompany him, he set off in the dark alone. He reached Dundee, about twenty-
five miles distant, during the night where, exhausted, he managed to persuade a
local Boer farmer to ride on with his message for a fee of £20. Having slept for a
while, Gardner was up at dawn, borrowed a horse and continued to ride to Utrecht
by a shortcut over the hills. He arrived at the town at the same time as his Boer
messenger who had gone the long way round via Newcastle. A relay of two more
messengers took the warning on to Wood, who received it late on the 23rd (at
about the same time as the people of Luneburg received the news by native
runner). Gardner, after his rather gallant ride, returned to Helpmekaar.[1] Wood,
having received timely warning of his now vulnerable right flank, retired to Tinta's
Kop.

Within days of Isandlwana Chelmsford was desperately looking for local
reinforcements to replace his losses and to repulse the expected invasion. Of his
original five columns, totalling more than 15,000 men, over half were gone due to
casualties, desertions or disbandment.

He was still hoping that the Swazis and the Boers would come to his aid; but
the Swazis would not budge and the Boers were now contemplating a good-
neighbour policy with the Zulu rather than the British. They believed that they
had been betrayed by the boundary award and now that Britain had been
humiliated they were going to enjoy seeing her struggle. As far as the award was
concerned, however, Sir Bartle Frere was ready to perform a complete volte-face, as
Chelmsford informed Wood in a letter dated 28 January. 'Sir Bartle Frere,' he
wrote, 'is going to inform the Dutchmen (Boers) in the Utrecht and Wakkerstroom districts that the boundary award is torn up, and that they will in future be
considered as under the British Government – and you are quite at liberty to let
them know of this decision at once.'

The Boers, for their part, did not want anything to do with the British Government – especially not to be subject to it. There were reports coming in of
kommandos assembling in the rural areas of the Transvaal – but they had revolt in

mind now that Chelmsford was fully occupied with the Zulu. The Boers of the
Orange Free State, who until a short while earlier had seemed a likely source of
500 mounted volunteers, now wanted nothing to do with Britain or her war. Frere
had sent as his deputy one of Chelmsford's staff officers, Captain Ernest Henry
Buller, [2] to negotiate, but he returned empty-handed. The OFS Executive, it was
reported by one of the newspapers, 'declares itself unable to call out a kommando,
unable to allow advertising for the purpose – in fact declares its total inability to
help us in any way'. And in the Disputed Territories, not far from Wood's camp, a
number of armed Boers came upon some cattle, recently captured by British
soldiers from the Zulu, and herded them back into Zululand on the grounds that
the animals, being where they were, would bring the Zulu down upon them.

Chelmsford saw his salvation in Wood and Buller. Five days after Isandlwana he
wrote to Wood: 'My best thanks are due to you and Buller – I feel confident that
you two are going to pull me out of my difficulties', and eight days later concluded
another letter with '. . . best love to Buller – you two will have to pull me out of the
mire'. They would do their best but they would also have their share of disaster.

1. Later he was slated for his efforts by the jealous, gossiping Major Clery.
2. Not to be confused with Colonel Redvers Buller.

4
DISASTER AT THE INTOMBI

*'. . . A fearful and horrible sight presented itself and the stillness
of the place was awful.'*

Major C. Tucker, 80th Regiment

Chelmsford determined to lavish upon No. 4 Column all the troops he could find.
Mounted men were his first choice as it had become plain that only cavalry could
manoeuvre against the enemy with any advantage. He wrote to Wood: 'My idea is
that our only chance of making any real impression in Zululand is to reinforce your
column to the fullest extent with mounted men and that I will endeavour to do.'

In England, two cavalry regiments, the 17th Lancers and the 1st Dragoon
Guards, were shortly to embark for Natal, but it would be many weeks before they
were ready for active service. Consequently, horsemen needed to be acquired from
local sources. Wood's mounted men at that moment consisted of the FLH, many
of whom would shortly take their discharge, and the Burgher Force. Over the next
few weeks Wood's command was to increase to over 700 horsemen and it is
unlikely that a more mixed bag of cavalry would ever be seen again. In the
meantime Wood acquired additional infantry – taken from Rowlands who was
still very much out of favour; during the month of February he was to become a
commander without any troops.

Although Rowlands was senior to Wood, Chelmsford schemed behind his back.
'Kindly send Rowlands full instructions and remember that he is on no account to
interfere with your independence,' he wrote to Wood and continued:

> I have told Rowlands that if the Swazis refuse to advance, he must be prepared to
> send you his mounted men and even his infantry should you ask for them. . . . I think
> it would be wise for you to summon all the Derby Force into your district placing
> them where you think most desirable – Rowlands will not like it but it can't be
> helped. . . . I hope you thoroughly understand that Colonel Rowlands is in no way
> entitled to interfere with your military command – pray carry this meaning of mine
> out to the fullest extent. . . . I am quite prepared to order him away if you find him a
> nuisance. Rowlands being wanted in Pretoria will leave you all his troops absolutely

at your disposal. . . .[1] One line to congratulate you on getting rid of Rowlands . . . make what distribution you like of the 80th men they are now entirely under you. . . .

The road from Derby to Utrecht, which crossed the Intombi River at Meyer's Drift, would shortly become a busy thoroughfare. In the meantime, the days immediately after Isandlwana, Wood and his command were busy enough keeping the flag flying for the whole of the British army in Natal.

There seemed no better way to let the enemy know that at least some of the British force still had teeth than by the continual burning of his dwellings and stealing his cattle. But first a secure and fortified base must be found for Wood's troops and Tinta's Kop was not the best location. Wood decided to move ten miles due west to a high but gently sloping ridge called Kambula, named after a former local chief who lived in the area, which commanded the countryside for miles around. Water was plentiful and firewood obtainable in a number of wooded kloofs three miles away. Wood fortified the highest elevation of this ridge with a stone redoubt and laagered his wagons in a manner to accommodate both men and beasts in time of attack. To the north of Kambula, fifteen miles away, lay the Zunguin Nek from where they had watched, several weeks earlier, the splendid drill manoeuvres of the abaQulusi warriors; and beyond Zunguin, just out of sight, was Hlobane Mountain.

Once established at the new base, Buller and his mounted men lost no time in taking the offensive. Twenty-five miles distant from Kambula was the Makulusini military kraal, a depot and rallying point for the abaQulusi. This was Buller's first target.

An hour before dawn on 1 February, Buller led out 116 officers and men of the FLH accompanied by Piet Uys and thirty-one of his burghers. By seven o'clock they had reached the northern slopes of Zunguin where a halt was called, the horses unsaddled and breakfast made. Shortly after eight o'clock they marched again, picking up the wagon track that Potter had used when supplying the Makulusini kraal with goods from his store. Buller's force would certainly be under observation from Hlobane Mountain, the base of which was two miles to the north. At noon, Uys judged them to be only five miles short of their destination and Buller ordered his force into a fast canter. Leaving a rearguard of thirty men, the rest swept over a ridge and down its rugged slopes into the kraal. The attack was a complete surprise; the Zulu garrison fled and every hut was destroyed. Some 300 head of cattle were taken and a number of the enemy killed. Buller's force escaped without a single casualty. 'The Makulusini kraal has been until now a rallying point for the most determined opponents of the British Government and its destruction will have a good effect on all friendly and neutral natives,' wrote Wood the following day in a letter to Chelmsford. Writing of Buller, one of his admiring officers commented:

He would do some dashing act like burning of the Makulusini military kraal, an exploit hardly heard of at home; with a small force of 120 men [it was actually 148] the colonel burnt a large kraal in face of an enemy several times as numerous; its opponents were a regular drilled regiment, but he brought off his force without any loss of life. It was a sight to see him standing on some eminence in the hottest fire, calmly looking through his telescope.

If Buller's officers admired him, and undoubtedly many did, then Buller admired Piet Uys. Almost every report that he wrote concluded with a sincere compliment: 'Throughout the day I received the greatest assistance from Mr Piet Uys ... without his assistance we would never have got to the place ... our movements would not be possible without the aid of Mr Piet Uys whose knowledge and courage are both remarkable.' It was an odd friendship; Buller, the Eton-educated Devonshire squire, and Uys, the rough frontiersman, but a deep friendship did exist and there seemed to be no one whom Buller respected more.

Over the next few days Buller and Uys, accompanied by their men, were raiding in all directions and on 10 February attacked the lower slopes of the Hlobane fortress, burning huts and capturing another 500 head of cattle. But the British were not going to have it all their own way: they had aroused the hornets nesting in the Tafelberg. That night a combined force of freebooters, led by Mbelini and Manyanyoba, stealthily skirted the fort and laager at Luneburg and set about the destruction of the local Christian natives. Soon the sky was red with burning huts. By morning the raiders were back across the Intombi River leaving many dead and taking hundreds of captured cattle with them.

Schermbrucker and his small garrison at Luneburg set out in pursuit but on foot there was no chance of drawing level with the raiders. Retaliation was essential but Buller's FLH was no longer as strong as it had been. Many of the troopers, having enlisted in the middle of the previous year, were now due for discharge and most took it. Chelmsford, in writing to the Secretary of State, regarded their departure with sorrow:

> I regret that nearly half the volunteers serving under Lieutenant-Colonel Buller are leaving him. They have done good service. But the loss of the services of mounted men such as these is much to be deplored at this moment. Mounted men are found to be an absolute necessity in this country and I trust the effort of His Excellency the High Commissioner, to obtain them from the Free State and Cape Colony will be successful.

Over seventy of the FLH resigned. As they made their way to Pietermaritzburg, where they were to be paid off, their progress was marred by murder. As one newspaper reported: 'We regret to learn that a couple of men of the FLH have disgraced themselves and thrown discredit on their corps by a serious crime....' When the contingent reached a wayside inn, called The Rising Sun, situated on the

Onderbroek Spruit between Ladysmith and Colenso, two of their number were seen to run from the inn by the back door carrying a box. A native girl gave the alarm and the owner, by the name of Doig, quickly discovered his cash-box had been stolen. Mounting his horse, he dashed after the two thieves, catching up with them as they were about to climb in a wagon with their comrades. An altercation followed during which Doig was struck down and subsequently died of his injuries. However, the honour of the regiment was upheld by the rest of the men who promptly arrested the robbers and handed them over to the nearest magistrate for trial. The newspaper concluded that the FLH 'are a fine lot of fellows'.

Notwithstanding the depletion of his force, Buller would not idly await the replacements which were already on their way from the Cape *en route* for Kambula. With diminished numbers he intended to wreak vengeance on the Tafelberg marauders. But he would find his protagonists skilled and resourceful enemies and their stronghold impregnable against the small force at his command.

On 15 February, with what was left of the FLH, he set out with Uys and his burghers for Luneburg, twenty miles from Kambula. On arrival he found that Lieutenant Schwartzkopf, of Schermbrucker's Kaffrarian Rifles, had already led a small retaliatory raid against Manyanyoba's stronghold four days earlier. Buller determined to mount another.

With thirteen of the FLH, thirty-three burghers, a few Kaffrarian Riflemen and 500 locally recruited natives of Wood's Irregulars, an inconclusive assault was made on the stronghold, during which thirty-four of the enemy were killed and as usual, a number of cattle stolen. But the stronghold was not taken. The death of thirty-four of their followers would give the bandit chiefs ample motive for counter-retribution.

Colonel Rowlands, not far away on the road to Derby, also attacked another Zulu stronghold at Tolaka Mountain. It was to be his last engagement before he was deprived of his troops. It was also an indecisive affair and he got little credit from Chelmsford for his efforts. Several of the enemy were killed and another 200 head of cattle went to join the swelling number of beasts to be sold as booty. A letter written on 6 March, composed by several colonial officers who took part in this action, was published in *The Times of Natal* twenty-five days later. It described in detail the difficulties of fighting in the mountainous bush-covered terrain, and particularly noted the bravery and dash of Charlie Potter, a local man and Rowlands's interpreter, who led part of the attack. The letter also openly criticised Rowlands for failing to follow up the success of the first day's operations, and accurately prophesied the conditions in which the disaster at the Intombi River would take place the following week: 'The feat could have been easily accomplished [the follow-up attack] and thrice the booty obtained, thus giving a thorough check to the Tolaka Zulus; but instead of an attack [as promised by Rowlands] at midday we marched to Luneburg ... had the success been followed up, this nest of thieves and murderers would have been cleaned out; instead of which the road from Derby to Luneburg has been, and continues to be impenetrable without a strong military convoy....'

While engaged at Tolaka Mountain Rowlands received a 'request' from Wood (who had wasted no time) for the 80th to be sent immediately to Luneburg. Major Charles Tucker, who commanded the regiment, was ordered to proceed with three companies while Rowlands followed with the remainder of the men. As the two separate columns made their way south-west to the Intombi Valley, they took the opportunity to raid, capture cattle and burn kraals, leaving a trail of devastation in their wake. A number of captives, mainly women and children, were offered their release but such was the state of the countryside, with the crops destroyed and homes burnt, that rather than accepting their immediate freedom they preferred to remain captive and become a British liability.

All this raiding and counter-raiding was taking place in a relatively small area. The distance from Wood's camp at Kambula in the south to Luneburg in the north was no more than twenty-five miles, with Hlobane Mountain, the Zunguin range, the Makulusini military kraal, Meyer's Drift and the two strongholds of Mbelini and Manyanyoba above the Intombi River, scattered in between. The area was extremely volatile and the road between Derby and Luneburg, along which all the supplies for the 80th would have to come, had become fraught with danger.

Amidst all this activity a new and influential character was about to make his presence felt. Wood had scored a diplomatic success in enlisting Piet Uys and his burghers and was now about to achieve another; this time none less than Cetshwayo's brother.

Between the north-eastern border of the Disputed Territories and the Lebombo Mountains lay the source of the Mkuze River. This was the country of Hamu (Oham) and his people, stretching as far as the borders of the Transvaal and Swaziland. Hamu was a full brother of Cetshwayo – in fact he was Mpande's first son and as such was, in Zulu custom, unable to succeed his father as king, but he was a prince and an influential member of Cetshwayo's council. Like all the male members of the Zulu royal family, he was an enormous man standing well over 6 feet in height and weighing over 270 pounds. He was considered brave and outspoken. At the time that Cetshwayo was fighting to establish his claim to the throne, Hamu had given him his full support. At the bloody battle of Ndonda-kusuka, in 1856, he had commanded a wing of Cetshwayo's victorious army. But the two brothers did not sit easily with one another; suspicion and envy divided them. As Cetshwayo once remarked, 'Hamu is the man that has for a long time during my reign tried his best to dethrone me and get my place.'

Of the two, Hamu had experienced more contact and dealings with the white man, often wearing European clothing. He enjoyed the goods he obtained by trading and, perhaps, appreciated the power wielded by the white civilisation; at any rate Hamu had not wanted war, and in council had voted in favour of handing over Sihayo's sons and complying with British demands. He had reason to be apprehensive of a foreign invasion for his territory would be the first to encounter the enemy. Nevertheless he and his faction had rallied to their king, his warriors suffering heavy losses at Isandlwana and retiring from the field with their share of the booty.

Perhaps as a result of the casualties sustained by the Zulu army at Isandlwana, Hamu became convinced that his people would ultimately be defeated; for it was after the battle that he decided to defect.

The correspondent for *The Natal Mercury*, J.M. Rathbone, who was attached to No. 4 Column, questioned a number of Hamu's people and came to the conclusion that Hamu had contrived to murder Cetshwayo after Isandlwana but that the would-be assassin, when confronted with his victim, collapsed and confessed all and threw himself on Cetshwayo's mercy. Cetshwayo in turn tried to lure Hamu to his presence with sweet words and gifts, but his wily brother was too old a hand at the intrigue of the royal court and decided it was time to leave.

Hamu was described as the most popular of the royal princes, rich in cattle and commanding 6000 warriors – not a position to relinquish without real cause. That the British might make him king in his brother's stead would have been reason enough; and perhaps he thought he could contrive such a possibility.

On 24 February, a white man rode into Kambula camp carrying a flag of truce. It was Hamu's emissary and a more unsuitable choice would have been hard to find. Hamu had several white trader advisers living in his territory, among them James Rorke, whose father (also James Rorke) had given his name to the now famous drift across the Buffalo River. There was also Herbert Nunn and a man called Calverley whom Hamu had chosen as his messenger. The military correspondent of *The Scotsman*, a Glasgow newspaper, described the scene: 'We saw the face of a white man carrying in his hand a flag of truce. On his nearer approach he was discovered to be an Afrikaner (Boer) bearing the name of Calverley. The colonists who were with us instantly recognised him as a man of doubtful reputation who had several times been "wanted" by the authorities.'[2]

What damned Calverley was not only the rifle and water bottle that he carried (for both had been looted from the slaughtered 24th Regiment at Isandlwana) but to top it all, he was riding the horse of none other than Lieutenant Coghill who had met his death, carrying the regimental colours, at Fugitive's Drift. The volunteers and soldiers alike saw these items as proof of participation if not in the actual battle of Isandlwana, then at least in the orgy of looting that followed, and many were all for lynching him on the spot. It was probably Wood's intervention and threat of the severest punishment on anyone molesting the man that saved his life.

Calverley brought tidings that Hamu wished to surrender with his people, and wanted to negotiate terms. As far back as November there had been subtle overtures of such an eventuality: Chelmsford had instructed Wood that Hamu must be told, '... he who is not with us is against us, and that if he remains passively in his kraal whilst we are advancing he must not be surprised if we take him for any enemy – I have no intention of remaining neutral inside the Zulu border'.

In no uncertain manner Wood told Calverley that the only terms available were unconditional surrender. Waiting until well into the night, lest Calverley should be accosted, Wood sent him back to find his master who was now in great danger for Cetshwayo had determined to catch Hamu before he reached the British. Forewarned, Hamu slipped through the net of warriors that guarded the drifts leading out of Zululand and, with many of his followers, found temporary sanctuary with the Swazi king. A message was sent to Captain McLeod, the British political agent to Swaziland, and it was to him that Hamu surrendered. On 4 March, he and 700 of his followers were taken to Derby and from there proceeded along the wagon track to Luneburg, thirty-eight miles distant, crossing the Intombi River at Meyer's Drift. Buller and a mounted force had gone out to meet him and acted as escort through the Intombi Valley, all arriving safely at Luneburg on the 7th.

A convoy of wagons, escorted by the 80th Regiment, which left Derby at about the same time as Hamu's party, was less fortunate. The wagons were transferring supplies for the 80th from their old depot at Lydenburg to their new quarters at Luneburg. The transport carried fresh mealies, tinned food, biscuits, weapons (including a rocket battery) and 90,000 rounds of Martini Henry ammunition. Believing its progress through the Transvaal relatively safe, it had been unescorted as far as Derby. Thereafter it had set out again unescorted but with a promise of a suitable force meeting it on the road. On the morning of 1 March, 'D' Company of the 80th Regiment, under the command of Captain Anderson and accompanied by Lieutenant Daubeney, marched out and met the convoy.

It had been raining for days and the condition of the track was appalling: the wagons, often up to their axles in mud, had to be manhandled almost every step of the way. After four days of hard labour, Anderson, his men and the convoy, were still some five miles from Meyer's Drift. It was then that Anderson received a note from Major Charles Tucker commanding the 80th at Luneburg. The exact contents of the message are unknown but it seems that Anderson assumed he had been recalled; so leaving ten wagons of the convoy where they were, he and his men marched back to Luneburg.

The progress of the convoy had been carefully monitored by the warriors of Mbelini and Manyanyoba, whose strongholds were near by, and as soon as the escort marched away a party of pillagers descended to loot the unprotected wagons, sending the drivers and voorlopers fleeing in the direction of Derby. Hardly had the robbers started their work when some forward scouts of Hamu's party appeared on the scene and drove them off. But it was a temporary measure for no sooner had Hamu's warriors departed than the looters returned, pillaging a number of stores and making off with more than forty of the transport oxen.

When Anderson arrived at Luneburg without the convoy, Tucker was appalled, but instead of sending him back Tucker ordered Captain David Moriarty, with 106 men of all ranks, to recover the wagons. Moriarty marched out of Luneburg just as Hamu and Buller arrived and by the time Moriarty's relief force reached Meyer's Drift, four and a half miles out of Luneburg, the Intombi River had risen and was found to be impassable. A camp was therefore pitched on the Luneburg bank and Moriarty set about building a raft which was a rickety affair of barrels and planks lashed together with ropes. Ferrying a few men at a time, most were transferred to the opposite bank, leaving thirty-five on the Luneburg side under the command of Lieutenant Lindop. Once safely across, Moriarty and the rest of the men set out to recover the abandoned wagons, only to find most had been looted.

It was not until early in the afternoon of the 11th, four days after Moriarty had set out from Luneburg, that the last of the wagons were brought to the Derby side of Meyer's Drift. The men were now in a wretched condition, having been wet through for days and without any means to dry their clothing or cook food. Moriarty was, therefore, pleased to see that in his absence two of the wagons which had been left at the drift had been transported to the Luneburg bank. However, the Intombi was again in spate, running at seven knots and quite impassable. Moriarty had no option but to spend the night where he was and decided to form his wagons into a laager of sorts. This was the fifth night in succession that Moriarty and his men had spent on the road and as they had survived so far without a laager they did not take great pains with the one they were about to make. A successful laager must be a tightly packed construction – not like Moriarty's slack affair with gaps between each vehicle. His laager was laid out in the shape of an inverted 'V' with its feet resting on the river's edge; but by late afternoon the Intombi had subsided again, rendering the river side of the laager open and defenceless. Nothing was done and the lesson of Isandlwana, so recent and severe, had not been learnt.

Neither was Moriarty an inexperienced soldier. He was forty-two years of age, had seen service in India, had marched against Sekhukhune and had been with the 80th along the Zulu border for almost three years. He should have known that being immobile under the wings of such hawks as Mbelini and Manyanyoba, there could be no room for complacency.

In the late afternoon Tucker rode over from Luneburg to see how things were. He inspected the laager and whilst disapproving of its sloppy arrangement, or so he said later, did nothing about it. Tucker was accompanied by Lieutenant Henry Hollingworth Harward, whose unhappy duty it was to relieve Lieutenant Lindop, who had been stationary on the Luneburg side of the river ever since Moriarty had crossed six days earlier. Harward crossed the river on the raft and hearing that some cattle had strayed, went off in pursuit. He found them and recovered the herd in the nearby hills, killing two natives in the process. Harward returned to the camp with the cattle plus some goats that had belonged to the dead natives. He had hoped to sleep in Moriarty's tent but was ordered back across the river.

Tucker and Lindop eventually rode off back to the fort, leaving Harward to inspect his little command, on the Luneburg bank, of two wagons, several tents and thirty-five men. His senior NCO was Sergeant Anthony Booth, a man of fifteen years service who had held his rank for over seven years. He was 5 ft 6 in tall, (about average height in Queen Victoria's army) and had been a tailor by trade before enlisting.

Toward evening some German settlers passed by the camp and with heavy Teutonic humour offered to build a bridge over the river for the sum of £5.

On the opposite side of the drift, Moriarty and his men prepared to settle down for the night. The river had receded further and several tents were pitched in the space that had been left between the last wagon and the river bank – a move more to keep the transport animals inside the laager than the enemy out. Moriarty, disdaining to sleep inside the laager, had his tent pitched beyond the apex of the top wagon.

The morrow was the day the Governor of Natal had declared as one of humiliation. It is doubtful if the sleeping soldiers were aware of this and they would have cared little had they known. There were sixteen wagons to get across the river, which would be an humiliating task in itself. Moriarty would have been well aware of the standing order that a camp such as his should be 'guarded by outlying pickets of infantry thrown at short distances to the front, flanks and rear' – but only a single sentry was posted on either side of the river.

Mbelini had been trained as a warrior since childhood, though not in the warfare of large armies. His training had been one of stealth and surprise attack, typified by an impi that travelled at night, hid by day and fell upon its unsuspecting target at first light whereupon the victims, men, women and children, would be mercilessly slain. Looking down from the lofty Tafelberg, Mbelini saw below him a situation that was well suited to his type of warfare.

Combined with Manyanyoba's warriors, Mbelini had a force of almost 1000 men. Only a few firearms, sufficient for the first surprise volley, would be taken; to ensure complete silence the remainder of the force would carry only a stabbing spear and a knobkerrie per man. Shields would be left behind and all would strip naked. In the early morning Mbelini's war party started to descend the mountain, making their way toward the sleeping camp three miles away.

At 4.30 am before first light, the sentry on the Luneburg bank was alarmed by a single shot coming from the direction of the opposite camp. The shot also awoke Harward who ordered Sergeant Booth to shout across the river and alert the other sentry, for as yet no one had stirred on the opposite bank. Booth bellowed an order but there was no response – perhaps the sentry was already dead? After more shouting by Booth, a man finally emerged from one of the tents and after a few moments called back that the camp had been alerted and the men were to dress but could remain in their tents. Satisfied, the men on both sides of the river returned to their slumbers.

Booth, however, was uneasy and got himself dressed. Then he buckled on his ammunition belt and climbed up into the commissariat wagon. In company with another man, and in an anxious mood, he lit up his pipe. He chatted for half an hour or so and just as it was beginning to get light both men were startled by another shot from the opposite bank. Booth ducked out of the wagon and to his horror saw that the laager across the river, less than 100 yards away, had been surrounded by hundreds of warriors. As he watched, the attackers fired one volley into the tents at point-blank range and then swarmed through the laager, stabbing the soldiers as they bolted terrified from their tents.

Moriarty, outside the area of the wagons, was one of the first to die. Revolver in hand, he charged from his tent, shooting three warriors at close range before he went down with an assegai in his back and a bullet in his chest, reputedly shouting, in his Irish accent, as he fell, 'Fire away, boys, death or glory! I'm done!' Those who managed to escape from the tents were caught up in the nightmare mêlée of maddened cattle and frenzied warriors – all in an area of little more than half an acre. Isandlwana in miniature, all over again.

A lucky few made it to the river, which was still roaring along at seven knots, and swimmer or not they plunged in, hoping to be swirled across to the opposite bank. Josiah Sussens, a civilian wagon conductor, described his escape as he called to his friend Whittington to get out of their wagon:

> He immediately came out and jumped down, but was caught almost as soon as he got to the ground, he was assegaied on all sides. The poor fellow shrieked out but without avail ... I ran down between the oxen and made for the river which was about sixty yards off. I found Zulus shooting and stabbing the people in all directions. The sight was a most horrifying one and one never to be forgotten. As soon as I got to the river I jumped in and made a dive, as swimming was too dangerous, the Zulu standing on the bank, and at the edge of the river, as thick as thieves, throwing assegais and aiming their guns wherever they saw a head. I came up about the middle of the river, but the moment my head was out, I saw several Zulu pointing their guns and ready to fire. I therefore dived again and came up on the other side, the river was very full at the time and a strong current running. In crossing I had torn off my shirt, the only garment I possessed and, therefore, when I landed I was entirely in a state of nudity.

As soon as Booth saw the attack, he organised his men and they fired volley after volley across the water. At so close a range they killed a number of the enemy but could not stop the slaughter on the opposite bank. Including civilian conductors, drivers and voorlopers, there had been almost 120 with Moriarty, of whom only twelve managed to cross the river and survive.

Mbelini, having completed the carnage on the north bank, diverted his warriors'

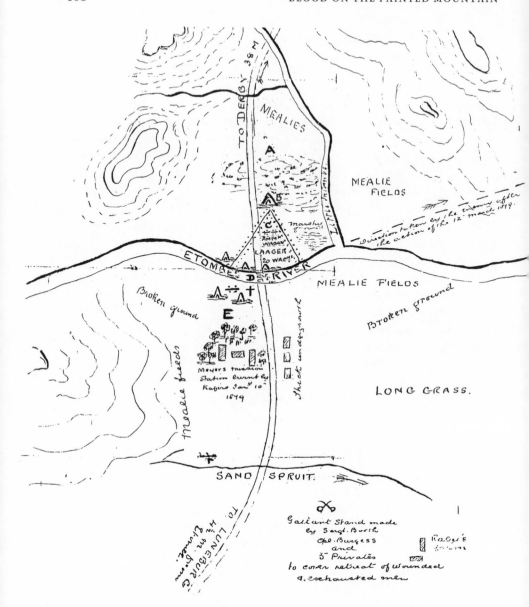

4. THE BATTLEFIELD AT INTOMBI RIVER
(Caption on facing page)

attention to Booth and his men who were keeping up a determined covering fire. Warriors were soon swarming across the river and as they did so Harward mounted a horse belonging to another man (most probably one of the conductors) and galloped away to Luneburg, leaving Booth and the rest of his command to their fate.

The day after the battle Booth described the ordeal in a letter to his wife: 'I commanded the party on this side as Lieutenant Harward saddled his horse and galloped away leaving us to do the best we could. When I saw all our men across, about fifteen in number, and all as naked as they were born, I sent them in front and we retired firing at the enemy.'

Mbelini's men had now crossed the river in large numbers and Booth was in danger of being surrounded; he kept his head, however, and retreating slowly, succoured the wounded and exhausted men who had joined him. He retreated to high ground and there took up a stand at a deserted farmhouse. At that point four men left him, hoping to gain Luneburg by a shortcut, but alas they were overtaken and killed.

In the meantime Harward had galloped into Fort Clery where he dismounted, stumbled into Major Tucker's tent and, having woken his CO with a start, burst out, 'The camp is in the hands of the enemy, they are all slaughtered, and I have

Caption to Map 4 (on facing page): The battlefield at Intombi River where a predawn attack by Mbelini and his warriors caught a British convoy of the 80th Regiment asleep in their tents. The map was probably drawn the day after the battle, by Major Charles Tucker who commanded the 80th at nearby Luneburg.

Key:
A. Rising ground behind which the enemy to the number of 4000, collected at 5 am on 12 March, during a thick misty rain, when with a [indecipherable on the original] followed a charge they attacked the laager defended by only 60 men of the 80th Regiment.
B. Tent occupied by Capt. Moriarty and Dr. Cobbin.
C. Spot where Capt. Moriarty fell after killing 2 of Manyanyoba's sons.
D. Drift 10 feet deep owing to 5 days incessant rain, it is to be feared that some of our men must have been lost therein.
E. Camp commanded by Lieut. Harward. The 30 noncommissioned officers and men here gallantly secured the retreat of some of our men from the other side.
F. At this spot one wounded man and in the spruit 4 of our men were found dead. These brought into Luneburg and buried that night by torchlight.
+39 noncommissioned officers and men buried here three hours after the engagement.
Below the crossed swords: 'Gallant stand made by Sargt. Booth, Cpl Burgess and 5 privates to cover the retreat of wounded and exhausted men.' The stand was made at Rabe's deserted farmstead. (Staffordshire Regiment Museum)

galloped in for my life!'. Harward then fell into a dead faint across Tucker's bed.

With commendable haste Tucker mounted every man for whom a horse could be found and, ordering 150 infantry to follow, led his horsemen down toward the river. On the way he passed Booth and his party who, despite casualties, had kept his men together and a tenacious enemy at bay.

As Tucker's force approached they could see a dense mass of Zulu across the river moving off toward Mbelini's stronghold. When they reached the devastated camp Tucker recalled, '... a fearful and horrible sight presented itself and the stillness of the spot was awful, our men were laying about all over the place, some naked and some only half clad ... all the bodies were full of assegai wounds and nearly all were disembowelled.' But the mounted men could not follow, the current being too strong for the horses. Mbelini had made a particularly audacious attack; his timing ensured that the flooded Intombi prevented pursuit by the Transvaal Rangers and the Border Horse who, having left Rowlands's column, had been in Luneburg since the beginning of the month.

A badly shaken and disgruntled Sussens described his reception when, with Sergeant Booth's party, he stumbled into Fort Clery:

> Arriving in a state of nudity with the exception of a soldier's overcoat, got from a native on the road, I applied to the authorities for some blankets to sleep under but was refused. They said they had none ... to add to our annoyance two wounded Zulu were brought in (one on my cartel) and were put into a nice tent and covered with blankets whilst we had to take our chance as best we could underneath the wagons.

A mass grave was dug on the south bank of the Intombi River and the dead, with the exception of Moriarty and a twenty-eight-year-old civilian surgeon named Cobbin, who rated individual graves in the local cemetery, were piled in. Booth maintained in the letter to his wife that the Zulu crept back across the river that night, dug up some of the dead, and skinned them. This could well have been true, the skin being used by witchdoctors to make powerful muti (medicine).

For weeks after the battle the bodies of missing men were found in the river and along its banks as the water rose and subsided with the rains. Out of a total of approximately 150 personnel, both soldiers and civilians that had camped on the banks of the Intombi, only fifty or so survived.

In addition to the loss of human life, 225 pounds of gunpowder, a number of rifles and 90,000 rounds of ammunition had been lost.[3]

The press, after lamenting the loss of brave soldiers, was soon questioning the competence of their officers. Understandably, Lord Chelmsford was furious as incompetence and complacency were clearly the cause of the disaster – and there was no doubt that Moriarty was the chief culprit, with Tucker next in line. But if blame was to travel higher up the ladder, it would rest with Wood, for he had taken the 80th under his command two weeks previously. Perhaps even more damning was a letter he had received from Chelmsford as far back as December regarding the perils of the Derby/Luneburg road. 'I am anxious to move the troops from Derby by the direct southern route,' Chelmsford had written, 'if it could be done with due regard to proper military precautions – if you say it is not the best road for them to take I shall be quite satisfied.' Wood had little to say with regard to the disaster that followed at the Intombi River. In his autobiography it was dismissed in one paragraph in which he concluded, 'I went over at daylight [13 March] to the scene – forty miles distant – to enquire into the disaster, and to ensure our system of security being adopted for the future, returning in the afternoon to camp, as I had arranged a long ride for the next day.'

Nevertheless, apart from Sergeant Booth being awarded a well earned VC, there appeared to be no repercussions to affect anyone's military career either adversely or beneficially. It even seemed as though Harward's hasty departure from danger would be overlooked. Yet this was not to be. Eight months later, after Sir Garnet Wolseley had taken over Chelmsford's command, Harward was brought back from England under arrest to face a charge of 'misbehaviour before the enemy and shamefully abandoning a party of the regiment under his command when attacked', and other lesser charges relating to the incident. Much to Wolseley's chagrin (and no doubt the surprise of the army in general) Harward was found not guilty on all charges on the basis that he went to procure reinforcements, which, by their arrival, or the imminence of their arrival, warded off destruction for the party that he had abandoned. He was released and ordered to return to duty. Wolseley was appalled: what with Isandlwana there had been too many officers riding away from the heat of battle while their abandoned men fought on. Wolseley had to abide by the court's decision but added his own adverse comments to the verdict, writing that had he not done so it would have been 'tacit acknowledgment that I concurred in what appears to me a monstrous theory, viz; that a regimental officer who is the only officer present with a party of soldiers actually and seriously engaged with the enemy, can, under any pretext whatsoever, be justified in deserting them and leaving them to their fate'. He added some further damning remarks with which the Field Marshal Commander in Chief, the Duke of Cambridge, agreed, causing them to be read at the head of every regiment in Her Majesty's service. Wolseley confided to his diary that he would have liked to have seen Harward hang and would have volunteered to do the deed himself!

Unquestionably, Wood was anxious to get away from the scene of the Intombi disaster as he had arranged a long ride for the next day. At the time he was much occupied with the defection of Hamu, for although he had the prince and many of his followers safely ensconced at Kambula, there were still another thousand or so hiding in caves near the source of the Mkuze River. Unless Wood could secure their escape and conduct them safely to the British lines the propaganda benefits of Hamu's surrender would be completely lost.

Early in the morning of 24 March, 360 mounted men and 200 of Hamu's warriors (all of whom had fought against the British at Isandlwana) marched off deep into Zululand.

Wood himself accompanied the expedition. The horsemen were led by Buller, and Mr Llewellyn Lloyd, who had commanded the disastrous Zulu Police during the Sekhukhune campaign, was in charge of Hamu's warriors. He also acted as Wood's political officer and interpreter.

The rescue mission took the force forty-five miles across rugged terrain and they arrived at their destination sixteen hours later. Much of the night was spent in collecting all those who wished to join Hamu. By nine o'clock the following morning a great cavalcade of humanity and cattle was ready to move. Wood's gamble had come off. Not only would their journey be a safe one but the number of fugitives would increase *en route* for three women successfully gave birth and, within no time at all of producing their babies, were up and going again, much to Wood's amazement.

Kambula proved to be too far to reach that day; consequently the whole cavalcade bivouacked on the banks of the White Umfolozi River. The following day Wood sent ahead to Kambula for every mule wagon that was to be had, and into these he piled the children who had walked so far the previous day. Nevertheless there was insufficient room for all and as the march started the hardened FLH could be seen conveying small black bodies fore and aft on their horses. Even the fearsome Buller, who had declared he would have 'nothing to do with verminous children', was seen with a nursery-full of little Zulus clinging to his saddle.

The return route took them past Hlobane Mountain, where once again the abaQulusi were waiting. They opened fire but the distance was too great for any damage to be done. It was rumoured that after his Intombi success, Mbelini had taken up residence on the mountain which was now the most powerful Zulu base for miles around. Its garrison, the abaQulusi, as Wood had witnessed some weeks before, was a disciplined and well-drilled regiment. The Hlobane stronghold would have to be dealt with. It certainly could not be left intact when the invasion resumed.

But first there was a score to settle with Mbelini for his brilliant success in destroying Moriarty's convoy. Wood must have wondered what Hamu's secret thoughts were and would he have defected had he known there would be another bloody British defeat? Worse still, it was a defeat right on Hamu's doorstep and executed, not by drilled regiments of the Zulu army, but by a gang of freebooters. If there were any other chiefs dithering between loyalty and defection (and there had been one or two), Mbelini's victory would now ensure their continued loyalty to Cetshwayo.

Despite their arduous journey to Hamu's territory and back, Wood had all his mounted men on parade again the following morning.

With 300 horsemen and 500 Swazis of Wood's Irregulars, he set out for

Luneburg and the Intombi, thirty-five miles distant to the north-west, 'to destroy crops of one of our most troublesome foes'.

Luneburg had become a frontline target. There was no other white settlement that had been subjected to terror tactics and attack as had Luneburg, whose people had real cause for panic – but had not done so. Over the past three months the white inhabitants had been shut up in their laager and in consequence had suffered the ravages of disease. The Hermansburg and Meyer's mission stations had been destroyed, as had a number of homesteads, many Christian blacks had been killed, cattle stolen, crops destroyed and, to cap it all, almost a company of the 80th slaughtered only four miles from the Luneburg laager. Wood hoped that his visit and the punitive action he proposed to take would do much to restore local morale.

Recently, both Buller and Rowlands had attempted to storm enemy mountain strongholds with little success. Wood, therefore, did not intend to attack Mbelini's fortress without infantry support. Perhaps he listened to Piet Uys expounding his theory that the easy way to beat the Zulu was by relentlessly destroying his crops and burning his dwellings. In any event the destruction of the enemy's crops was the course that Wood decided to pursue.

He first visited Pastor Filter and his wife, the leaders of the German community, seeking to reassure them with his show of force. The Filters' son Heinrich, a youngster of about seventeen years, was serving on Wood's staff because of his useful local knowledge and language ability. Wood offered to post the boy back to Luneburg to be close to his parents, but Mrs Filter would not hear of it, replying that the boy was at Wood's service.

Having shown the flag in Luneburg, the punitive force crossed the Intombi, passing the massed grave of the 80th, now twelve days old, at Meyer's Drift. Wood described what followed: 'We spread out over the basin of the Intombi River, cultivated by Mbelini's tribe ... we destroyed all the crops we could, and after two long days work returned, on the evening of the 26th [March] to Kambula Hill.'

On the return journey, Hlobane Mountain would have been visible to the south-east and Wood's spies assured him that Mbelini had left the Tafelberg and now resided on the southern slopes of Hlobane. Wood had contemplated an assault on the mountain for some weeks. As he was now under pressure from Chelmsford, who was planning an attempt to relieve Eshowe, it could be an opportune time; Mbelini's presence on the mountain made it a doubly desirable conquest. As virtually all the mounted troops that had been promised had arrived at Kambula, Wood determined to assault the Painted Mountain without delay.

1. Sir Bartle Frere, apprehensive of an uprising of the Transvaal Boers, had requested Rowlands's presence in Pretoria.
2. Calverley is a mystery figure. He is described here as an Afrikaner but his name is

English. There is little doubt that he was one of two brothers whose widowed mother, Susannah Calverley of Durban, apprenticed both of her boys to be bound for five and seven years respectively to one Jacobus Johannes Uys (elder brother of Piet Uys) as general servants. Their apprenticeship papers, dated 1863, stipulated that they were to be cared for as children of Uys, taught to read and write, understand accounts and to be paid one heifer a year each. At the time of Hamu's defection the older brother, Henry, would have been twenty-six years old and John twenty-four. Having lived with the Boers for all their adult lives they would have been taken for Afrikaners and, being locally raised, instantly recognised by many of the volunteers. A popular legend at the time was that the Zulu army at Isandlwana had been led by white men, their faces blackened with burnt cork. Calverley, carrying spoils from the battlefield, gave substance to the legend. But such rumours were nonsense. The Zulu army needed no white men to lead it and certainly none of Calverley's ilk.

3. The Woolwich Arsenal would soon be working overtime to replace the enormous quantity of arms and ammunition that had been lost. In less than eight weeks the enemy had acquired 600,000 rounds of ammunition, two cannons and approximately 1000 breach-loading rifles. Badly needed replenishments were on their way but the vessel, the SS *Clyde*, which at the time of the Intombi River disaster was steaming southward for the Cape, would shortly sink after going aground at Diaz Island. All her cargo, consisting entirely of government stores for the troops in Natal, would be lost, including 150 tons of ammunition, rifles and Gatling guns.

5

THE HORSEMEN ASSEMBLE

'By the time they reached the column, thoroughly hardened and seasoned, and as men of ruined fortune are proverbially reckless of life, they were well suited to the work before them.'

W.H. Tomasson
(With the Irregulars in the Transvaal and Zululand)

The volunteer horsemen were a heterogeneous gathering and a number of contemporary descriptions have survived. W.H. Tomasson, who was himself a volunteer, did not have too high an opinion of his comrades, describing their ranks as consisting of 'broken gentlemen, of renegade sailors, of fugitives from justice, of scum of the South African towns … almost every European nationality was represented; there were a few, a Greaser, a Chilean, several Australians and a couple of Canadian voyageurs from somewhere in the Arctic regions.'

Another contemporary scribe, apparently much to his detriment, made the acquaintance of a particular unit of horsemen and left them with the opinion that 'if they fight as well as they thieve, they will be of great execution amongst the Zulu'.

'They are undisciplined and disrespectful to their officers,' was yet another opinion, 'fearfully slovenly and various drunks and winebibbers that ever took a carbine in hand.' A description of their officers was hardly more flattering: 'The volunteer officers, some zealous, some sluggish, some cantankerous were, as regard any knowledge of duty, for the most part quite useless.' In conclusion it was generally acknowledged that 'it needed a thoroughly masterful man, like Colonel Redvers Buller, to bring these desperadoes into subjection'.

It is likely that some units had their own individual style of uniform. The FLH and the Imperial MI certainly did, whereas the burghers wore their everyday attire. By the time the force set out for Hlobane, most uniforms had been reduced to remnants and the men dressed as best they could with consideration to climate and comfort. Major G. Tylden, in his book *Armed Forces of South Africa 1659–1954*, described the irregulars as wearing 'a white helmet with a puggree hanging well down behind, jacket black or dark blue, braided and worn with a neckcloth', but this would have been an officer's attire and even then more the exception than the rule. Archibald Forbes, the war correspondent of the *London Daily News*, commented that 'those droll irregulars never took much pains, neither smartness nor uniformity was a desideratum. The fellows dressed how they liked ... the only uniform accoutrement was the bandolier in which cartridges were carried.'

There were now eight different mounted units attached to No. 4 Column. In order, more or less, of their date of arrival at Kambula, they were: Frontier Light Horse; Burgher Force; Kaffrarian Rifles (they had recently received horses); Imperial Mounted Infantry; Natal Native Horse; Baker's Horse; Transvaal Rangers and the Border Horse – sometimes called the Border Lancers.

The Frontier Light Horse had served the longest with Wood, they had been raised in Kingwilliamstown in 1877 by Captain Frederick Carrington of the 1/24th Regiment and were initially known as Carrington's Horse. Due to change of command and early service on the Cape Colony frontier, the unit was renamed the Frontier Light Horse. It had always been commanded by good officers and now that Buller had been promoted to take command of all the mounted units, Captain Robert Barton, a special service officer seconded from the Coldstream Guards, was in charge. A number of reinforcements had arrived during February and March and the FLH was again over 200 strong. Although there may have been little in the way of uniform for the new recruits there never seemed to have been a shortage of wide-brimmed felt hats with mimosa-coloured puggrees, worn by everyone from Buller down to the newest recruit.

The Burgher Force, commanded by Piet Uys, comprised approximately forty men, many of whom were related to their commander, four of them being his sons, and all were recruited from the area of the Disputed Territories. Their local knowledge was invaluable and generally they supplied their own guns and rode their own horses. There were one or two English-speaking burghers among their number, but most were Boers speaking only Dutch and Zulu. The landrost of Utrecht, Adrian Rudolph, was a member. According to most contemporary evidence, they would accept neither pay nor emolument but 'served solely to restore peace and prosperity to the land'. They did, however, demand their share of the cattle booty and in addition Wood had promised them farms when the war was over. They could also, hopefully, expect generous compensation for their families in the event of death on active service.

Uys was fifty-five years of age and had a lifetime's experience of the frontier. Having considerable land holdings in the Utrecht area, he was particularly interested in seeing peace restored. He actually wore a white helmet and a frogged jacket, as described by Tylden, on active service, but the rest of his burghers wore their battered workaday clothes with bandoliers. They were well mounted and equipped: a small force but a formidable one.

The Kaffrarian Rifles of Commandant Schermbrucker were the longest-residing unit in the Disputed Territories, having guarded the frontier settlement of Luneburg for over three months. From a foot unit they had recently been elevated to the status of horsemen, the unit having received '110 capital horses' during the middle of March. The correspondent of *The Transvaal Argus*, who recorded this piece of news, snidely concluded that the unit would 'soon learn to ride under the mild persuasion of their commandant'. Their number had also been increased by the arrival of fifteen white NCOs from Chelmsford's disbanded NNC, who had originally been recruited at bargain rates of pay from the Cape. Because they could speak neither English nor Zulu, Chelmsford, noting that they were 'foreigners', dumped them on Schermbrucker – presumably they spoke German. Schermbrucker's position, and that of the men under his command, seems to have been unique, being directly responsible to Chelmsford himself.

When it was decided that the Kaffrarian Rifles should be mounted, they were ordered to march to Kambula. Schermbrucker wisely requested Wood for an escort of mounted men, pointing out that a company of infantry marching between Luneburg and Kambula could be met by an overwhelming Zulu force (how right he was, almost prophesying the disaster at Intombi River two weeks later). Wood replied by letter, in a patronising vein, to the effect that Schermbrucker need not be nervous while he was in command at Kambula. To make matters worse, Wood neither put his confidential letter in an envelope, nor sealed it in any way. Schermbrucker took immediate offence and replied in blistering form:

I have the honour to acknowledge receipt of your dispatch marked 'confidential', which was handed to me open and without envelope . . . the observations which I had the honour to make yesterday were dictated only by that sense of responsibility which devolves upon a commanding officer in regard to his troops . . . having done so I am relieved of that responsibility . . . I need hardly say, that I, alone, would ride from here to Cetshwayo's kraal at any moment I might be required to do so; my own life being my own property.

Schermbrucker also criticised Wood's knowledge of the area with heavy sarcasm, pointing out that the enemy 'would be between Luneburg and Kambula, if my map of Zululand is correct, and not behind your column'. He concluded his letter by reminding Wood that the boots he had requisitioned for his men two months earlier had still not arrived and in spite of many men now being barefoot he would march for Kambula without delay and without escort.

The Kaffrarian Rifles were *en route* for three days and Wood, alerted to their arrival and perhaps in an effort to make amends, had the regimental band of the 90th LI march out and lead the gallant little unit of 106 men into camp. Mr Rathbone, the correspondent of *The Natal Mercury*, describes the scene with Schermbrucker highlighting the plight of his bootless men:

On arrival at Kambula the Kaffrarian Rifles, headed by the band of the 90th Regiment, marched to their camping ground in first rate style. A very remarkable sign of the wear and tear which this corps has undergone since they set foot on shore at Durban, presented itself to all beholders in the utter absence of boots and stockings from the feet of the foremost section; the men marched, however, with firm step and easy gait, nevertheless, barefoot.

It had been Wood's intention to scrap the Kaffrarian Rifles as a unit and use the men as replacements for the FLH; but he had reckoned without Schermbrucker and his unique terms of appointment.

Once arrived at Kambula, Schermbrucker immediately wrote to Chelmsford reminding him that his appointment was that of 'Commandant under the Lieu-tenant General' and if he and his men were posted to the FLH he would in effect be reduced to the rank of a captain without any chance of independent action in the field, which his military spirit would forbid him to accept. He then offered to resign, concluding, 'I would scorn the idea of withdrawing from the battlefield before I frankly explained my position and found that it was inevitable to do so. . . .' Schermbrucker won the day, the Kaffrarian Rifles lived on, and his bootless soldiers went in search of the '110 capital horses' that had been earmarked for them. They now had twenty-five days in which to learn to ride but, unfortunately, their mounts were still *en route* from the OFS and it would be another week before they arrived!

The Imperial Mounted Infantry had been formed by transferring infantry men from their parent battalions, such as the 1/13th and the 2/24th, to the mounted force. Most of the men had previous equestrian experience, mainly that of being a groom. Their attire was an adaption of an infantryman's uniform; they wore a normal red serge jacket (with parent regimental buttons and badges), helmet and waist belt, cord breeches, boots and gaiters; and to give them a bit of swagger and some appearance of a horseman they also wore a pair of hunting spurs. When mounted, a Swinburne-Henry carbine was slung over the left shoulder, the small of the stock resting on the right hip and fastened, when not required, by a small strap to the waist belt (the carbine was also carried in various forms of 'rifle buckets' slung from the saddle). Later in the campaign they were also issued with swords which were attached to their saddles.

There are numerous illustrations of the IMI looking spruce enough to ride escort down The Mall, but due to the exigencies of the service they became as rough a lot as any of the volunteers. Wood had inspected them the previous Christmas before they rode over to join Chelmsford prior to Isandlwana, and wrote: 'a more ragged crew was perhaps never got together, except professional beggars on a stage. I was much dissatisfied, for the first horse I looked at was about to get a sore back, his saddle cloth being twisted up under the saddle. Many of the men had only ten rounds of ammunition. . . .' An even more disparaging description has survived, that 'their uniform was a red coat, more or less tattered, trousers and leggings ditto, with a battered helmet. They looked like a cross between a groom out of place and a soldier after a night in cells and a big drink.'

By the time they reached Kambula on 14 March, the Mounted Infantry were the most work-worn and most unhappy of all the mounted men. They had been on active service, more or less, for almost two years, riding thousands of miles in every kind of weather. They had recently experienced the dispiriting catastrophe of the Sekhukhune campaign and the daylight horror of the Isandlwana battlefield where forty-eight members of the unit who had remained in camp were slaughtered. Their new and unpopular commanding officer, Lieutenant Colonel Cecil Russell, had since that fateful battle avoided any active duty along the Zululand border and had sulked in safety at Helpmekaar, pleading unfit horses. Two weeks after Isandlwana, Russell wrote that the Mounted Infantry wanted to disband, the men wishing to return to their regiments. Chelmsford responded by writing to Wood, 'It will be some time before you get any mounted men from Helpmekaar. Between ourselves, Russell appears to have lost heart and allowed his men to get out of hand. . . .' Wood recognised the malady and in replying to Chelmsford said '. . . all down the Helpmekaar way are like beaten children. I could have forgiven a week, but now it is time to cheer up . . . all Helpmekaar wants stirring up. . . .'

The previous commander of the IMI, Lieutenant Edward Stevenson Browne of the 1/24th, who had been with the unit since its inception, and was now reduced to second-in-command, was made of sterner stuff and would have made a better showing. Russell had many critics, even among his friends, and now he was with Wood and under the direct command of Buller, he would have to buck up – and so would his mounted infantry.

The Natal Native Horse, Edendale Troop, was formed entirely of Christian blacks, except for two or three white officers, all of whom were of the amaGwane tribe and had lived for many years at the Edendale Mission near Pietermaritzburg. The Zulu were their traditional enemy, Shaka having dispossessed them of their land and cattle sixty years earlier. At that time and in order to survive and re-establish themselves, they had fought with their neighbours, the amaHlubi, but in the end both tribes had been forced to flee their traditional territory and each eventually settled in the foothills of the Drakensberg near Ladysmith. The Hlubi Troop also formed part of the NNH but they had little in common with their former amaGwane enemies of the Edendale troop, except a hatred of the Zulu.

The ancestral land of the amaGwane had been in the vicinity of Wood's present camp, so riding to Kambula was like returning home – in fact their association with the area was reflected in the name of their troop sergeant major, Simeon Kambule. Like the Boers of the Burgher Force, they had provided their own horses, saddlery, uniforms and equipment – but unlike the Boers they had received no promises of compensation or land. Furthermore they were paid less than half the rate the white volunteers earned, which was grossly unfair as there were few white men who were their equal. The injustice of such discrepancy went unnoticed, as is indicated by Tomasson's assessment of their worth: 'They were courageous and possessed the merit of being cheap, finding their own horses and getting three pounds per month.'

Many years later, the son of Sergeant Major Kambule described the troop's departure from Pietermaritzburg on their way to Isandlwana: 'We were all proud of them as they marched through the city. Sober, clean and well made men in the fullness of their strength' [a rather different picture from the drink-swilling ruffians as described in other volunteer units]; 'Their equipment was of the best and perfect in every particular.' Nor was this their first engagement as allies of the British. Many members of the troop had served against the Bushmen in 1862, and again with Durnford in 1873, against Langalibalele. Kambule's father, Elijah, who had been Durnford's chief scout and interpreter, was killed at the top of Bushmen's Pass at the same time that Durnford had been wounded.

Their conduct at Isandlwana had been praised by many, including Chelmsford, but there were whispers that they had left the field early and had deserted Durnford. The evidence outweighs this accusation, although it is also more than likely that as soon as they saw the disintegration and flight of the British infantry, they lost no time in departing; the Victorian concept of dying a gallant death for the sake of glory would simply not have occurred to them. On the other hand they were the only unit to have made a disciplined and fighting retreat from the field.

After Isandlwana the Edendale Troop spent some time on patrol work in the Ladysmith area, falling under the control of a local bully-boy named Thomas Carbutt. He had recently raised a unit, yet to be recognised by the government or to see active service, which he grandly called 'Carbutt's Border Rangers'. They were described as living on a habitual diet of rum and unleavened bread cooked in ashes. When the Edendale Troop requested different rations, Carbutt is reported literally to have kicked some of them across the parade ground! Having reported the matter to the local magistrate, the troop departed to find Wood's column, where they were put under the command of Lieutenant William Francis Dundonald Cochrane, a special service officer seconded from the 32nd Regiment. Like the men of the Edendale Troop, Cochrane had been at Isandlwana with Durnford, serving as his transport officer, and had escaped across Fugitive's Drift. Another escapee from Isandlwana later to be attached to the Edendale Troop was Lieutenant Charles Raw who, it will be remembered, discovered the Zulu army on top of the Nqutu Plateau.

Wood described the Edendale troopers as men who never made an unfounded complaint, nor an unreasonable request. Everyone who encountered the unit would always remember them for the wonderful harmony of their singing as they conducted their evening prayers. Even the worst of sinners, it was said, paused to listen.

Baker's Horse had a long trek in front of them as they set out from East London for Kambula, a journey which commenced with a very uncomfortable sea voyage. The unit had been raised during the Ninth Frontier War, finishing its service at Kokstad where it was ordered to march to East London and disband. It had been raised by Captain Francis James Baker, a man in his early thirties who had seen previous service fighting in Burma with the Ceylon Rifle Regiment. More recently he had served in England with the Royal Anglesey Militia, a volunteer regiment, which he left in 1877 in order to sail to the Cape.

Hardly had Baker disbanded his men in East London when he received a telegram from Chelmsford asking him to raise the unit once again, and proceed with all haste to Northern Natal: easier said than done. Baker decided to raise the men locally in the Eastern Cape, but equip and horse them when they reached their destination. By 7 February the first detachment 'of fifty men of the proper class, being young strong fellows, admirably adapted for the work before them', as the local paper enthused, set sail for Durban aboard SS *Dunkeld* with Lieutenant W. Pickering in charge. Fourteen days later, the second detachment of fifty men went aboard the SS *Venice*. 'They went off in a lighter towed by a tug which for some time did not make much headway, her screws frequently out of the water in tossing seas ... however, the brave fellows managed to board the steamer eventually,' reported *The East London and Eastern Province Standard*. Three days later a further fifty-seven men were on their way and despite their steamer, RMS *Africa*, departing in the early hours of the morning, their embarkation was cheered by throngs of wellwishers. The departures of Baker's Horse were becoming a jolly social event in East London which, before long, would be replaced by a morbid scrutiny of its casualty roll. One account of their departure says that they were suitably clad, implying that had been issued with uniforms. Their nickname, 'The Canaries', is believed to have been derived from the 'bilious colour of their jackets'.

Having arrived safely at Durban, each detachment was dispatched to Pietermaritzburg, fifty-seven miles inland, where the men drew equipment and arms. Then commenced another footslog of 170 miles to Utrecht, via Estcourt, where they were at last to be mounted. They made the overland trek sleeping rough and with little protection from the elements. One volunteer was to recall: 'As everywhere, the weaker went to the wall, succumbed to climate; fever and dysentery, and rheumatism thinned out the weakly ... drenched with frequent thunderstorms and then frozen, it will not be wondered that many sank.' The whole journey from East London to Kambula took an average of thirty-six days. It was unfortunate for those who could not ride, for they had no time to learn. The attempt to master their unbroken horses in so short a time proved a memorable experience.

The Transvaal Rangers were the most heterogeneous unit amongst a most extraordinary diverse gathering of horsemen. Recruited mainly from the human flotsam and jetsam of the Kimberley diamond fields, their ranks contained numerous nationalities, many of whom were coloured men. It was the Transvaal

Rangers that Tomasson had so disparagingly described as 'a forbidding lot of mixed Hottentots and scum of the diamond fields as was never collected together outside a prison wall'. Indeed, perhaps they were, if appearances were any indication, yet under their able leader there was no unit in the forthcoming battle that would acquit itself with more esteem than Raaff's Transvaal Rangers. Many men had already experienced the dangers and tedium of African campaigning, having fought unsuccessfully against Sekhukhune in the Transvaal. Their leader, Commandant Pieter Raaff, had accompanied Rowlands and had served with the Lydenburg Rifles. He was a slim, dapper man, dressing in the mode of a country gentleman, riding a beautifully groomed and accoutred horse, but wearing, incongruously, a Prussian-type steel helmet complete with spike, which must have glowed with heat under the Zululand sun. A photograph survives of Raaff, seated among his officers, all armed to the teeth, while he carries nothing but a riding crop.

The unit's strength was approximately 150 mounted men. They had formed part of Rowlands's No. 5 Column, but had been acquired by Wood as soon as he had received Chelmsford's approval to strip Rowlands of his troops. They had ridden down from Derby and had been encamped at Luneburg since the beginning of March. Years hence, Raaff would still be fighting colonial wars and would play an important role in the ill-fated Shangani Patrol during the Matabele War. He was also an articulate man, once describing the typical British officer of the time as 'class conscious, snobby, usually badly trained, often inexperienced and inefficient, yet always incredibly brave, often stupidly so'.

The Border Horse had also been part of Rowlands's command and, like the Transvaal Rangers, had been acquired by Wood. Their commander, Colonel Frederick Augustus Weatherley, was a flamboyant character and a horseman of much experience. He had studied for more than four years at the Austrian Military Academy and had served in one of that country's crack cavalry regiments. On returning to Britain he obtained a commission in the 4th Light Dragoons and fought in the Crimea. Some accounts have Weatherley charging with the Light Brigade at Balaklava but these are incorrect as he only joined his regiment ten months after the charge had taken place: nevertheless he saw plenty of action in the latter stages of that conflict. During the Sepoy Mutiny, while serving with the 6th Dragoons, he took part in numerous campaigns against the rebels in northern India. It was at that time that he met and became a friend of Sir Bartle Frere.

A fellow officer, writing home from India, described Weatherley as being patronising, a name-dropper and married to a 'flashy' little woman who went on campaign with her husband 'carrying a revolver, riding like a man and laying about the natives with her riding crop'.

At the age of thirty-seven, and now the father of two sons and a daughter, Weatherley had sold his commission in the 6th Dragoons and retired to Brighton for a number of years before leaving for South Africa at the end of 1877. He had acquired land near Lydenburg (possibly encouraged by Sir Bartle Frere), and was also involved with the Eersteling Gold Mining Company.

Whilst briefly campaigning with Rowlands, he met a dubious character who claimed to be The Gunn of Gunn, an ancient Scottish title, but was, in fact, a trickster and a charmer who had recently been released from gaol. He proposed that Weatherley, who had only been in the country for less than a year, take Shepstone's place as Administrator of the Transvaal! To this end he produced a petition, with almost 4000 forged signatures, which he presented to the government. The document was unmasked, The Gunn departed with Weatherley's wife and, in a scandal that rocked prim Pretoria, Weatherley divorced her, gaining custody of all the children. He then decided it was time to leave the capital, so set about raising a unit of sixty volunteer horsemen, mainly from the English settler community of the Transvaal for service in Zululand, taking both his sons along with him.

The unit, the Border Horse, was supposedly raised as lancers, but there seems to be no evidence that lances were ever carried. The unit did, however, in true cavalry tradition, carry a regimental flag or guidon, which had been finely stitched by the ladies of Pretoria. It was emblazoned with a strange-looking lion's head above a scroll bearing the regimental motto 'Be Vigilant'. The Border Horse eventually departed the Transvaal, riding down from Pretoria along the Derby road to join Wood's camp at Luneburg. The unit arrived on 2 March after a journey of more than three weeks. Ten days later they were to witness the butchered bodies of the 80th at the Intombi River ... and would be wise to heed the words of their own motto.

The horses ridden by the irregulars were as varied a lot as their riders. All were locally bred in southern Africa and although there had been much talk of acquiring suitable mounts from overseas, nothing came of it. One gentleman tried to motivate the importation of cavalry horses from Uruguay, describing them as 'averaging fifteen hands in height, dashed with Arab blood, having great hardiness, endurance and specially handy over bad ground'; the estimated cost, landed at the Cape, was £15 each – about twenty-five percent cheaper than locally purchased horses which, the same gentleman pointed out, 'required about two years training to be efficient steeds'. Many of the irregulars would be lucky if their mounts received two weeks' training before they rode them off to Hlobane.

A cavalryman's foremost weapon was, in fact, his horse. Without a well-trained mount he could not pursue or close with the foe or have the opportunity to use the other weapons in his arsenal such as sword, lance, pistol or carbine. The better trained his horse, immediately responsive to leg or rein, the safer the rider's life and the more efficient his role as a horse soldier. The horse that shied or bolted from danger, or from the sounds of gunfire or a screeching enemy, was a liability and had no place in a cavalry unit.

Among Wood's horsemen, especially those in the older established units such as the FLH, Burgher Force and NNH, there must have been many who rode mounts well schooled and trained for their masters' work – but there were those less fortunate who would be going into battle astride a horse that was hardly accustomed to having a saddle on its back. A member of one unit later recalled how a troop of 120 horses 'were put out to graze without knee halters; exercise is what they wanted so the whole lot galloped off and scattered far and wide and it was more than a fortnight before they were recovered'.

It was not always the best-looking horse that was best for the job. Buller, the commander of all the irregulars, had a favourite mount by the name of 'Punch', who was described as a 'fiddle-headed, brindled, flat-sided, ewe-necked cob ... perhaps the very ugliest horse of his day and generation in all South Africa but he was also amongst the most valuable'. Another officer of Wood's staff, Captain Henry Hartford, described purchasing a pony and emphasised the importance of having a gun-proof mount rather than a good looker. 'I bought a very nice animal, and a splendid shooting horse into the bargain. His colour was against him being a flea bitten red skimmel but for real worth he could not be beaten.'

All very well for the officers purchasing their own ponies, but the allocation of the troopers' mounts was a very different matter. One correspondent reported the arrival of a herd of remounts as 'a grand sight – buck-jumpers, kickers and bolters of all description!' Amusing no doubt as long as one was not required to ride them.

Describing the mounting of Baker's Horse. Tomasson wrote:

> The mode of selection was primitive in the extreme. The horses were driven into a stone enclosure, called a kraal, every man then went in with a halter and from the plunging, kicking mass, selected what suited himself. The result being with men who did not know about horses, absurd; some large men got small horses and vice versa ... the knowing ones got ponies as a rule, short wiry, and thick little brutes that could wear down any big horse by sheer dint of superior prowess of endurance ... the men, many of them knowing little about riding, had to be taught; they learnt by dint of falling off ... the falls were many, as riders were bad and the horses young and untaught.

No doubt, many a volunteer was given to wonder whether learning to ride was not more dangerous than an actual Zulu encounter would be!

The Royal Artillery, under the command of Major Edmond Tremlett, consisting of twenty officers and men, would accompany the horsemen, taking with them two rocket tubes on pack horses. They were dubious weapons which were supposed to strike the unsophisticated enemy with terror. The staff of the Royal Arsenal at Woolwich had come to this conclusion, but had obviously not experimented with the weapon on the Zulu. It will be remembered that the rocket battery which accompanied Durnford at Isandlwana was easily overrun and the gunners slaughtered. Not the sort of contraption to take up a precipitous mountain!

Wood's Irregulars, the 1st and 2nd Battalions, each over 500 strong, under the command of Commandants White and Roberts, also accompanied the mounted men. Although on foot, once on the mountain or traversing rough ground, they were as fleet as any horseman. They were mainly Swazis, wearing traditional feather headdresses and, like the Natal Natives who made up the rest of Wood's auxiliaries, they were clad in a mixture of traditional attire and cast-off army uniforms which were in great demand. One war correspondent wondered at the number of native stores selling old army gear and on investigating he found on sale 'the uniforms of British Grenadiers, French Chasseurs and Austrian Hussars, all laid out in every form of tempting display'. This strange mixture of fashion was the natives' 'strutting out garb' and was discarded entirely at the first sign of battle, the men preferring to fight little more than naked. Unlike the defunct NNC of No. 3 Column, who had had only one firearm between every ten men, all of Wood's Irregulars were armed with a gun of one sort or another from antiquated Brunswick or Baker rifles to new Martini Henrys. By and large they were men of splendid physique, the Swazis in particular being equal in strength, speed and stamina to their Zulu counterparts. Like the British soldier, they were each paid a shilling a day.

Hamu's Warriors were the last addition to Wood's forces and they numbered approximately 200 under the command of twenty-four-year-old Lieutenant Cecil Charles Williams, a special service officer of the 58th Regiment, who was assisted by Calverley, Hamu's white adviser. They were of course pure Zulu and many must have washed their spears in the blood of British soldiers at Isandlwana. Now that they had defected they would be branded as traitors and better they might die cleanly in battle than fall into the hands of Cetshwayo's army, for they would find no mercy there.

6
HLOBANE AND DEVIL'S PASS

'It immediately became apparent that a catastrophe was inevitable.'

Major William Knox-Leet
1/13th Light Infantry

'Then an awful confusion took place – horses fell on top of the rocks, broke their necks and legs – you saw horses on top of men ... and thought it was all up with me.'

Lieutenant Alfred Blaine
Frontier Light Horse

Wood had viewed an attack on Hlobane Mountain with considerable misgivings. Early in March he had told Chelmsford that Buller wanted to assault the stronghold, but mentioned he was against the idea, believing it could cost the lives of half an infantry battalion if he tried. Towards the latter part of the month, for three good reasons, he began to consider an assault on Hlobane as vital: he could not leave the stronghold in his rear when he advanced into Zululand; Mbelini must be seen to be utterly routed or destroyed; and he had recently received intelligence from Hamu's spies that the Zulu army was to join up with the forces on Hlobane, using it as its base, and from there wipe out Wood's column and capture the traitor Hamu. Then followed the final motivation ... the letter from Chelmsford requesting Wood to make a diversion while he attempted to relieve Eshowe. Colonel Pearson and his men were still besieged and Chelmsford wrote of them:

> They have rations up to the 4th April only, so it is high time that a convoy and column went to their relief – it seems almost certain that we shall be attacked and I have been anxious therefore to make my column as strong as possible so that we may read the Zulus a severe lesson – if you are in a position to make any forward movement about the 27th of this month, so that the news of it may reach the neighbourhood of Eshowe about the 29th, I think it might have a good effect.

With reinforcements that had either come out from England, or had been diverted from other parts of the Empire, Chelmsford had assembled a relief column of five British infantry battalions, a naval brigade of sailors and marines drawn from three warships lying in Durban harbour, volunteer cavalry, mounted infantry, artillery, Gatling guns and a strong force of the now reinstated NNC. Altogether there were almost 4000 whites and 2280 blacks – double the number of infantry of the original No. 3 Column with which Chelmsford had marched to Isandlwana two months earlier, and twice as strong as Wood's column. Chelmsford was taking no chances on this occasion. On 19 March he wrote again to Wood:

> I write to say that you are perfectly free and unfettered, and that any offensive operations which you think fit to undertake will not only meet with my approval, but will be heard of by me with pleasure. No. 1 Column is about to assume the offensive and if No. 4 can follow suit, I shall be delighted. . . . Reports say that all the Zulu army that Cetshwayo can collect is now, or will be in a few days, out or about Eshowe – we shall have a hottish encounter if this is the case.

Chelmsford was wrong: the Zulu army would not be at Eshowe but at Hlobane to inflict another British disaster.

Hamu's spies had been correct and persisted with their reports of the Zulu army advancing towards Hlobane, giving the date of its intended departure from Ulundi as the 26th or 27th, the regiments wishing to be cleansed by their witchdoctors before departure.

Despite these reports, it was apparently during his return from laying waste to Mbelini's country in the Intombi Valley that Wood finally made up his mind to raid the Painted Mountain, and thereafter wasted no time.

Despite the arduous riding of his volunteers over the past two weeks, Wood decided there would be but one day of rest; the move against Hlobane would commence on 27 March. He also decided that he would take only horsemen supported by Wood's Irregulars and Hamu's warriors. His two regiments of British infantry would be left behind to guard the camp.

Wood divided his attacking force into two columns, one under the command of Buller, the other under Russell.

The first column consisted of Commandant Piet Uys and thirty-two burghers; 158 men of the FLH under the command of Captain Robert Barton, seconded from the Coldstream Guards; seventy Transvaal Rangers commanded by Commandant Piet Raaff; fifty-four Border Horse commanded by Colonel Augustus Weatherley; eighty men of Baker's Horse commanded by Lieutenant W.D. Wilson; eight men of the Royal Artillery with rocket tubes carried by pack mules, led by Major Edmund Tremlett; and two companies of Wood's Irregulars commanded by Major William Knox-Leet of the 13th LI. Buller's second in command and staff officer was Captain the Honourable Alan Gardner of the 14th

Hussars, the man who had made the lone ride from Isandlwana bringing news of the disaster to Wood. Buller's total force, all ranks, numbered 408 mounted men and 280 native auxiliaries.

Russell's column comprised eighty-two men of the Mounted Infantry, commanded once again by Lieutenant Edward Browne of the 24th Regiment; forty-one men of the Kaffrarian Rifles who, presumably, had learned to ride in two weeks, and were led by Commandant Schermbrucker; seventy-one men of the Edendale Troop of the NNH under the command of Captain Cochrane, most of whom had survived Isandlwana, as had Cochrane himself; eleven men of the Royal Artillery with rocket tubes under Lieutenant Arthur Bigge; 240 men of Wood's Irregulars commanded by Commandant Lorraine White, and almost 200 of Hamu's Zulu warriors under the command of Lieutenant Cecil Charles Williams of the 58th Regiment. Also accompanying this column was Calverley, acting as an interpreter. A total of 206 cavalry and 440 native auxiliaries.

Wood's plan was to assault the eastern and western slopes of Hlobane simultaneously. A contemporary description of the mountain, which rises 1500 feet above the plain, gives some idea of the formidable task: 'It was strongly protected by krantzes and terraces, huge masses of boulders and scrub, intersected with stone walls, backed up by caves and fissures in the mountain itself, accessible only by footpaths from the plains below.' A more unsuitable target for horsemen would be hard to conceive. For once they reached the plateau (three miles long and over a mile wide in parts) they would still find the going almost as difficult, with precipitous slopes and its wide acres, sown from one end to the other with masses of rocks and boulders projecting through the soil – a surface as dangerous as could be found for a speeding horse!

The human defenders were no less formidable. The estimate of their numbers given later by the British varied considerably from 1000, presumably a low figure to excuse the folly of the attack, to over 4000, presumably to justify the defeat. The true number of abaQulusi on Hlobane more than likely exceeded the higher figure, for it will be recalled that in January, Wood and his staff had witnessed from afar several regiments drilling below the Hlobane, whose number they had put at 4000. Since then Wood had mentioned on several occasions rumours of additional troops arriving from Ulundi. Add to this the certainty of Mbelini's followers crossing with him to the stronghold, and the number of armed men on the mountain probably exceeded 5000 (Schermbrucker estimated them at between 6000 and 10,000).

Buller had been given the task of assailing the eastern end of the mountain. As it was more than ten miles further from Kambula, he left camp early on the 27th. His plan was to march in the direction of the Mkuze River, bivouacking for the night four miles south of Hlobane. By so doing he hoped to deceive the abaQulusi (who would be watching from their eyrie) into thinking that he was going to bypass the mountain and strike off into Zululand, as he had done on past occasions. But the enemy were not deceived for they could also see Russell's column, half a day's march behind Buller but following in his tracks. That the first force intended to attack their stronghold from the east and the second from the west appeared a simple conclusion to the British manoeuvres. But the abaQulusi were, nevertheless, confused. Buller was on a collision course with the advancing Zulu army; could it be that the British were really unaware of its presence, not fifteen miles to the south, heading towards Hlobane?

Russell's task was to ascend the western slopes of Hlobane, by way of the Ntendeka plateau, also referred to as the lower plateau, and arrive on the summit, thus trapping the abaQulusi and their cattle between the two British columns. That was the plan but when put into effect it would not work as conceived. What could not be appreciated from below was the steepness of the 150-foot ascent that linked the lower plateau with the summit. It was, in fact, little more than a rock face of massive boulders down which an agile man with time to pick his way might descend with safety. Before the day was out the descent would, however, for good reasons become known as 'The Devil's Pass'.

Wood had a poor opinion of Russell's qualities as an officer of irregular horse; he was not made of the right stuff. It was an opinion that was justified in many respects as after Isandlwana Russell's morale seemed to collapse. Even Chelmsford, who had asked for him to be sent out from England as a special service officer, commented on his lack of zeal in a letter to Wood: 'Between ourselves, Russell appears to have lost heart and allowed his men to get out of hand....' Wood had found fault with Russell the moment he arrived at Kambula. Having led his men to the camp via Newcastle to avoid any danger – a detour of over thirty-six miles – Wood commented: 'Precautions should, of course, be taken, but this shows an excess of caution, to a cavalry man lamentable....' As soon as Russell arrived, Wood requested his removal. But for the time being Chelmsford was prepared to stick by his friend, and replied rather curtly, 'I quite appreciate what you say about Russell – I do not at present, however, see my way to giving him more congenial employment.' Captain Robert Barton, commanding the FLH, confided to Wood that Russell would 'take any berth to avoid serving under Buller – even the Remount Depot'. Prophetic words, for that is where he would end up.

Russell's column, having a shorter distance to travel, did not leave camp until noon on the 27th, then rode as far as the base of Zunguin where it bivouacked.

In the early evening, Wood, accompanied by three staff officers, an escort of eight mounted men of the 90th LI and seven mounted Zulu, arrived to spend the night.

Wood had decided, once his columns were in motion, to play the role of roving observer in the forthcoming battle. As will be seen, with so small an escort, he was very vulnerable and somewhat of a liability to his commanders. He spent much of the evening at Russell's camp in conversation with Piet Uys and Charlie Potter (recently appointed a captain in Wood's Irregulars but having already seen service in Rowlands's column) whose father had owned the nearby trading store that bore his name; Wood had lately dismantled the store, moving it to Balte Spruit to house his supplies. The Potters, senior and junior, were businessmen and while the father tried, for obvious reasons, to persuade Lord Chelmsford that the wagon route past his store was a first-class road (which it was not), the son had sold his services as an interpreter and guide at much above the going rate! But as young Potter had actually been up on the top of Hlobane on a number of occasions, and had first-hand knowledge of the few tracks up and down, his services would be invaluable.

Perhaps Uys had a premonition of impending doom for, as the conversation of the evening drew to a close, he turned to Wood and offered to care for his children if Wood were killed on the mountain, requesting Wood to do likewise in a reverse situation. Potter, it seems, did not get involved – perhaps he had no children or was, as a businessman, still considering the advantages or otherwise of such a pact. With or without a premonition of doom, it would have been in his interest to have joined, for on the following day both he and Uys would die on the mountain.

Buller's men, having settled down in their bivouac, got their cooking fires going by stoking them with timbers from a nearby kraal.[1] Their aim was to deceive the enemy into thinking they were set for the night. However, Buller was soon on the move again and the whole column quietly made its way through the starlit African night toward the black mass of Hlobane.

The abaQulusi had also been building fires; for much of the night three huge beacons had been blazing on top of the mountain which should have given the British some indication that other Zulu forces were not far distant; indeed, over 20,000 Zulu warriors were at rest not five miles to the south behind Nyenbe Hill. Unaware of this mighty army, Buller and his men slept fitfully; fully accoutred and carrying 100 rounds of ammunition per man, they dozed, each with the reins of his horse tied around his hands.

At 3.30 am the column was roused, and as best they could in the darkness, the men mounted up and prepared to ascend the mountain. The only route up this eastern end was a narrow rocky path – never designed to accommodate an army of mounted men. With Uys and Raaff leading, the column set off with the troopers riding four abreast. But the way was too precipitous and soon the whole force dismounted. Men then started to stray either side of the narrow pathway into long grass and boulders that impeded every step. For two hours and more they climbed and stumbled upward, forever being jostled and trampled in the darkness. Just before dawn a violent electrical storm descended on the mountain, illuminating the landscape with great sheets of lightning and drenching the sweating men in a downpour of icy rain. Above them, the abaQulusi also braved the elements to witness the struggling line of horsemen whose progress was so conveniently illuminated by the storm.

For all the trials of the ascent Buller had timed it well and, as the day dawned,

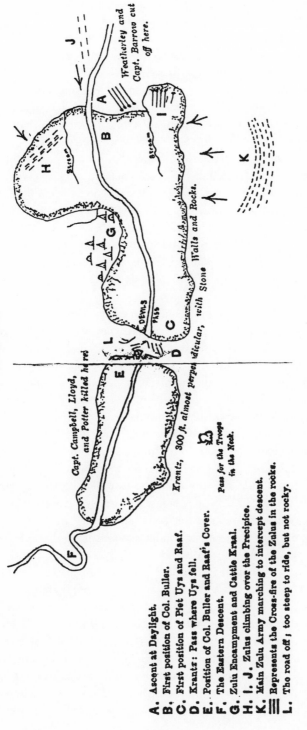

5. HLOBANE

Weatherley and Capt. Barrow cut off here.

Walls and Rocks.

Krantz, 300 ft. almost perpendicular, with Stone

Capt. Campbell, Lloyd, and Potter killed here.

Pass for the Troops in the Neck.

A. Ascent at Daylight.
B. First position of Col. Buller.
C. First position of Piet Uys and Raaf.
D. Krantz: Pass where Uys fell.
E. Position of Col. Buller and Raaf's Cover.
F. The Eastern Descent.
G. Zulu Encampment and Cattle Kraal.
H. I. J. Zulu climbing over the Precipice.
K. Main Zulu Army marching to intercept descent.
≡ Represents the Cross-fire of the Zulus in the rocks.
L. The road off ; too steep to ride, but not rocky.

A contemporary sketch of Hlobane by a 'Combatant', which appeared in a local newspaper shortly after the battle. Although the map has several inaccuracies, it is one of the few diagrams that correctly show abaQulusi reinforcements (at J) advancing from the top of the adjoining Intyentika plateau to cut off both Buller's and Weatherley's retreat.

the leading ranks approached the plateau only to find the abaQulusi were not unprepared. Just below the summit, on the left of the column, cliffs formed a horseshoe-shaped recess, something like an amphitheatre, and from the rocks and krantzes about its base, the abaQulusi set up a withering fire. Several men and horses were hit and soon the pathway was cluttered with dead bodies. The men of Wood's Irregulars, being far more agile than the dismounted horsemen, were immediately brought forward and 'many swarmed up the hill with praiseworthy courage and rapidity,' as Knox-Leet was to recall. Running up the centre of the amphitheatre was a low ridge and Buller ordered Lieutenant George Williams[2] and his troop of the FLH to take possession. Williams captured the ridge but having done so was shot through the head while chatting to Gardner about a mutual acquaintance he had met when at Oxford. Nevertheless Williams's troop continued to lay down a fire which sent the enemy scurrying for cover, allowing the column to proceed to the summit without further loss. Williams's body and those of several dead troopers were abandoned where they fell. It was not quite the surprise attack that Buller had planned; furthermore, one of his units, the Border Horse, who had been dragging their feet since the previous afternoon, were missing. The time was 6.00 am.

At the other end of the mountain the hour of six found Russell and his men well on the way up to the lower plateau. Shortly they would arrive at the bottom of Devil's Pass which Russell and his horsemen were supposed to climb in order to link up with Buller. To Russell's eye, that of a formal cavalry officer, it was out of the question for horses and he made no attempt to tackle it. Instead he ordered his mounted troops to support Hamu's warriors and Wood's Irregulars in rounding up hundreds of cattle which were to be herded back to the British camp at Kambula. Once this task was underway, Russell sent Browne, and twenty men of the mounted infantry, to climb the pass on foot and make contact with Buller. So far Russell had encountered no opposition, although it was clear from the sound of distant rifle fire from the east that Buller had engaged the enemy. Indeed, on reaching the plateau, Buller had got another hot reception; the abaQulusi, concealed among the rocks and scrub, were killing men and horses as they breasted the summit. Buller again ordered the FLH to skirmish and clear the enemy, and in doing so an Austrian adventurer, Lieutenant Baron von Stietencron, was shot dead. He had been a man of considerable military experience and his death was a great loss to the column; he had served as adjutant to Marshal Benedek during the Austro-Prussian war of 1866 and had been with the FLH throughout the Ninth Frontier War and the Sekhukhune Campaign. Nevertheless the Zulu opposition was pushed back – if only temporarily, from the vital area that would afford the British invaders a relatively safe descent. From where Buller stood he could see only two ways down the eastern end of the mountain: the first was the route they had just ascended and, about a quarter of a mile further to the north-east, a likely looking place where the plateau joined the Intyentika Nek;[3] the second was one of the routes that Potter had described to Wood the previous evening.

Buller's immediate objective was to secure both lines of retreat. He ordered 'A' Troop of the FLH to hold the first area at all costs, while men of Baker's Horse were sent to secure the position above Intyentika Nek. The remainder of the column then pushed on into the plateau, spreading out in all directions, looking for Zulu to fight and cattle to plunder. As they did so the abaQulusi seemed to evaporate before them: for Hlobane abounded in natural hiding places. The enemy slipped behind rocks, into crevices and down on to ledges there to wait, watch and return. Mbelini, the master tactician, hardly daring to believe the enemy still remained ignorant of the Zulu army, was ably exploiting the British advance, luring the troopers deeper on to the plateau; that they were able to round up cattle virtually unopposed would have caused a surge of unease in more prudent men!

The troopers of 'A' Company, left behind in the whispering silence of the early morning with the scattered bodies of men and horses near by, took up position north of where they had emerged from the plain. The inaccessible edge of the cliffs would protect their rear and flanks. They lay in a line behind a makeshift defence of boulders; at the end of their right flank, however, where the cliff turned into the plateau, their line was vulnerable and exposed. They had been left to defend a position that could not have been held by twice their number and, as the tail end of Buller's column disappeared into the undulations of the plateau, the abaQulusi emerged from their places of concealment; working their way from rock to rock, they began to encircle the isolated men who had been left behind.

About the same time (around 6.30 am) Wood, complete with staff and escort, having left Russell's bivouac area three hours earlier, was trotting along the southern slopes of Hlobane about a mile from where 'A' Troop was being encircled. It was a pleasant morning and Wood and his party were enjoying the ride. The imminent prospect of danger and battle bore the younger officers along in an exuberant and talkative mood – no doubt accentuated by their ignorance of warfare. That they were members of Wood's staff at all was due more to having the right connections than experience for the job. Thirty-year-old Captain The Honourable Ronald Campbell, Coldstream Guards, was Wood's chief staff officer. In common with Chelmsford and Buller, he was an old Etonian and in addition second son of the Earl of Cawdor. Well connected indeed, but he had only been in Africa for four months and had not seen active service before. Lieutenant Henry Lysons, Wood's orderly officer, was twenty years old and had arrived, fresh from England, a few weeks earlier to take up his first posting with the 90th LI. His father, Major General Sir Daniel Lysons GCB, was Quartermaster General at the War Office. The last member of Wood's staff was his civilian interpreter and political officer, Llewellyn Lloyd, who, as mentioned, had commanded the Zulu Police during the Sekhukhune campaign and had been twice wounded. His father was not only a retired major general in the British army but also a member of the Natal Legislative Assembly.

Apart from eight mounted men of the 90th LI, Wood also had an escort of seven native horsemen led by none other than Mtonga who, being half brother to the Zulu king, was perhaps the best connected of all! It will be recalled that Mtonga had fled Zululand years previously, finding refuge with the Boers at Utrecht. The correspondent of *The Natal Mercury* had recently described him as being 'the same pertinacious codger that he was when a boy'. The only men who had no connections – but fair experience – were the eight hardened soldiers of Wood's personal escort. However, as one of them would win the Victoria Cross and another the Silver Medal for Distinguished Conduct before the day was out, they too would have connections in the future.

As this small, but distinguished, cavalcade rode along they could hear the sound of rifle fire echoing down from the mountain. Young Lysons and Lloyd had been chattering so loudly that Wood wondered whether the Zulu up on the plateau would hear them. Breaking into Wood's silence, one of the young men asked him what he was thinking. Wood replied, rather morbidly, that he had been thinking which of them might be writing to his wife with bad news, or whether he might be writing with ill tidings to their families – indeed as would be the case before the day was out. If the enemy up on top had not heard the chattering, an ambush party of abaQulusi, concealed in a labyrinth of rockfalls above them, certainly had.

The abaQulusi had also seen Weatherley and his Border Horse riding west and about to bump into Wood heading east. The Border Horse had not kept up with Buller's column and had been missing since the previous evening. Wood and his escort had been following the clearly defined trail left by Buller's advance; a pathway of trampled grass, littered here and there with bits of equipment and dead horses – an easy trail to follow but unaccountably missed by Weatherley and his men.

What passed between Wood and Weatherley when they met is not recorded, but it must have been obvious that the Border Horse, riding downhill away from the firing, were heading away from the battle. Perhaps it can be assumed that Weatherley's men, all of them volunteers, whilst willing to engage in the odd skirmish for cash and cattle, were not prepared to risk their lives in a frontal attack on a strongly held natural fortress. The fact that Weatherley had two of his sons with him, the younger only a boy of fourteen, may also have influenced the matter. Followed by Wood, the Border Horse moved off as ordered but hardly had they got underway when the abaQulusi above them opened fire and the troop came to a sudden halt. Wood, followed by his escort, pushed through the Border Horse and, observing that the shooting was coming from the base of the cliffs, immediately led the way off the track and up toward the enemy. He continued to lead his horse while the rest of the ponies were herded into an abandoned stone-walled cattle kraal. On foot the party advanced upward toward a jumble of rocks from where the marksmen were shooting, but at a hundred yards they were pinned down by an intense and well-directed fire from three sides.

The Border Horse, now 200 yards behind, returned the abaQulusi fire, causing Lloyd to remark that the salvo would impair the enemy's aim. Hardly had he uttered these words when a warrior stood up from behind a rock, not fifty yards away, and shot Lloyd, who fell to the ground mortally wounded, exclaiming, 'I am hit! Very badly, my back is broken.'

Wood tried to lift him but Lloyd was too heavy a load, and when Wood was seen to stumble, Captain Campbell rushed forward, lifted Lloyd and carried him back to the safety of the cattle kraal where the rest of Wood's escort had also taken cover. Wood, however, did not retire; still leading his horse, he started to advance when a warrior, concealed below a boulder, fired at point-blank range, killing Wood's horse instantly. As the animal buckled and fell, it crashed sideways into Wood, bringing him down beneath it. Wood struggled out and instructed Campbell to go to Weatherley and order him to clear the rocks from which the fatal shots had been fired. Weatherley was some way below but sufficiently close for Wood to hear Campbell give the order three times. Weatherley, however, refused to move, whereupon Campbell shouted to Wood, 'Damn him! He's a coward!' Then running forward, Campbell called, 'I'll turn them out.' Inspired by Campbell and infected by the danger, excitement and the shock of a dead comrade, others of Wood's Escort rose up led by young Lysons who, desperate to test his courage, yelled, 'May I go?' Wood, equally carried away, yelled back, 'Yes! Forward the Personal Escort!' In a mad rush a half-dozen men, including one or two of the Border Horse, made for the jumble of rocks. Campbell in the lead scrambled up and peered down into a black recess from which the shots had come. Momentarily unable to adjust his eyes from bright sunlight to pitch darkness, he could see nothing, but immediately below him an abaQulusi marksman, hidden in his deep cavity, was close enough to touch. He poked the muzzle of his rifle at Campbell's head and pulled the trigger.

Campbell was killed instantly and his body fell about the rocks. Young Lysons, aghast, pushed past and shoulder to shoulder with Private Edmund Fowler of Wood's Escort, opened fire into the recess, driving the abaQulusi marksmen back into their labyrinth. The exuberant assault party of a few minutes earlier pursued the enemy no further. They gathered up Campbell's body and dragged it down the rocky slope to where Wood had remained with the mortally wounded Lloyd, who was now dead. More men, too, were hit and dying; the Border Horse were suffering casualties and a number of the horses of Wood's escort had also been killed by the aggressive and accurate Zulu fire. On the exposed mountainside, Wood tried to lift the bodies of his dead staff officers on to the back of his spare pony but the task was beyond him. Wood's bugler, Private Alexander Walkinshaw, who like the rest of the escort was returning the enemy fire, saw Wood struggling;

6. HLOBANE

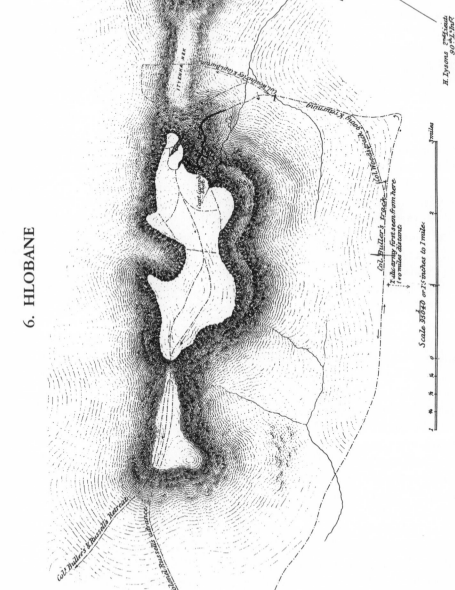

A map of Hlobane drawn by Wood's orderly officer, twenty-year-old Lieutenant Henry Lysons, who was present at the battle. Wood was well pleased with the sketch and sent it to the Intelligence Branch of the War Office where it was printed later in 1879. Mysteriously, the drawing seems to have been copied identically, except for the omission of some detail and different spelling of the mountain, by Lieutenant Slade of the Royal Artillery who put his name to it. (Natal Archives)

running forward, Walkinshaw told him to hold the restive horse, and swung the bodies on to its back.

Unlike the dead of the FLH, who had been left where they had fallen, Campbell and Lloyd were to be buried as Wood's first priority. It then occurred to him that the small prayer book which he had borrowed from Campbell only that morning was still in the saddle of his dead horse, fifty yards up the mountain. The book, a parting gift to Campbell from his wife, was something that Wood felt he must retrieve. Turning again to his trusty bugler, Walkinshaw, whom he later described as one of the bravest men in the British army, Wood instructed him to climb back up the mountain and remarked, 'Whilst I do not want you to get shot for the saddle, you are to take all risks for the sake of the prayer book.' With a commanding officer who would casually risk a man's life for the acquisition of a prayer book, Walkinshaw needed all the courage that he could muster. However, with unhurried stride and with fortune following the brave, he pulled the saddle with its wallets from under the dead horse, while the bullets hummed around him, and then nonchalantly returned to Wood with the saddle balanced on his head. Wood's party, carrying its dead, retreated back to where Weatherley and his Border Horse were still firing away at the abaQulusi.

Wood was evidently a kind and affable commander and was fond of the two young men who, with more prudence and less heroics, might still have been alive. He could justifiably have felt responsible for their deaths and was, no doubt, assailed with self-recrimination. Wood had held Lloyd in the highest esteem and had only two days earlier written to Sir Bartle Frere, ' I am anxious to bring to your notice the name of Mr Lloyd, who has been of the greatest assistance to me. To personal energy, he adds a knowledge of the Zulu, their language, character and every attribute of a humane English gentleman.' Later he wrote, 'In Mr Lloyd . . . I lose an officer I cannot replace.' Campbell he had held in the same high esteem, but with greater affection, for Campbell had idolised Wood; so much so that Campbell's wife, on hearing of her husband's death, wrote:

> I can only say that proud as I always was of my dear Ronald, I am prouder than ever now to think that he risked his life to save such as you, and the thought of his glorious soldier's death is such a grand thought that I shall ever love to dwell upon it . . . I cannot imagine with what joy he must have made that last dash forward to carry out your order.

Much emotion, therefore, must have been astir in Wood's breast. Nevertheless, there was a battle in progress and Wood was still nominally in command. Whatever his depth of remorse, the dead should either have been taken along or their interment deferred until time and the enemy permitted. But Wood could not bring himself to leave the bodies behind to an almost certain fate of mutilation by the enemy, and as a number of horses had been killed there were none spare to

carry dead men off the mountain. Consequently he set about the burial of
Campbell and Lloyd on the spot. To dig a grave in the rocky terrain was no easy
matter – and quite impossible where the bodies lay. So Wood, his escort and the
Border Horse, retreated downhill 300 yards to where the ground was soft enough
to dig; but there was no shovel. Not to be thwarted, Wood ordered his Zulu escort
to dig with their assegais. An assegai, however, makes a poor spade and the
digging of the graves was a long and laborious task that would cause further
casualties before Campbell and Lloyd could be laid to rest.

The time was now about 6.45 am, and at the eastern end of the mountain
Russell and his men had been rounding up cattle but had still not encountered any
enemy opposition. Browne and his twenty mounted infantry, accompanied by
Calverley and Potter, had climbed Devil's Pass to the top of the plateau where all
was quiet, although distant firing could be heard to the east. Browne decided to
hang around and await the arrival of Buller.

Buller and the rest of his column, after leaving the detachments of the FLH and
Baker's Horse to guard their escape route, had turned west into the plateau, which
was like another world compared with the slopes below. Although they stood on a
mountaintop, one only had to ride a few yards in from the edge and the whole
countryside beneath disappeared from sight so that all sensation of height was lost;
they might have been riding across a moor at sea level. This was the grazing
ground of the abaQulusi cattle, serving, too, as a natural fortress in times of attack.
In its centre a perennial stream flowed and a waterfall plunged over the south-
eastern rim. The abaQulusi, however, did not live on this high place – it was far
too exposed to the elements, especially to vicious electrical storms, to be a
permanent home. They preferred the lower slopes with its kinder climate and
many caves. From afar the plateau might have appeared ideal terrain for horsemen,
but in fact the surface resembled a sea of rocks punctuated by grass. It was
fortunate that Buller's men were mounted on surefooted Basuto-type ponies, for
the going on the plateau would have lamed or brought down almost any other
breed at a pace faster than a walk – and the majority of the column would be
riding for their lives before the day was out.

The column had spread out in groups, probing for cattle, right around the lip of
the mountain. Little opposition was encountered although from the sound of firing
back at the ascent, the rearguard was still hotly engaged. There was reputed to be
over 4000 head of cattle dispersed around the mountaintop and before long
Wood's Irregulars were herding immense numbers of captured beasts toward the
descent where Browne waited to make contact with Buller.

Whilst his men were busily engaged in cattle-lifting, Buller sent two of his
officers – Major William Knox-Leet of the 1/13th LI and Major Edmund Tremlett
of the Royal Artillery – on ahead to seek a way back at Russell's end of the
mountain. This was obviously the preferred route which, if feasible, would enable
Buller to sweep the cattle and the enemy westward, bottling them up in a trap at

the top of Devil's Pass where Russell, it was presumed, lay in wait to slaughter the abaQulusi and shepherd the livestock. Then it would be down on to the lower plateau and the plain below, and back to Kambula for supper. That was the plan and, as far as Buller was concerned, it seemed to be going well.

One glance down Devil's Pass was enough to convince Buller's two scouts that this, emphatically, was no route for horsemen. A change in plan was clearly required: rounding up all the cattle and men, and retracing their steps right across the plateau and back down the way they had come, seemed to be the only option. It would add another ten miles to the return journey, rendering supper at Kambula out of the question. Had Mbelini conceived the whole thing he could not have contrived a worse predicament for his enemy.

Below the summit Wood's escorts were still trying to dig a grave with their assegais. They were not left unmolested, for part of the abaQulusi force that had hampered Buller's ascent was now making its way around the base of the cliffs. Weatherley and his men were still with Wood and were suffering casualties. The gravediggers had reached a depth of about 4 feet when the approaching abaQulusi were seen and, with no more ado, the bodies of Campbell and Lloyd were hastily bundled into the trench. But Wood would not have it: the grave was too short for the dead men's legs to lie straight. He estimated the abaQulusi to be about a third of a mile away and at that distance he judged them to be poor marksmen and not much of a threat; so the bodies were removed and digging continued – no doubt with added urgency. Fortunately, assistance was at hand; some of Buller's men, scouting on top of the cliffs, looked down over the plateau rim, and seeing Wood's predicament, opened a vigorous fire on the approaching warriors, driving them back the way they had come. No longer harassed by the enemy, Wood satisfied himself that his dead companions were interred with dignity and read an abridged version of the burial service from Mrs Campbell's prayer book. The day was now well advanced and once again Wood ordered Weatherley to follow Buller's track to the plateau. The Border Horse headed up the hill, leaving their casualties behind, '. . . only six men dead and seven wounded,' as Wood subsequently wrote; presumably he regarded the number as trifling, but to Weatherley it accounted for almost a quarter of his force.

It had been Wood's intention to join Buller on top of the mountain but he now changed his mind. Instead of following the Border Horse up to the plateau, Wood and his escort about-turned and commenced riding west, back the way they had come, in the direction of Russell's column. Three hours had elapsed since Wood's small cavalcade had first come under fire. It was now well after nine o'clock.

At the eastern end of the plateau, toward which the Border Horse were now ascending, 'A' Troop had continued to hold at bay ever-increasing numbers of ever-bolder abaQulusi – and at the other end of the plateau the tranquillity of the early morning was no more. Wood's Irregulars and Hamu's men, rounding up cattle, were no longer undisturbed, for all along the north-west rim the abaQulusi were emerging from their hiding places, climbing up from below the crags and krantzes. Every baboon path seemed to be alive with warriors intent on preventing Buller from joining up with Russell. Clearly it was time to depart – but not before the enemy had been contained. The Burgher Force and the Transvaal Rangers, Buller's most experienced units, were ordered forward and, skirmishing with a quiet skill, forced the enemy back over the plateau edge. Buller decided that if the descent from the plateau at Russell's end was not possible for horsemen, it was feasible for cattle and herders, and that was the way the auxiliaries and booty would have to go. Russell and his men would be there to see them down and escort them back to Kambula. Unhindered by cattle and herders, Buller and his horsemen would retrace their steps and go down the mountain by the same route as they had ascended early that morning.

He promptly set about gathering his scattered cavalry. 'A' Troop of the FLH and the contingent of Baker's Horse which had been holding the descent area for most of the morning, at some cost in dead and wounded, had mistakenly been withdrawn only a short while before. Now 'A' Troop was sent back at top speed to retake its old position while the contingent of Baker's Horse remained with Buller.

Although it was time to go, Buller was conducting a withdrawal, not a retreat. He ordered Barton, who commanded the FLH, to take 'C' Troop and follow 'A' back to the descent area, and then continue to Kambula, burying the bodies of Williams and von Stietencron on the way. There was still time for such formalities, or so it seemed up on top of the plateau where nothing of the surrounding countryside could be seen. Russell, however, was better placed: from his position on the lower plateau, now congested with cattle and men, he had a bird's-eye view to the south. And in that direction he saw movement. First it had looked like a dark cloud scudding swiftly over the hills – but there were no clouds! All too soon the truth was revealed. There, five miles away, and advancing at an awe-inspiring pace, was the mighty Zulu army. Having left Ulundi three days earlier, it had marched via the White Umfolozi *en route* for Kambula, but had been diverted the previous evening, by the abaQulusi beacons, toward Hlobane.

The spectacle was frightening, but hardly a surprise, even though the enemy had arrived a day earlier than predicted by Hamu's spies. What, then, had happened to the British scouts? Wood's last action before mounting his horse for the attack was a brief note to Chelmsford saying, 'I am not very sanguine of success. We do not know how steep the eastern end may be, but I think we ought to make a stir here, to divert attention from you, although, as you see by our last reports, it is asserted that you have only coast tribes against you, and that all Cetshwayo's people [the Zulu army] are coming here' – and here they were. Despite all their foreknowledge, Wood and Buller had been caught napping; worse still, they had disregarded one of their own cardinal rules – no screen of watchdog scouts or vedettes had been posted – an omission indeed, as only a couple of weeks earlier Wood had again slated Russell for posting his scouts only a half a mile out, holding up as a shining example Buller's vedettes which were posted as far out as eight miles or more. In his autobiography Wood was to state: 'From December 1878 I had the native scouts twenty miles in front of our force, and patrols six miles out an hour before daylight....' and went on to comment that the natural vision of his native scouts was extraordinary and surpassed only by the telescope. It is, therefore, inexplicable that vedettes had not been posted straddling the route from Ulundi. From Nyembe Hill, which was less than two miles from the site of Buller's bivouac, the Zulu army would have been visible early the previous day.

This was the greatest of the many British blunders involved with Hlobane and it is remarkable that no one was held responsible, for the posting of scouts should have been as routine as watering the horses. Tomasson, who was with Baker's Horse, defended Buller on the issue, writing: 'History says, some mistake as to the placing of the vedettes took place, but not by anyone under Colonel Buller's orders.' Perhaps scouts had been posted but had shirked their duty as unpleasant things were inclined to happen to lonely vedettes. In an incident reported by a local newspaper, one man of a vedette had become separated from the rest of the party, when he was surprised by about fifteen Zulu who seized the mane of his horse and tried to pull him from the saddle. However, putting his spurs in, the scout managed to get clear but was shot at from all sides:

> One bullet entering his left thigh going through part of the saddle lodged in his right thigh ... another went through the sleeve of his right arm and carried away two fingers; another hit the butt of his carbine near the lock thus saving him from instant death, another passed through his helmet and assegais flew around his retreating horse. He, however, came out of his peril and on riding back to camp was loudly cheered for his pluck and bearing.

At the bottom of Devil's Pass Russell scribbled a frantic note to Wood, whom he assumed to be up on the plateau, warning him of the approaching army, and his messenger began forcing his way up the pass against the descending tide of bellowing cattle, dust and screeching herdsmen. The man could not find Wood and some time elapsed before he came upon Buller to whom, in the absence of Wood, he delivered Russell's warning. But by now it was stale news. Buller, alerted by his own men on the southern lip of the plateau, had sighted the Zulu army not long after it had come into Russell's view. Buller had also seen an additional impi of some 2000 warriors approaching along the crest of Intyentika Hill toward the nek of the same name, opposite 'A' Company's position. This impi of the abaQulusi was, due to its elevation and proximity, a greater threat at that moment than the main army. A glance was enough to convince Buller that to continue his withdrawal across the plateau would end up with them all drowning in a Zulu tide. There was nothing for it: the precipitous descent at Russell's end was their only option. But what of Barton, who had set off to bury the dead and return along the southern route? If he were not warned he would ride headlong into the advancing army. Buller at once sent two troopers chasing after Barton directing him to 'drop Lieutenant Williams's body and retreat at once to camp by the "right side" of the mountain': a carelessly worded order that would result in great tragedy. As the messengers rode away as best they could across the boulder-strewn terrain, Buller gazed after them searching the plateau for some sign of Wood and his escort. Unless they were with Russell they would be in grave peril.

As for the abaQulusi and Mbelini, the course of events could not be going better. A few days earlier the correspondent of *The Port Elizabeth and Eastern Province Standard*, writing of the Ntombi disaster and Mbelini's success, said of him and his followers:

> They were thoroughly acquainted with every krantz and ravine, in fact with every inch of their country, lightly armed and unencumbered with army impedimenta, accustomed to long marches, they possessed all the successful qualifications for the successful accomplishment of similar stealthy movements. Added to these advantages they seem always well posted up with regard to military operations on our side and they 'feel' their European enemy with the greatest nicety.

The correspondent had come close to prophesying what was taking place at that moment on the Painted Mountain.

Having completed the burial service of Campbell and Lloyd, and having ordered the Border Horse up on the plateau, Wood was meanwhile proceeding westward at a leisurely pace. Apart from Lieutenant Lysons and his personal escort, Wood's party now included a badly wounded NCO of the Border Horse who could not proceed with the rest of his unit. As the small cavalcade ambled along Wood stopped occasionally to administer brandy to the wounded man, while Mtonga and his Zulus rounded up stray sheep and goats to herd back to Kambula. Although closest by far of all the British force to the advancing impi, Wood and his party were completely oblivious of its presence and continued to ride steadily in its direction. None of his commanders had the faintest idea of his whereabouts.

Russell and his subordinates, still up on the lower plateau, continued to watch in fearsome fascination the magnificent deployment of the enemy. Some had seen it happen before. Were they destined, having escaped from Isandlwana, to be subjected to a second terrible ordeal? Cochrane and his Edendale Troop of the NNH had fought at Isandlwana and survived; the mounted infantry had been the first to witness the awful savagery of a Zulu victory. Many must have been the prayers silently muttered by the Isandlwana veterans, as they watched those same Zulu regiments that had overwhelmed the British camp deploying to encircle the southern slopes of Hlobane. The haunting memory of Isandlwana would now adversely influence the action of Russell and his column. Schermbrucker and his Kaffrarian Rifles were the only mounted men with Russell not to have experienced

Isandlwana, but they had seen sights almost as harrowing at the Intombi River.

Three and a half miles away at the other end of the plateau, 'A' Company of the FLH, after being mistakenly withdrawn, had, after a stiff fight, retaken possession of the eastern escape route. Thereafter they had witnessed the passage of Weatherley and his Border Horse as they climbed on to the plateau where they went searching for Buller. As 'A' Company was left alone once more to guard the pass, the enemy, suddenly possessed with fresh aggression, rose up and came at them fearlessly. The abaQulusi had not only seen the great army to the south but were at that moment about to join hands with the vanguard of the 2000-strong impi from the opposite plateau. 'A' Company, whose view of the surrounding country was completely obscured by the plateau rim, were probably the only troops on the summit who were still unaware of the arrival of the Zulu army – and it was only when they saw the different coloured shields of the impi from the opposite hill advancing toward them that they realised they were about to be overwhelmed. A survivor of the troop, Lieutenant Alfred Blaine, recalled, 'We saw at once it would be all up with us if we did not act quickly,' and act quickly they did: another survivor, George Mossop, a trooper of the FLH and a mere lad of sixteen years, whose only love in his life was his Basuto pony 'Warrior', described his departure: 'As one man we rose like a covey of partridges and ran for the horses ... a loud whinny from my pony drew me to him like a magnet ... the Zulu were upon us, and their stabbing spears became busy ... my pony's head was pointing north-east. He bounded away in that direction and I let him go.'

The British rearguard disintegrated, and Buller's disciplined withdrawal of only half an hour earlier began to descend into the abyss of a rout. On the plateau the two messengers had overtaken Barton who, on reading Buller's message, completely misinterpreted its intention due to its ambiguity. When Buller had written, 'Retreat at once to the camp by the right side of the mountain', he had assumed Barton would be riding toward Kambula and that 'the right side of the mountain' would signify the north side away from the Zulu army – either that or Buller had employed military terminology that Barton did not understand, for it was not unusual for an attacking force to describe the flanks of its objective as left and right, facing it from the front. If 'the right side of the mountain' had been used in that context, its meaning to Barton would have been equally uncertain had he tried to apply it to an objective as vast as Hlobane. When Barton received the message he had yet to see the Zulu army; and it has been surmised that he took Buller's note to be a confirmation of his previous order. Yet it could not have been a misunderstanding as simple as that. Clearly there was a new ring of urgency and warning in Buller's note: 'Drop the body ... retreat at once'. Moreover, what of the messengers themselves? Arriving at all speed, they would surely have bawled their news of the advancing Zulu army; and had they not, Barton would certainly have wanted to hear their first-hand intelligence of the situation back on the plateau. One way or the other, he must have been appraised of the advancing army. That being the case, it is strange that he did not question his own immediate assumption and conclude that Buller's message was not a confirmation but a countermand. However, it is a riddle without a solution, as all those who could have supplied an answer would be dead within the hour.

If there was blame to be allocated for the disaster that would shortly result from the misunderstanding, Buller, unlike other of his fellow officers, was ready to accept it entirely. In his official report which he wrote the following day and which would, in due course, be printed in *The London Gazette*, he admitted his careless wording was the cause of many deaths. Buller was made of the 'right stuff' and his reputation needed to be saved – as would other reputations before the day was over.

Wood and his party, including the herded sheep and goats, had travelled about five miles along the base of Hlobane since they had left the grave of Campbell and Lloyd. They were well over half-way to the spot where Wood expected to rendezvous with Russell, when Mtonga, following a stray goat, rode a little higher up the slopes, giving him a view over the undulating ground to the south. There, not two miles away, silent, vast and moving at a fearsome pace, was the Zulu army. Mtonga shouted, waving his arms, and Wood joined him at a canter. They had been riding on a collision course with the advancing army which had already deployed into attack formation of five columns. Wood's thought was to warn Russell and he scribbled a note: 'Below the Inhobane 10.30 am 28.3.79. Colonel Russell there is a large army coming this way from the south. Get into position on Zunguin Nek. Signed E.W.'

Since sighting the advancing army Russell had already withdrawn his men off the mountain to the plain below, taking up a position between the base of the lower plateau and the south-eastern edge of the Zunguin range. It was the very position to which Wood intended him to move, but it was not the Zunguin Nek. One way or another, Wood had his place names confused, for the Zunguin Nek was, as would be expected, a saddle in the Zunguin range itself and was situated six miles to the north-west. The saddle was on the route to Kambula and the British columns had marched through it the previous day. The consequences arising from this mix-up would be as disastrous as the ill-worded directions that Barton had received from Buller.

Wood tore the message from his notebook and sent Lysons, his one remaining staff officer, galloping off to find Russell. Wood and the rest of his party, although hampered by the wounded NCO, pressed on as fast as they could. They had been seen and a detachment of the Zulu army had set off in pursuit.

Young Lieutenant Lysons was having an exciting day, a day seemingly straight out of the pages of an adventure story. What could be more gallant than to be a lone courier galloping across the face of the Zulu army – a *beau sabreur* indeed! Lysons pulled in his sweating horse and handed the note to Russell who scanned it while keeping an ever-anxious eye on the advancing enemy. He waved and

Above: The 'field farmers' forge' at Kambula Camp, shoeing horses of Colonel Buller's irregular cavalry. The rocky terrain in which the troops operated necessitated the horses being constantly reshod. (Africana Library, Johannesburg)

Right: Colonel Redvers Buller, VC, in the campaign dress that he wore during the Zulu War. His daily apparel, like that of his horsemen, could never be described as formal uniform. (Talana Museum, Natal)

Below: An officer of the Frontier Light Horse. He carries a British issue light cavalry sword, Pattern 1853. The weapon was 3ft long and weighed 2lb. Swords were issued after the battle of Kambula. (John Young collection)

Right: A proud and strict disciplinarian, Commandant Friedrich Schermbrucker raised his corps of the Kaffrarian Rifles in the Eastern Cape. The men were recruited from ex-German mercenaries who had been settled around the East London area by the British Government after the Crimean War. (Killie Campbell Africana Library)

Lower right: A rare photograph of an aged colonial volunteer who was apparently involved in every major action of No. 4 Column from January 1879 through to the final battle of Ulundi, and was twice wounded. He stands proudly next to his trusty steed, 'Lady', and was most likely an officer or senior NCO of the Frontier Light Horse. (Killie Campbell Africana Library)

Above: Men of the Edendale Troop, Natal Native Horse. The exact date of the photograph is uncertain but it is probably the occasion, on 15 December 1881, when Evelyn Wood presented the troop with a flag and battle honours. The seated native officer in the left foreground, wearing a bead-covered 'deerstalker hat', is more than likely Sergeant Major Simeon Kambule with the ribbon of the Distinguished Conduct Medal pinned to his jacket. (John Young collection)

Right: An NCO and a trooper of the Ixopo Mounted Contingent from Southern Natal displaying a comprehensive arsenal of weapons including a cavalry carbine and bandoleer of ammunition, a quiver of throwing spears and a knobkerrie. As was the custom with some tribes, the NCO rides with his big toe only in the stirrup iron and wears his spurs strapped directly on to his bare feet. (John Young collection)

Above: Commandant Pieter Raaff with his officers of the Transvaal Rangers. An officer of a rival unit of Irregular Horse described, rather unfairly, the Rangers as 'a more forbidding lot of mixed Hottentots and scum of the Diamond Fields ever collected together outside a prison wall'. (Africana Library, Johannesburg)

Left: The flag of the Edendale Troop, NNH, presented to the unit in 1881, was acquired for safe keeping by the Killie Campbell Africana Library in 1959. Present at the ceremony was Alfred Kamulo whose father fought at Isandlwana whilst serving with the troop. (Killie Campbell Africana Library)

Right: The flag of the Border Horse made by the ladies of Pretoria. The unit was virtually annihilated at the battle of Hlobane, but must have been reformed to take part in the Sekhukhune campaign eight months later. The flag until recent times was displayed in a Pretoria museum but now seems to have been lost.

Right: An abaQulusi warrior on top of Hlobane Mountain waits out in icy rain the arrival of Colonel Buller's attacking column.

Right: An abaQulusi sniper fires on an advancing British column, emptying the saddles of two horses, while cavalry skirmish with warriors in the background. The original caption to this picture called it a narrow escape for Colonel Wood who, presumably, is the mounted officer in the foreground. (Killie Campbell Africana Library)

Above: Men of Wood's Irregulars (with their officer adopting a strange position in the front row). As can be seen, they were men of superb physique. Not 'tame natives' from Natal, but true mercenaries, hired from the Swazi kingdom. It was written that they were 'fine stalwart fellows ... inveterate foes of the Zulu'.

Below: Colonel John Cecil Russell, 12th Lancers, who commanded the western assault column on Hlobane. His interpretation, rightly or wrongly, of Colonel Wood's orders was largely responsible for the rout of Buller's forces and the disaster of Devil's Pass. (Regimental Museum of the 9th/12th Royal Lancers, Derby City Museum and Art Gallery)

Below right: Captain William Francis Dundonald Cochrane was one of the six imperial officers to escape from Isandlwana. He survived to fight at the battles of Hlobane, Kambula and Ulundi at which he commanded the Edendale Troop of Natal Native Horse. (Natal Archives C2063)

Right: The grey-bearded Induna on the right is Mahubulwana, a chief of the abaQulusi. (Natal Archives)

Below right: This sketch of the burial of Campbell and Lloyd, presided over by Evelyn Wood, has usually been ascribed to Wood himself. It was, in fact, drawn by his mother, Lady Emma Wood, which explains the otherwise inexplicable inaccuracies of the burial scene – especially the two angelic-featured young men disposing of a single corpse, and Wood wearing his Ashanti War uniform and sword. (Killie Campbell Africana Library)

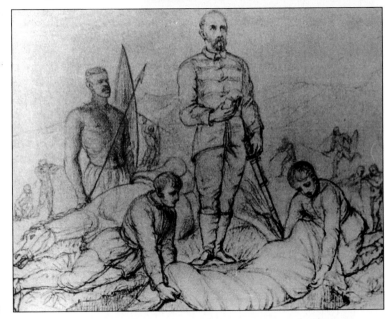

Below: A sketch of the slopes of Hlobane Mountain drawn by Lieutenant Slade in 1880. The jumble of rocks in the right of the picture contained the 'cave' from where the hidden sniper shot Captain Campbell and Mr Lloyd. (Killie Campbell Africana Library)

Above: This unfortunately blurred print from a contemporary lantern slide, although completely inaccurate in terms of the terrain, nevertheless conveys the awful panic and confusion of Devil's Pass. (John Young collection)

Above: This present day photograph, looking down Devil's Pass on to the lower plateau, gives some idea of the fearsome terrain that Buller's column had to negotiate while being attacked from all sides. Wood and his escort spent much of the day on Zunguin Mountain which can be seen in the background across the plain.

Below: 'Did you think that I would leave you dying,
When there is room on my horse for two?
Climb up here Joe, we'll soon be flying,
we can go just as fast with two.'
So ran the words of a popular Victorian song. Saving a comrade's life in the face of a savage foe was the epitome of Victorian valour. Here Buller is portrayed rescuing Captain D'Arcy on Hlobane for which he was awarded the Victoria Cross. (John Young collection)

Col Sir Redvers Buller saving Capt. D'Arcy at the Battle of Inhlobani Mountain, March 28th 1879.

Right: In the middle of this picture can be seen the jagged northern edge of the Intyentika Nek over which a number of the Border Horse and FLH were pushed or thrown to their deaths.

Right: Colonel Weatherley, clutching his young son, Rupert, attempts to cut his way off Intyentika Nek while, in the background, the men of the Border Horse and Frontier Light Horse, vastly outnumbered, are slaughtered by abaQulusi warriors. Apart from some small inaccuracies, the sketch truly portrays the horror of the massacre. The inset picture, on the other hand, is highly inaccurate, bearing no resemblance to Evelyn Wood. (Rai England collection)

Opposite page, top left: Major William Knox-Leet of the 13th Light Infantry who won his VC at Hlobane for rescuing a dismounted officer of the FLH. (Royal Archives, Windsor)

Opposite page, top right: Only six men of the Border Horse survived the battle of Hlobane. One was Captain Dennison, seen here twenty years later as a major during the Anglo-Boer war.

Opposite page, bottom: The regimental band of the 13th Light Infantry at Kambula camp. Spit and polish had become a thing of the past. (Africana Library, Johannesburg)

Below: The Commissariat Department of the 90th LI. Lieutenant Quartermaster Joseph Newman, who, as a young sergeant, was 'conspicuous by his gallantry' at the Relief of Lucknow during the Indian Mutiny, smokes his pipe and has his pet terrier on his lap. (Africana Library, Johannesburg)

Bottom: Boredom of camp life at Kambula was relieved by various sports organised by Wood. Races and tug-of-war were among the favourites. Here the Swazis of Wood's Irregulars compete at spear-throwing. (John Young collection)

Opposite page, top: The bakery of No. 4 Column, which was situated just outside the camp at Kambula and was overrun during the Zulu attack. Colonel Wood made a point of always having plenty of fresh bread for his troops. The bakers look as rough as their bread! (Africana Library, Johannesburg)

Opposite page bottom, left and right: The commanders of the opposing armies at Kambula, Colonel Evelyn Wood VC, CB, and Tshingwayo ka Mahole Khoza. In these pictures they are very likely dressed exactly as they were when fighting the battle. (John Young collection)

Top: This present-day picture was taken from the position of Wood's redoubt. In a hundred years the battlefield of Kambula has hardly changed. Buller's attack on the Zulu right horn and its premature charge would have been just to the left of the picture. A: The waterhole and often boggy ground in which some of the horsemen encountered difficulties and were slain by the Nkobamakosi. B: The rocky outcrop to which the Nkobamakosi Regiment retreated after its abortive charge. C: The defeated Zulu army was pursued across the plain for 8 miles toward the Zunguin Nek. D: The main body of the Zulu army would have been positioned where the trees now stand. (Author)

Above: Melton Prior, the war artist who drew this sketch depicting the 90th LI repulsing the left wing of the Zulu army, was not present at Kambula on the day of the battle. The height of Kambula Hill and the redoubt is exaggerated, as is the depth of the ravine from which the Zulu army attacked time and again. The action portrayed is at the height of the battle but the drawing, unfortunately, fails to convey the drama of the occasion and the vast number of warriors involved. The main laager is to the far right of the picture; the unlimbered guns of the Royal Artillery are in action below the redoubt; the cattle laager stands above the ravine and the struck tents of the British camp are scattered on the ground behind the firing line of soldiers.

Left: Lieutenant Edward Browne, who assisted in saving the life of his commanding officer, Colonel Cecil Russell, won the only Victoria Cross that was awarded at the battle of Kambula. (South Wales Borderers Museum, Brecon)

Below: Commandant Scherm-brucker, astride his orderly's horse, helps Captain Moore aboard while his orderly, Larsen (not seen in the picture) attempts to escape on foot. Unfortunately, Larsen was overtaken by the Zulu and speared to death while the other two escaped.

Right: Lord Chelmsford came in for a great deal of criticism when he returned to England. Here, in a cartoon of 1879, looking carefree and youthful, his handling of the campaign is held to question by an enquiring public.

CLEANING HIS BOOTS.

' SO FAR AS I AM CONCERNED, THE WAR IS OVER.'—*Lord Chelmsford, after the victory of Ulundi.*

Below: Much of the battlefield of Hlobane has seen little change. With the aid of a diagram drawn by Lieutenant Slade in 1880, the remains of the stone cattle kraal (right of the picture) where Wood sheltered his ponies and Lloyd was shot, was located 114 years later. The 'cave' which sheltered the hidden Zulu sniper was also found in the undergrowth above the kraal. (Author)

Above and below: Part of the deputation of over 200 Zulu leaders which petitioned the Natal Government for the return of their king from exile. As will be seen from the key to the picture, the deputation consisted of many members of the Zulu royal family and other powerful leaders. (Natal Archives C870/1)

No. 2 Part of *ZULU DEPUTATION* to the *NATAL GOVERNMENT*, to entreat for the bones of *CETSHWAYO* that they may bury them in Zululand, that is to pray that Cetshwayo may return to Zululand under any conditions that may please the English. The whole party consisting of over two hundred.

Present in Picture No. 2.	Rank, Position, &c.	Under which of Sir G. Wolseley's 13 Chiefs.
1 Ndabuko Maduna. son of Mpande (King Panda).	Only brother of Cetshwayo by the same Mother, in the eye of the people Regent for his young nephew, Dinuzulu, the elder son of Cetshwayo representing on this occasion the major part of the tribes, now placed under Mfanawendhlela, and also the major part of the tribe of MKosana. son of Vundhlana. now placed under Mgitshwa.	Zibebu.
2 Shingana, son of Mpande.	A younger half brother of Cetshwayo, late Induna of the u'Dhloko regiment.	
3 Ngeongewana. son of Mgundane.	Uncle of Cetshwayo.	Faku, son of Ziningo.
4 Makoba, son of Mapita.	Represents the left side of the House and Tribe of Mapita.	Hamu.
5 Ndabezimbi, nephew of Mapita		Zibebu
6 Nyosana, son of Masiputa.	Masiputa was Prime Minister to Mpande.	Hamu.
7 NKungane, son of Mbonda.	Uncle of Cetshwayo, on mother's side.	
8 Ndabankulu, son of Lukwazi.	Represents Seketwayo, and, in token thereof, brought down Seketwayo's Letters' Patent,—ie,. his appointment as chief signed by Sir G Wolseley, &c.	Seketwayo.
9 Mholo.	Chief Induna of eku Buseni Kraal. one of 10 large Kraals filled with people who had been saved by Cetshwayo, from being killed as *abatagati* (malefactors).	Zibebu.
10 Mahubulwana.	Chief Induna of, and represents aba Qulusi Tribe.	Hamu.
11 Magadeni.	The late Chief Induna of the isi Xepe Military Kraal.	Ntshingwayo.
12 Dhlambulu.	An Inneeku (Household or civil officer) of Cetshwayo.	Zibebu.
13 Mgobe, son of Mbopa.	Mbopa is brother to Mpande's mother.	Gaozi.
14 Magelana. 15 Dabuka.	} Inneeku's of Shingana.	Faku, son of Ziningo.
16 Mgwazeni.	Uncle of Cetshwayo, on Mother's side.	
17 Ngatsha.	Induna of the aku Buseni Kraal.	Zibebu.
18 Madhlenya.	Represents Maboko, son of Masiputa, and the major part of his Tribe.	
19 Mapetu.	Son of MKosana, who is with Cetshwayo at Cape Town.	Mgoiana.

shouted for his officers to join him, read the note aloud and posed the question as to where precisely was the Zunguin Nek? Where exactly did Wood wish them to take up position? Six miles away, in the opposite direction to the advancing Zulu army, appeared to be the popular opinion of the officers present.

It is interesting to surmise who those officers may have been. Browne, commanding the mounted infantry, was not present; he was still up on the Hlobane plateau, as were the local experts Potter and Calverley. White, of Wood's Irregulars, was far out of sight trying to save some of the captured cattle and urge his men away to Kambula. Bigge of the Royal Artillery was present, and having been on the Zunguin Nek during the operation of 24 January, must have known the correct location. Cochrane and Raw of the NNH would have been with Russell but as fairly recent arrivals may have had no firm opinion. On the other hand, Schermbrucker and his officers, who had been in the area the longest of all, would definitely have known the exact location. But what is more important, which of these officers, having agreed on the position of Zunguin Nek, would have had the fibre to assert that Wood had obviously mixed up his names and that by speeding away to the north-west, they would not only leave their own native auxiliaries at the mercy of the enemy, but also their comrades who were still on top of the mountain?

There is no record of an altercation between Russell and those officers present except for Schermbrucker who is reported to have objected to the proposed withdrawal. What is pertinent is that those who could have added their weight to Schermbrucker's objection (if indeed he made one), Cochrane and Raw, did not do so. Although not particularly senior, they were experienced officers; but, like Russell, their dominating experience was that of the horror of Isandlwana. In any event, Russell ordered his whole column to retire, his instructions being delivered to White just as the native auxiliaries were running out of ammunition, having been fiercely engaged with the abaQulusi who were trying to retake their cattle. White sent one of his officers, Lieutenant P.F. Darcy,[4] galloping after Russell with the request that he be allowed to remain behind and help his men. Darcy, having caught up, began to deliver his message but was curtly interrupted by Russell who said, 'Tell Commandant White to leave the cattle and push on as fast as he can.' In doing so White would also have to abandon his men.

At the opposite end of Hlobane, and still up on the plateau, Barton, with 'C' Troop of the FLH was following Buller's orders to retreat at once to Kambula, and was mistakenly making toward the eastern descent when he met with Weatherley heading in the opposite direction. Presumably Barton told Weatherley the operation was over, that the rest of the troops were on their way down and that he, Weatherley, would be wasting his time to cross the length of the plateau: better they join forces and retreat down the mountain together. In any event, that is what happened and down they went, pushing past the abaQulusi straight toward the Zulu army which, at that moment, might well have been just outside their line of vision. They did not have far to go before they almost ran headlong into the advancing mass of warriors that threatened to squash them against the mountain if they did not alter course. There was no option other than to return the way they had come, but not up on to the plateau. They would go slightly north, fight their way through the abaQulusi, over Intyentika Nek and, with luck, find Potter's track down the northern side of Hlobane and cross the plain back to Kambula. There were about eighty of them, roughly thirty FLH and fifty Border Horse. They must have known that they did not have much of a chance: the Zulu army behind them, precipitous heights to the left and the right, and then an uphill charge against 2000 elated warriors. The going was also to their disadvantage: long grass and stony – but worst of all, their horses were knocked up and tired. Furthermore, about Weatherley's neck hung a heavy yoke of self recrimination, for what had he been doing bringing his fourteen-year-old son, Rupert, on this horror expedition?

The little body of horsemen walked and trotted, just fast enough to keep their distance from the army behind. As they neared the summit of Intyentika Nek they formed into an extended line for what would be a parody of a cavalry charge.

Pathetic though it may have been, it was a gallant charge against great odds and one in which only a handful would survive. Here were all the ingredients for an epic Victorian painting. Alas, it would not even be done the honour of a scribbled sketch. They were now being fired upon from all sides. There was no point in waiting and with a faint cheer they kicked their tired mounts into a semblance of a gallop toward packed ranks of abaQulusi straddling the nek. What had started as a charge disintegrated into an 'every man for himself' ride for freedom. As they crashed into the enemy, down went men and horses, to be stabbed again and again long after they were dead. A few of the horsemen, clubbing with upturned carbines at heads and grasping hands, broke through and found themselves on the left of the nek and the track heading north to the plain below. Down this they scrabbled and slithered, hanging on to their saddles for dear life, for to be dismounted was instant death. But the majority of those who broke through were headed off to the right where the nek descended in sweeping ledges, terminating in a sheer drop of several hundred feet to the boulder-strewn valley below.

It was toward this final plunge that the Border Horse were herded and, dead or alive, were clutched by many hands and tossed into the void. There was one exception: the only soldier ever to have been taken prisoner during the Anglo-Zulu War and to have survived was captured on Intyentika Nek. The story of his captivity and escape has been the subject of much speculation but there is no doubt that he was captured on Hlobane and reappeared, half naked and starving, many miles away eighteen days later. He was a Frenchman by the name of Grandier, serving in Weatherley's Border Horse.[5] He later described his capture:

We were descending the Hlobane, when we met a large force of Zulu about the place where we had met Colonel Wood in the morning. We fell back, Colonel Weatherley giving orders to fire volleys. We crossed the Intyentika Nek, being assailed on all sides by the enemy. The horses were much exhausted. I was nearly the last and had put a comrade on my horse. I was running alongside, when a Zulu caught hold of me by the leg. They did not attempt to assegai me, but took me to Mbelini's kraal which is on the south side of the Hlobane and about half way up.

Prisoner or not, Grandier was more fortunate than most of his comrades. Over a hundred years later their bones would still lie scattered on the rocks below the cliffs. Weatherley and his young son were among those who perished on the nek. A survivor told how the boy, having been dismounted, was for a few moments saved by his father who, swinging his old Crimea sabre, kept all at bay until they both died 'under a flurry of assegais'. Although no Victorian artist produced a painting of this worthy scene, Major Waller Ashe, when painting a word portrait in his book *The Story of the Zulu Campaign*, published a year after the battle in 1880, rather overdid it even for a patriotic Victorian readership when he wrote:

Nothing could be more sad than Weatherley's death. At the fatal hour when all save honour was lost, he placed his beloved boy upon his best horse and kissing him on the forehead, commended him to another Father's care above, and implored him to overtake the nearest column of the English Horse, which seemed at that time to be cutting its way out. The boy clung to his father and begged to be allowed to stay by his side, and share his life or death. The contrast was characteristic. The man, a bearded, bronzed and hardy sabre with a father's tears upon his cheek, while the blue-eyed and fair haired lad, with much of the beauty of a girl in his appearance, was calmly and with a smile of fondly light loading his father's favourite carbine. When the two noble hearts were last seen the father, wounded to death with cruel assegais, was clasping his boy's hand with his left, whilst the right cut down the brawny savages who came to despoil him of his charge.

Perhaps twenty of the fugitives, including Barton, got over the nek and down on to the plains below. Many were wounded and fortune would not ride with them. The first warriors from the main Zulu army, mounted skirmishers of the Umcityo Regiment, now came cantering up the nek. As Barton and his party reached the plain they glanced back at the mountain; the Umcityo were silhouetted against the skyline, urging their horses down the slope in hot pursuit.

At the other end of Hlobane, still haunted by the spectre of Isandlwana, Russell and his men rode away, leaving Wood's Irregulars and Hamu's warriors to escape as best they could. Worse still, they had deserted their mounted comrades in their moment of great peril. Fourteen years later, Schermbrucker wrote an account of his experiences at Hlobane in which he grossly distorted the wording of Wood's order to Russell, and glossed over Russell's desertion and his own collaboration in it. Schermbrucker changed Wood's terse order – 'Get into position on Zunguin

Nek' to a long-winded: 'A message was instantly dispatched to Colonel Russell to apprise him of the approach of an overwhelming Zulu army with instructions to communicate, if possible, with Colonel Buller; both columns, Buller's and Russell's, to retire from the mountain without a moment's delay and hurry by the shortest route and the highest possible speed to reach the camp.' Schermbrucker went on to say that it was never clear from Wood's order whether or not Russell was intended to assist Buller's column and even if he had, it would not materially have affected the actual issue! He then described for his readers the horror of watching Buller's men being butchered down Devil's Pass, but gave no explanation as to why Russell did not go to their rescue – not one shot, it seems, was fired in their support despite the enemy being within rifle range.

Schermbrucker offhandedly concluded, 'Colonel Russell's column, formed at the foot of the mountain, were directed to proceed to the camp at Kambula.'

Up on the plateau blind panic had, with the exception of a courageous few, seized upon all of Buller's men.

Knox-Leet described the scene as Buller and the majority of the mounted men were pursued across the plateau by a large force of running warriors:

> Buller came up and said we had better mount our horses and get down the krantz [Devil's Pass] on to the lower mountain at once . . . with so many men and horses to get down the operation at any time would have been an extremely difficult one, but with the enemy pressing on it appeared impossible. . . . I looked at once to this lower mountain expecting to see Lieutenant Colonel Russell's force ready to cover our retreat, but not a man was to be seen and it immediately became apparent that a catastrophe was inevitable.

The Zulu army was upon them. Russell had deserted and a savage and awful death was imminent. The only way of escape was Devil's Pass and all fled there helter-skelter to be the first down. But merely to reach the pass was for many a ride in the face of death. Young George Mossop, separated from his comrades of 'A' company and all alone, was galloping west on his Basuto pony across the plateau when:

> . . . suddenly the ground dipped into a hollow, and scattered about were some three or four hundred Zulus, who sighting me, began shouting and pointing their spears while they formed a half moon, which covered a considerable distance cutting me off . . . I think my horse realised the predicament . . . he was pulling hard to get away in the direction of the running Zulus who had almost completed their formation . . . cut off on all sides, it did not matter where I galloped, and I gave the horse its head . . . he became a wild animal, all his instincts urging him to break away from the enemies who surrounded him . . . when we were about fifteen paces from the enemy, a few on our right rushed in to support those immediately in our front, leaving a narrow gap in their line. Like a hare with a pack of dogs behind it, the horse swerved and darted into the breach. . . .

Young Mossop lived to fight another day – but as will be seen, the ordeal was far from over for him and 'Warrior', his little horse.

Including the native auxiliaries, there were still in the region of 500 men and over 300 horses on the plateau with no way down but via Devil's Pass – and around its narrow rim the conglomeration of men and horses pushed and shoved. There was neither discipline nor restraint, only noise, fear and desperation. For all that, Devil's Pass was negotiable. Given time and patience, a rider leading his horse could scramble from top to bottom with every hope of a safe landing; but there was no time and it seemed none had patience. In their favour, however, it must be remembered that few of the men were soldiers: they were civilians with little or no military training – some were fine horsemen and good shots but, lacking discipline, were unable to stand firm. Lieutenant Alfred Blaine of the FLH, writing in a letter three days later, described the scene most vividly:

> Then an awful confusion took place – horses fell on top of the rocks broke their necks and legs – you saw horses on top of men I was under my horse for about two or three minutes and thought it was all up with me. We shouted to the men not to hurry, but to take it coolly. The kaffirs got in amongst us and assegaied our fellows. We could not hit them even with our carbines for we were too jammed up.

Tragically, there was no immediate reason for fear and panic: the Zulu army was still far enough away to be outdistanced and the abaQulusi, who had engaged Barton and Weatherley, could have been kept at bay long enough for the column to have withdrawn in an orderly fashion.

The arrival of the Zulu army also had a marked effect on the conduct of the abaQulusi. They became reckless with courage. Leaving their hiding places among the rocks and krantzes, they rushed in upon the congested mob; even a few abaQulusi women, spears in hand, went into battle. But not all the British force had lost its head. A few courageous men about-turned and formed a rearguard. Lieutenant Browne of the Mounted Infantry (who had remained on the plateau), Commandant Raaff and Lieutenant Everitt of the FLH, to name but a few, and a small number of troopers from the latter unit, got themselves behind the rocks. Maintaining a steady fire, they kept the advancing abaQulusi in check until one of the defenders yelled to cease firing, believing the enemy to be their own allied natives of Wood's Irregulars! (Buller later attributed most of the British loss to this tragic mistake.) The firing stopped and, although for no longer than a few hesitant moments, it was enough: the enemy sprinted across the gap and, now within stabbing distance, they set about the rearguard. That was the end of any organised resistance on the plateau and it was then every man for himself and God help the wounded.

Some of the first down were the men of Piet Uys's Burgher Force whose departure was disparagingly described by Captain Cecil D'Arcy of the FLH as

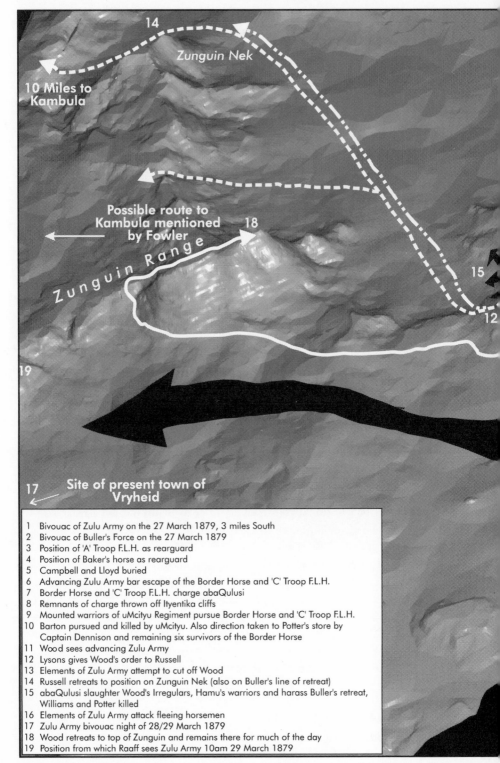

14
Zunguin Nek
10 Miles to Kambula
Possible route to Kambula mentioned by Fowler
18
Zunguin Range
15
12
19
17 Site of present town of Vryheid

1 Bivouac of Zulu Army on the 27 March 1879, 3 miles South
2 Bivouac of Buller's Force on the 27 March 1879
3 Position of 'A' Troop F.L.H. as rearguard
4 Position of Baker's horse as rearguard
5 Campbell and Lloyd buried
6 Advancing Zulu Army bar escape of the Border Horse and 'C' Troop F.L.H.
7 Border Horse and 'C' Troop F.L.H. charge abaQulusi
8 Remnants of charge thrown off Ityentika cliffs
9 Mounted warriors of uMcityu Regiment pursue Border Horse and 'C' Troop F.L.H.
10 Barton pursued and killed by uMcityu. Also direction taken to Potter's store by
   Captain Dennison and remaining six survivors of the Border Horse
11 Wood sees advancing Zulu Army
12 Lysons gives Wood's order to Russell
13 Elements of Zulu Army attempt to cut off Wood
14 Russell retreats to position on Zunguin Nek (also on Buller's line of retreat)
15 abaQulusi slaughter Wood's Irregulars, Hamu's warriors and harass Buller's retreat,
   Williams and Potter killed
16 Elements of Zulu Army attack fleeing horsemen
17 Zulu Army bivouac night of 28/29 March 1879
18 Wood retreats to top of Zunguin and remains there for much of the day
19 Position from which Raaff sees Zulu Army 10am 29 March 1879

The battle of Hlobane showing the movements of all the forces involved on 28 March 1879.

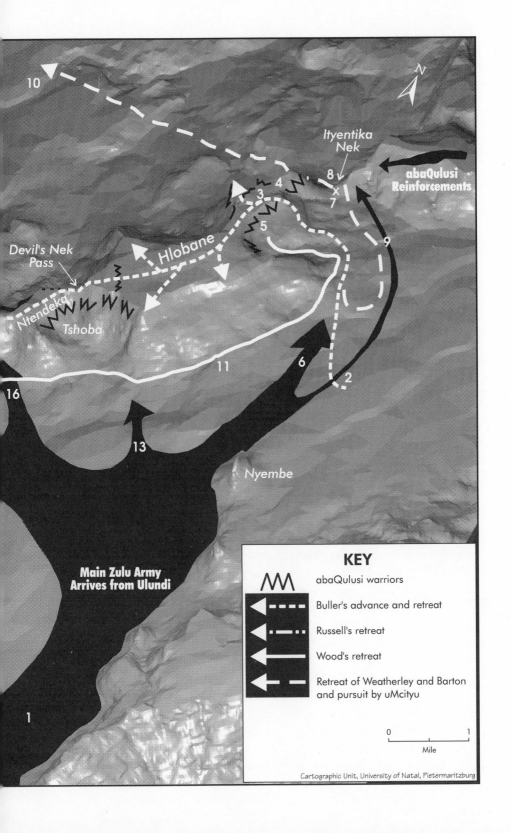

10

Ityentika Nek

8
X
7

abaQulusi Reinforcements

4

3

5

9

Devil's Nek Pass

Hlobane

Ntendeka
Tshoba

11

6

2

16

13

Nyembe

Main Zulu Army Arrives from Ulundi

1

KEY

abaQulusi warriors

Buller's advance and retreat

Russell's retreat

Wood's retreat

Retreat of Weatherley and Barton and pursuit by uMcityu

0   1
Mile

Cartographic Unit, University of Natal, Pietermaritzburg

'bolting as hard as they could go'. This was rather unfair as, unlike the rest of the white men on the mountain, the burghers all had families at no great distance and the defence of hearth and home had to take priority. Over fifty years later, one of the burghers by the name of Kritzinger would still remember how he and his friend Matthew Craig had seen the Zulu army descending from Enyati (Emyathi) hill across the plain, just as they were eating their breakfast. He also remembered how heartbreaking it was to abandon the captured cattle, which he numbered at 5000, and how on arrival at Devil's Pass they found the abaQulusi had built a stone wall around the rim of the drop which prevented the fleeing men from getting their horses over the edge. Kritzinger described the scene:

> I worked to the side away from the bunch of struggling men and horses, and I backed my horse up to the wall. He was a good horse and very quiet. I backed him to the wall and got him reared up and tipped him over the wall and he rolled nearly halfway down the slope lying on his side. I got my gun and followed down after my horse. Zulus were throwing assegais at the men on top and firing at us. I went to my horse and I had one spur left, I stuck this in my horse and he jumped and I had to run down the slope to get clear of him coming down after me.

Kritzinger managed to reach the lower plateau in safety and was about to ride off when a colonial officer threatened to shoot him if he did not stay and fight. Certainly Piet Uys and his four sons did not bolt. One of the reasons for Uys joining the British was to avenge the death of his father and brother killed by the Zulu forty-one years before. On that day the son, Piet Uys's brother, seeing his father surrounded by the enemy, had ridden back to the rescue – today the roles of father and son would be reversed in what was to be a tragic re-enactment. Uys, now at the bottom of the pass, looked back and on seeing his elder son, Petrus, unmounted and having difficulty with his horse, immediately turned back to the rescue. Uys's friend from Utrecht, Andries Rudolph, who was keeping Uys covered, saw a warrior leave a nearby mêlée and race up behind Uys, his spear raised ready to strike. Rudolph took aim but Uys was in between, masking the warrior, and before Rudolph could move his position the enemy plunged his assegai deep into Uys's back, killing him instantly. Rudolph then shot the warrior and escaped, as did all the Uys boys.

D'Arcy, who had criticised the departure of the burghers, supervised the descent of his own troop of the FLH whilst the enemy gave him 'awful pepper from Martini rifles'. Now it was his turn to make the descent and he had got halfway down when a stone 'about the size of a small piano' came bounding down after him, completely severing the leg of his horse. At the same moment another horse crashed into him from above and he found himself being squeezed to death beneath it. Struggling frantically, D'Arcy managed to extract himself, only to find the abaQulusi all around him, stabbing men and horses. Still burdened with his carbine and equipment, D'Arcy nevertheless managed to get to his feet and bounded downhill as fast as he could go.

Charlie Hewitt, a trooper of the FLH, had better luck. He and his horse got down intact but as he looked back at Devil's Pass he witnessed an awful sight: 'While I and the others were looking up at the struggling mass of horses, Zulus and volunteers, I saw the Zulus flinging some man clean over the end of the mountain down among the masses of rocks and bushes. I saw him come tumbling over and over and his arms and legs flying in the air.'

Young Mossop, due to his adventures on the plateau, arrived at Devil's Pass rather late and found that it was 'a complete jam' and that 'Zulus crawling over huge rocks on either side, were jabbing at the men and horses. Some of the men were shooting and some were using clubbed rifles and fighting their way down.' Mossop found a companion he knew well and years later recorded their conversation:

'Do you think there is any chance of pushing through?' I asked him, I was obliged to shout to make myself heard the din was terrific. 'Not a hope!' he replied and placing the muzzle of his carbine in his mouth he pulled the trigger. A lot of brains and other stuff splashed on my neck. It was the last straw – I gave one yell, let go the bridle of my pony, and bounded down the pass . . . my only thought was to get away from all these horrors.

The rout at Devil's Pass, which was Buller's immediate responsibility, was casually dismissed in his official report in one sentence: 'In such a descent a certain amount of confusion was unavoidable and this was increased by the Zulus crowding on our rear and flanks and commencing a heavy fire which killed a large number of horses.' He went on to blame the disaster on the man who yelled for the defenders to stop firing in the belief that the enemy were Wood's Irregulars, and Buller's superiors let it go at that.

Tarnished though the day had been by panic and flight, much of the esteem of Buller and his men would shortly be redeemed by selfless acts of bravery – acts that would turn the rout back from an impending massacre to the semblance of a retreat. Amongst the brave there was none braver than Buller himself, as the resilient young Mossop discovered when he landed at the bottom of the pass, more or less intact, but blind with fear. Mossop was about to flee on foot when he received a mighty clout upon the ear. It was Buller raging at all who descended the pass without a horse in the knowledge that the life of an unmounted man would be short indeed. It would seem that Mossop's fear of Buller's wrath was greater than his fear of the Zulu, so he struggled back the way he had come and discovered his beloved 'Warrior' still waiting on the rim. The abaQulusi were all around, stabbing every horse and man they could find, and again Mossop fled on foot. This time he ran to the southern side of the pass followed by 'Warrior' and together they went over the edge, bouncing and sliding down the almost sheer cliff face.

At the bottom of Devil's Pass the abaQulusi were swarming in from all sides, spearing and clubbing the remnants of the rearguard as they stumbled and fell over the jumbled rocks, all hope of escape now gone. Those of Buller's force who had survived the descent had fled the 300 yards across the narrow nek on to the lower plateau, but were still in great peril. The abaQulusi, frantic to kill all who had assailed their mountain, were already racing across the nek, while below the Zulu army was closing in on the southern slopes of the mountain. It was then that the horsemen rallied; inspired by dapper Commandant Raaff, of slight physique but of great courage, the stampeding colonials were halted, turned about and formed into line. They opened fire, covering the remaining men crossing the nek, one of whom was Buller who had stayed behind to see the last of his colonials off the plateau and had personally carried at least three to safety. The charge of the oncoming warriors was halted and before they could rally, the headlong flight of horsemen had ceased; they began to retreat in a semblance of order, keeping up a steady fire, and those who had a willing horse offered a stirrup and took a man up behind. Where there was no ride to be had, many a stronger man gave up his horse to a weaker or wounded comrade, then ran alongside, hanging on to a stirrup leather for dear life.

Meanwhile Mbelini's trap had almost closed; less than 900 feet below, the vanguard of the Zulu army had already reached the southern slopes of the plateau, cutting off all flight in that direction: another twenty minutes would see the base of the mountain completely encircled by 5000 warriors of the leading column. Buller and his men were left with the choice of two routes down, knowing that the abaQulusi would be trying to close with them every step of the way: either the gentle slope of the western side – which would lead them on a collision course with the enemy if not tackled with all speed – or the precipitous northern face, which would require a cautious and time-consuming descent. Either way, they had about five minutes in hand to beat the enemy to the base of the mountain.

Five miles to the north-west of Devil's Pass, far out on the plain, the remnants of 'C' Troop, FLH, and Weatherley's Border Horse were at a point of utter exhaustion. Of the twenty or so men who had escaped from Intyentika Nek down on to the northern plain, almost three quarters had been overtaken and killed by the mounted Umcijo warriors. Now it was to be Barton's turn. Somewhere in the flight from the mountain he had come across Lieutenant Poole of the Border Horse dismounted and alone. At the risk of his own life, Barton took up Poole on to his already exhausted horse and together they rode on, the Umcityu drawing nearer and nearer but cautious of Barton's revolver. They were now about eight miles from Potter's store which until a few days earlier had been a holding depot for Wood's Irregulars and, presumably, a place still manned and guarded to the extent that it could drive off a few mounted Zulu. But they would not reach their goal; Barton's horse with its double load finally collapsed. The riders sought escape in separate flight but Poole was quickly overhauled and killed. Although Barton still had his revolver, it would not fire and he waved it only as a threat. His pursuers closed in around him and drew his bluff: he pointed the gun and pulled the trigger but nothing happened. Barton stood alone in the silence of the plain watching the man who had just killed Poole. He walked toward Barton and stopped. Placing his rifle on the ground, the warrior gestured that he should surrender. His name was Chicheeli[6] and as his king, Cetshwayo, had given orders for a prisoner of some importance to be taken, he had decided to capture Barton. It was an easy decision as he had already killed seven white soldiers that day. The two men were now close to each other and Barton slowly put a hand to his head and raised his hat. At that moment another Zulu approaching fired at Barton, who fell mortally wounded. Chicheeli, believing the white man to be his prize and not to be killed by anyone else, stepped forward and speared Barton to death.

In due course Evelyn Wood wrote a letter of condolence to Barton's sister and next-of-kin, Mrs A. Childers, who, like Ronald Campbell's wife, was of the opinion that men dying on the battlefield enjoyed a glorious soldier's death. Mrs Childers, however, went a step further in believing that her two young sons could do worse than die early, provided they were killed in battle! She wrote to Wood: 'I wish nothing better for them than to follow in his [Barton's] footsteps as soldiers, even if it lead them to an early death.' Such was the support enjoyed by the officer class; it is doubtful if the rank and file held the same sentiments.

On the Ntendeka plateau the last few men down Devil's Pass were making a final exhausted bid to cross the nek. Wild with fear and on foot, they were pursued by the abaQulusi. The colonial firing line, inspired by men like Raaff and Buller, did its best to give them covering fire while a few gallant comrades rode forward among the warriors to pick them up. Forty years later Trooper Charlie Hewitt of the FLH recalled the scene:

> When all were down the mountain that it seemed possible to get down, and just before giving final orders to retreat, Colonel Buller spotted a crowd of our volunteers on foot racing for life with crowds of Zulus chasing them and all but on top of them and he asked some of us who still had horses fit to ride, to go back and give some of those poor beggars a hand to get away. So five of us rode back and each man managed to pick up one of the poor chaps on to his horse behind, and with two others hanging on to the stirrup straps we managed to dash out from the crowd of Zulus who were hotly chasing us.

D'Arcy of the FLH, whose horse, it will be remembered, had been killed descending the pass, described how he was rescued:

> Colonel Buller saved my life by taking me up behind him on his horse, then Blaine, who had been keeping the natives off in the rear for me (as after I had got my breath

I had got off the Colonel's horse) and he nearly cried when he met me, all the fellows thinking that I had been killed on top of the hill.

Lieutenant Alfred Blaine, also of the FLH, wrote to his cousin a few days later:

> A lot of us got down, and then we rallied our fellows and made a stand for a time, we retired fighting, the Zulus were the whole time within a hundred yards behind us, sometimes even closer. They did not fire much but were evidently trying to assegai. We lost no end of horses, and men jumped up behind others. Both Buller and myself were riding one for some time ... we retired well, but I shall never forget the kaffirs getting in amongst us and assegaing our poor fellows.

In the most gentlemanly manner, however, Blaine did not lavish praise either upon himself or his comrades, concluding his letter with a remarkable tribute to the abaQulusi: 'No men ever fought more pluckily than the Zulus, they are brave men indeed.' Words that should have long since been inscribed in stone, but regrettably there are no war memorials on the battlefield of Hlobane.

It was not only the officers of the column who excelled themselves in bravery. Twenty-year-old Corporal William Dommett Vinnicombe, a tough youngster bred on the frontier, was a transport rider fluent in Zulu who, because of his West Country name and origins, was quite a favourite with Buller, the Devonshire squire. Vinnicombe had dismounted to give his horse to two comrades, Wesley Francis and another man, when Buller saw him and yelled, 'Don't dismount, Vinnicombe!' But it was too late and in an act of bravado Vinnicombe, who was something of a long-distance runner, yelled back that the horse could carry two but not three and of the three he had the best legs!

Buller had begun to evacuate the wounded and those whose mounts carried a double burden, when Knox-Leet appeared out of the confusion of men and horses. He and Buller had actually been up on the Ntendeka plateau previously during one of the early cattle raids. On that occasion they had got up and down by the northern face, and Knox-Leet suggested they should now retire by this route. Buller agreed and shouted orders to the retreating men to that effect. However, it was too late as the column was already streaming down the gentler western side. Knox-Leet had not waited to see the result of Buller's shouted order; instead he plunged off north to lead the way down in that direction, little realising that he was alone except for one of his officers, Lieutenant Dunscombe of Wood's Irregulars. During the descent of Devil's Pass, Knox-Leet had already enjoyed a large share of luck. Several days earlier he had badly injured his knee competing in a tug-of-war at Kambula camp, and as a result could hardly walk. Coming down the pass, he had lost his horse and then a second one that he had been fortunate enough to catch. His present mount was an artillery pack-horse which had been carrying boxes of ammunition when he had grabbed its reins. Hobbling on one leg, he had cut off its load and clambered on to its back, riding on its pack saddle. He and Dunscombe had only gone a short distance when a large body of warriors appeared on the crest behind them. The abaQulusi immediately opened fire and with much shouting started in hot pursuit. At that moment a lone officer on foot, Lieutenant Metcalfe Smith of the FLH, sprinted over the rocks to join the two mounted men. Suddenly the boulder-strewn descent became perilously steep and ended abruptly in a sheer drop: they had taken the wrong direction. There was nothing for it but to return the way they had come in the face of the enemy.

Struggling back uphill, they were soon surrounded by yelling warriors who closed within a few yards but became hesitant of Dunscombe's revolver which he levelled and fired, quickly ducking a shower of throwing spears in reply, one of which impaled his horse. The animal faltered and, dismounting, Dunscombe raced after his companions on foot. In his heavy boots he had no chance, but before he was overhauled and stabbed to death Knox-Leet saw him turn and, at point-blank range, shoot down three of his pursuers. The abaQulusi, distracted for a few moments by Dunscombe's killing, allowed the other two fugitives to pull away but the effort cost Smith the last vestige of his energy. He was done and could go no further. He put his revolver to his head and was about to pull the trigger when Knox-Leet stopped him and with great difficulty managed to pull him up behind on to the pack saddle. The horse, with its double burden, staggered on and down over the rock-strewn ground as the abaQulusi closed in again. To their horror, the two riders spotted a second group of warriors racing in their direction from the valley below with the obvious intention of cutting them off. However, as Knox-Leet and Smith slithered around another precipitous face, they saw to their joy that they had almost come up with the rest of the column who were descending on their left. The ground suddenly became less steep and with a final effort the old pack-horse returned them to the comparative safety of their companions.

With the utmost good fortune, the column reached the plain just ahead of the Zulu army which had exhausted itself in its attempt to cut off its enemies. On seeing the mounted men riding away to the north, the mighty force of warriors pursued no further. Apart from its minor involvement at the east end of Hlobane and the mounted pursuit of Barton, the only men of Buller's column caught and killed by the Zulu army were a few unfortunates who had mistakenly descended Hlobane by the south side at a spot the abaQulusi called Tshoba. The whole credit for the British defeat thus far, apart from the intimidating effect of the Zulu army, belonged to the abaQulusi, and they were still far from being exhausted. For them the battle was not yet over.

Some 4000 head of cattle had been lifted by Wood's Irregulars and Hamu's men, and even though many had been abandoned, a great number were still being herded north toward Kambula. Although the auxiliaries had descended from the mountain earlier in the morning and went well ahead of the horsemen, they were now hampered by their booty and completely unprotected, as were most of their officers who had remained with them despite Russell's orders. The auxiliaries' greed for cattle was at that moment greater than their fear of the abaQulusi. To persuade them to abandon the captured herds was like asking a white man to burn his property and throw away his wealth, and the abaQulusi fell upon the scattered herders, slaughtering Wood's Irregulars and Hamu's warriors alike. Among those slain were Potter, Calverley and Lieutenant Williams, Knox-Leet's staff officer, who, by Wood's order, had been attached as guide to Russell's column. Williams had been highly thought of by Wood and specially commended by Buller for his fighting in the Intombi Valley.

In due course Wood wrote a letter of condolence to Williams's unmarried sisters. Unlike Barton's sister, however, their reply reflected no conception of their brother having died 'gloriously'. Instead, one of them replied, 'When I tell you that we are orphans you will understand what a great blank his death makes in our life.' Commandant Lorraine White, who had requested permission from Russell to remain with his troops and had been refused, stayed behind in any event and survived. He was later commended by Buller as having especially distinguished himself. Captain Alan Gardner, Buller's chief staff officer, who had survived Isandlwana and Fugitive's Drift, had another hair-raising escape. He was unhorsed on the nek and saved from imminent death by Adjutant Brecher of Wood's Irregulars, who rode in and snatched him up on to his saddle. Later he too caught an artillery horse and, cutting off its pack, rode it bareback to Kambula.

Not all the survivors from the plateau had been lucky enough to join up with the main column. A number had become separated and these lone fugitives were relentlessly pursued. Mossop was one who found himself alive but alone at the bottom of the pass. Apart from bruises and lacerations, he was suffering from shock and exhaustion whilst 'Warrior', although it was not apparent, had fatal internal injuries. To make matters worse, a broken saddle tree had ripped a jagged hole in the horse's withers which Mossop tried to pad with his shirt. Both boy and horse drank deeply from a stream, but on attempting to mount again Mossop found all his strength had evaporated and try as he might he could not get back into the saddle. He sank to the ground, assailed by weakness, until he saw a group of warriors silently approaching and almost upon him. Fear gave him strength and he was again on 'Warrior's' back. The game little animal took Mossop all the way back to Kambula but the next morning, when the boy went joyfully to feed his horse, he found him dead. Another lone youngster who survived was seventeen-year-old Heinrich Filter, the pastor's son from Luneburg. Having got off the mountain, instead of heading west for Kambula he turned north and arrived home the day after the dreadful news of the disaster had reached his parents, who had supposed him dead.

The abaQulusi, whilst enjoying an almost free hand in the slaughter of the auxiliaries, were cautious of closing with the remnants of Buller's column which still amounted to some 200 men who kept the enemy at a distance with regular rifle fire. As the survivors probably had less than 100 horses between them and a number of wounded, they could do little to help their native allies even had they been aware of their predicament.

Whereas a number of gallant men had risked their lives to save comrades and even strangers, some of the rescued responded in a despicable manner deserving of instant execution, by riding off with their rescuer's horse! Charlie Hewitt, who had saved a complete stranger, let the man, who pleaded exhaustion, ride while Hewitt walked. Having proceeded for a considerable distance in this manner, they stopped at a stream to drink and Hewitt suggested that it was his turn for riding, whereupon the stranger cantered off with his horse. The two burghers, Kritzinger and Craig, who still had mounts at the bottom of the pass despite having pushed them over the wall at the top, were bullied into making a pact with a fellow burgher, Elmans van Rooyen, who had no horse. The latter, a big man, commandeered the strongest mount while his two companions were left to ride the remaining animal, which was lame. Soon the trio were chased by a group of warriors, whereupon van Rooyen put spurs to his borrowed mount and galloped away, leaving his benefactors to their fate.

Fortunately, such acts of ingratitude and selfishness were the exception; by and large the horseless and the wounded were succoured and the column, keeping intact, slowly made its way toward Zunguin Nek and distant Kambula. When Knox-Leet caught up with Buller, he rode on for two miles in a vain effort to find Russell and bring him back to cover the column's retreat, and also to assist in protecting the auxiliaries, but Russell was waiting two miles further on, away from the action.

For the British, the attack on Hlobane, with the exception of Isandlwana, was the most disastrous engagement of the Zulu War. The official number of dead put out by Wood was eighty-nine colonials and two imperial soldiers. Subsequent research puts the number of colonials killed at closer to 130. The number of native auxiliaries who lost their lives has always been difficult to calculate as virtually all of Wood's Irregulars who survived deserted the same day, but given the circumstances, probably 200–300 were killed fighting to retain the captured cattle. Of Hamu's warriors at least fifty percent were killed.

What had happened to Colonel Evelyn Wood, the overall commander? The time had been 10.30 am when he had sent Lysons riding off with the misleading order to Russell, who had been approximately five miles distant with broken ground in between. A vigorous young rider like Lysons would have done the trip in about twenty minutes whereas Wood and escort, with the wounded man, would have taken twice as long. Therefore Wood should have arrived at the western base of Hlobane ten minutes after Russell's departure, but before the arrival of Buller and his men descending from the plateau. However, there is no record of either Russell or Buller seeing Wood until late that evening. In his official report written two days later, Wood stated that he and his escort had taken up a position on

8. HLOBANE

The battlefield of Hlobane Mountain, 28 March 1879, adapted from the drawing by Colonel John North Crealock. The sketch was made from Zunguin Mountain, from approximately the position taken up by Wood for several hours on the day of the battle. Crealock, using artistic licence, had diminished the distance between the two mountains, which appears in the sketch to be less than a mile in a straight line; it is, in fact, over five miles from Devil's Pass to the Zunguin plateau. Nevertheless, the drawing gives an excellent visual aid to understanding the battle and the terrain.

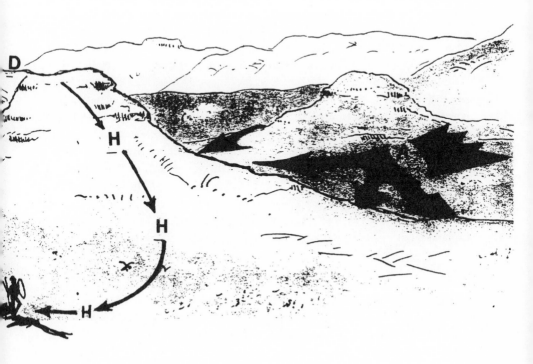

Key:
a) The Zulu army first seen at 9.00 am approaching from the south. b) Buller's column ascended the mountain in the early hours of the morning from the south. c) Devil's Pass. d) The Ntendeka or lower plateau. e) (i) Approximate position of Buller's rearguard made up of 'A' Coy, FLH and Baker's Horse. (ii) The advance of the abaQulusi from the adjoining Intyentika Hill toward the nek of the same name. f) Intyentika Nek. g) The direction of Barton's escape pursued by the enemy. h) (i) The direction of Russell's ascent in the early morning and subsequent descent and flight to Zunguin Nek. (ii) Buller's escape route after descending Devil's Pass and the lower plateau.

Zunguin Nek – that being his incorrect version of the nek's location. He did, in fact, occupy an elevated position at the south-eastern end of the range, about two and a half miles from the bottom of the Ntendeka plateau. From this vantage point he would have had a panoramic view of the dramatic scene below: Buller and his men fighting their way down the mountain; the abaQulusi pursuing the auxiliaries and the great Zulu army flooding across the plain, cutting off any possible contact with Buller, but taking little or no part in the engagement. Wood stated that at this juncture he sent a further message to Russell ordering him to return and cover the retreating auxiliaries – an order Russell complied with but too late to be of assistance. With little further reference to the events on Hlobane, Wood concluded his report by stating that he stayed on the Zunguin range until 7.00 pm. There we have an enigma, for with the entire Zulu army now threatening his camp at Kambula less then twenty miles away, with his mounted force in disarray and with his auxiliaries all but destroyed, what could he have achieved at such a crucial time, sitting on Zunguin for a further seven hours? In his auto-biography, written twenty-seven years later, Wood offers little more by way of explanation but does mention sending a messenger to Kambula:

> I now sent an order to the senior officer in camp, to chain up the wagons, and to continue the strengthening of the barricades. I wrote I had seen between 20,000 and 25,000 Zulus, and remained on Zunguin mountain until 7.00 pm, hoping to cover the retreat of any more of our men who might come up, being particularly anxious about Captain Barton, of whom we had had no news since he descended the eastern end of the mountain.

It would seem nonsense that the overall commander, with an escort of only fifteen men, should hang around on the mountain for the remainder of the day, on the remote chance that the odd straggler would make his way through the entire Zulu army to reach his position – especially so Captain Barton, who had descended Hlobane twelve miles to the north-east, going in the opposite direction!

Buller, having reached Kambula, seems to have had no idea of Wood's whereabouts and, despite his exertions of the last thirty-six hours, set out to find him, riding back in the dusk another twelve miles. Wood also recalls the meeting in his autobiography:

> I never knew until that day the depth of regard which Buller felt for me. I was sitting on the summit of the Zunguin range when he climbed up it, and, seeing me sud-denly, uttered so fervent a 'Thank God!' that I asked for what he was thankful, and he explained that he thought I had been cut off at the eastern end of the mountain.

Nothing further by way of explanation is offered in an article edited by Wood, if not written by him, which was published in 1914 in a fortnightly magazine called *British Battles on Land and Sea*. However, the account of Wood's movements as given by nineteen-year-old private Edmond Fowler of Wood's escort (who would be awarded the Victoria Cross for his earlier action when he charged the sniper's cave with Campbell and Lysons) was entirely different. On 9 April, two weeks after the action, Fowler wrote a letter home in which he vividly recalled the events of the day and concluded:

> After we had ridden about three miles we saw on our right front the whole of the Zulu army. The old man [Wood] says 'Gallop for your lives men' which we did, and a hard run we had of it for twenty-five miles. All the poor chaps that we left behind us were cut off and killed. We had a lucky escape, and when we reached camp [Kambula] and told the news it caused a great sensation.

Fowler's contradictory account indicates that Wood and his escort were first back to Kambula with news of the disaster, which is reflected in Fowler's remark that their news 'caused a great sensation'. If Wood did ride to alarm Kambula and gird up the camp's defences, only to leave again for Zunguin heights, he makes no mention of it. Either way there is little doubt that he spent much of the day inert on Zunguin, stunned by the destruction of so many of his horsemen.

Nevertheless, luck was still on Wood's side. He would get a second chance. The Zulu army had not come to Hlobane merely to support the abaQulusi in recapturing their cattle; it had come to destroy 'Somtseu's Impi' and to inflict another defeat of Isandlwana proportions upon the British. Wood hoped that with good fortune the outcome could be a classic set piece of colonial warfare: the enemy dashing itself to destruction upon the entrenched defences of Kambula and the fire power of the infantry decimating the Zulu army long before it could reach the British bayonets. In the wake of such a glorious victory, the result of the unfortunate skirmish on Hlobane would almost go unnoticed – especially so as virtually the whole of the butchers' bill was colonial or native. Yet someone must be held to blame and the unfortunate Russell was the obvious choice. That the column failed to send out scouts, that the Zulu army was not located, that Buller's ambiguous directions caused many men to ride to their deaths, that Wood ordered Russell to the wrong position and that the mountain was ever attacked in the first place with mounted men, would all be carefully overlooked.

At nine o'clock that night a message was received to the effect that some survivors from the mountain had reached the locality of Potter's store on foot. Without hesitation, the indefatigable Buller set out in the darkness and pouring rain to find them. Hours later he returned to camp with Captain Dennison, Lieutenant Cecil Poulet Mountjoy Weatherley [Weatherley's nineteen-year-old eldest son] and five men, the sole survivors of the Border Horse who had been caught on the Intyentika Nek – the unit had suffered seventy-seven percent casualties!

There was much to do at Kambula that night with the threat of battle on the morrow. Nevertheless, there was a flurry of report-writing as the various commanders took up their positions and justified their actions of the day. Exhausted or not, Buller wrote a factual account of what happened, although he clearly thought that his easy ascent to the plateau was due to his surprise attack rather than being lured into a trap. He was also courageous enough to hold himself largely responsible for the loss of Weatherley, Barton and their men; he wrote: 'By right I meant the north side of the mountain but Captain Barton must have understood me to mean the south side, and to my careless expression must I fear be attributed the greater part of our heavy loss on this day.' Wood, however, did not wish any discredit to attach to Buller or himself and crossed the paragraph out with the comment, 'Omit this from the Gazette.'

Buller had remarkably little to say regarding Russell's departure, merely stating:

> Our line of retreat was most difficult descending on to the plateau of the lower Hlobane mountain which had earlier in the day been occupied by Colonel Russell but which he had now left. On reaching camp I found most of the cattle we captured, some 2000 head, and which had been sent out before we left the mountain, had been abandoned by order of Colonel Russell only about 300 being brought in. . . .

Buller included in his report a unique tribute to his friend Piet Uys: 'Our loss was very heavy. Among them Mr Piet Uys whose death is a misfortune to South Africa. One so courageous and so sagacious I shall never see again, we had better lost a hundred men.'

Wood's official report mainly relates his own limited view of the day's events until he reaches the point of ordering Russell to the Zunguin Nek:

> Colonel Russell reports that he moved from the Hlobane to the Zunguin nek, but this is incorrect on the contrary, he went away six miles to the west[7] end of the range misapprehending the position of the nek, which is at the eastern corner of the range and for which Wood's Irregulars, the 1st Battalion and Hamu's men, were making driving the captured cattle. Colonel Russell ordered all the cattle to be abandoned and moved off very rapidly under the western end of the range. He thus uncovered the retreat of Hamu's people about eighty of whom were killed.

Unlike Buller, who admitted he was at fault with his directions, Wood stubbornly maintained for the rest of his life that he was correct. However, his error of direction did not exonerate Russell for his action in abandoning his auxiliaries and Buller's retreat. There was a degree of uncertainty as to the correct location of the Zunguin Nek and there is little doubt that Russell took advantage of Wood's mistaken instructions to flee before the advancing Zulu army. Wood had wanted to rid himself of Russell ever since he had arrived at Kambula and now determined to do so.

To support his case against Russell, he ordered Lorraine White and Darcy of Wood's Irregulars to add their comments. White wrote:

> When I was at the bottom of the last hill, a native from the 2nd Battalion of Wood's Irregulars, told me that the Zulus were taking the cattle away from them as they had no more ammunition. I sent Lieutenant Darcy to Colonel Russell, who was then on the first rise of road to the camp, to ask if I might remain and help them. Lieutenant Darcy returned to me and said, 'The Colonel says you are to leave the cattle, and push on as fast as you can.'

Darcy added a few lines, 'I went to Colonel Russell with the above order. He interrupted me before I finished speaking, and said "Tell Commandant White to leave the cattle, and push on as fast as he can".'

Russell, of course, also compiled a report in which he obliquely blamed Wood for Buller's losses, implying that he would have remained with Buller had it not been for Wood's order:

> I moved all my force down the hill, I told Commandant White to move his men at once to the Zunguin (as they were in very small numbers and would have only impeded the action of mounted men with whom I intended to remain near the Hlobane Hill, and join Colonel Buller if necessary). At this time I received a memorandum from Colonel Wood dated 10.30 am desiring me to 'get into position on Zunguin Nek'. I moved to that point and remained there until the last of Buller's force passed towards the camp.

As the last of the reports were signed by the light of a flickering oil lamp and the rain drummed down outside, Surgeon-Major O'Ridley was still busy in the hospital tent; however, his task would not take long as only five wounded men had lived to reach Kambula. The battle of the Painted Mountain was over for the moment, but none doubted that the fight that had started that morning on Hlobane would be brought to Kambula on the morrow.

---

1. In researching this book, the only thought for the ecology of the country that I have come across is one expressed by Trooper Fred Symons of the Natal Carbineers. The night before Isandlwana, when he was camped out, he commented that the NNC were not concerned about destroying huts to obtain firewood: 'They had not our scruples and pulled down the kraals for fuel. We had not yet reached that hardened state, and I never shall, for the destruction of one native hut means the destruction of about 500 saplings ... the man who burns a hut down, even in warfare ought to be condemned.' Symons did not know it then but the British would have no more scruples than the NNC. During the advance on Ulundi alone, one officer estimated that 20,000 huts were destroyed. Calculated at 500 saplings per hut, ten million saplings would be required to replace those dwellings that had been burnt.

2. Not to be confused with Lieutenant Cecil Charles Williams of the 58th Regiment and Wood's Irregulars.
3. Intyentika means 'Overhanging Rock'.
4. Not to be confused with Lieutenant Cecil D'Arcy of the FLH.
5. He was described as a tall, dark, wiry man of twenty-eight, a stonecutter by trade, and a native of Bordeaux.
6. As spelt by Wood, *From Midshipman to Field Marshal*.
7. Wood had his directions wrong: Russell went north rather than west.

7
KAMBULA

'You are not to go into the hole of a wild beast or else you will get clawed – wait until the soldiers come out of their laager and then fall upon them.'

Cetshwayo's orders to his warriors prior to
the battle of Kambula

'It was indeed a slaughter.'

An officer of Wood's Irregulars

The elevated position of the British camp at Kambula, straddling a flat-crowned ridge, commanded the undulating country for miles around in all directions. In the distance, hills with wooded kloofs, where firewood could be cut, rose up from the plains, and to the east the outline of the Zunguin range dominated the skyline. There was ample water, even for the vast herds of transport oxen, cattle and horses, for two springs rose from within 350 yards of the ridge, one to the east and the other to the west. The only bad feature of this defensive position was a shallow ravine, about 100 yards distant, that could provide shelter and a protected rallying point for a large force of attackers.

Unlike the disastrous camp at Isandlwana, which had sprawled across the plain for almost a mile, the Kambula defences were contained within an area of approximately seven acres. A redoubt constructed of stone and earth sods, oblong-shaped and not much bigger than a couple of tennis courts, commanded the crown of the ridge: a small fort but spacious enough to accommodate the commander, his staff, two companies of infantry and two 7-pounder guns of the Royal Artillery. The redoubt was further protected by a deep trench. About 150 yards to the west of this position was the main laager, its principal component being ninety or more transport wagons chained one behind the other into a lopsided 'square'. Low ramparts of sods to the height of the axle trees were built below the wagons and similar walls of mealie bags lined the outer face of the platforms above, providing each wagon with a two-tier firing platform for prone marksmen. The defenders were further protected by a trench running along the inside of the wagon wall which would give shelter to the ammunition handlers, supplies and wounded. This main laager would be defended by 1000 soldiers from the 1/13th and 90th Light Infantry, approximately 650 colonials of the various mounted units, a sprinkling of those Boers and Wood's Irregulars who had neither gone home nor deserted (amounting to less than seventy men all told) and about 200 armed wagon drivers and voorlopers. It would also contain the hospital tent, most of the column's supplies and ammunition, and close on 700 horses, saddled, bridled and ready for instant use, tethered to picket lines.

There was a further smaller laager of some forty wagons, chained and entrenched in the manner described, which was little more than a cattle pen, into which would be herded as many of the draught oxen and cattle as could be crammed in. It would be defended by a lone, and rather isolated, company of the 13th Light Infantry whilst the fire-power from the redoubt to which it was connected by a 50-yard-long palisade of 5-foot-high planks, would give added protection. Wood had ordered the construction of the palisade a day or so earlier, believing that it would delay an enemy charge out of the ravine against his command post. The crest of the ridge, between the redoubt and the main laager, would contain the remaining four guns of the Royal Artillery unentrenched, mobile and with harnessed teams of gun horses ready to move the 7-pounders in any direction at a moment's notice. Below the main approach to the ridge, broken glass, nails and other nasty objects had been strewn about forming a hazard for a barefoot enemy – and, in all directions, for a mile out and more, range markers had been driven into the ground ensuring accurate fire for both the artillery and infantry as soon as the enemy came within reach.

When the camp was not under threat, the men lived outside the defences, the tents, horse lines and kitchens being spread around the whole perimeter of the ridge. However, Wood's command was so well practised that within seventy seconds of the alarm being sounded – three long notes on the bugle – all tents could be struck and every man at his allotted position.

The camp had recently been moved from an earlier location a quarter of a mile to the east, the move being necessitated by fouling of the surrounding area by men and beasts alike. Although the military rules of hygiene had been enforced, latrines dug and the infantry marched in squads to perform the needs of nature, Wood found it impossible to persuade the burghers and the native auxiliaries to use such facilities; they preferred the privacy of the nearby bush. Add to this the excrement on a daily basis of 5000 animals of one sort or another, and it is hardly surprising that frequent moves were necessary.

Wood prided himself on having fresh bread available for his troops at all meal times and the camp at Kambula was no exception. The location of the bakery that had served the old campsite had not been moved, and it was now situated 300 yards to the south-east of the redoubt. The ovens, providing bread daily for over 2000 men, consumed fuel at a phenomenal rate and the wood-gathering parties

9. ONE OF COLONEL WOOD'S CAMPS
BEFORE THE MOVE TO KAMBULA

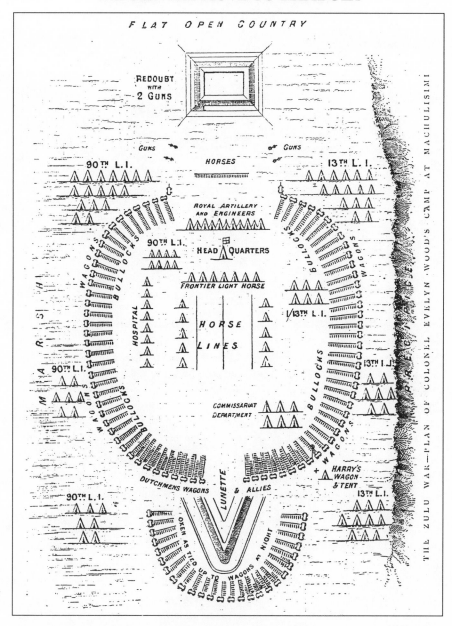

One of Sir Evelyn Wood's camps prior to the move to Kambula. An excellent diagram of a laagered camp with much interesting detail.

Wood's column was so well trained that all the tents could be down and the men at their posts within a minute of a bugle call. (Natal Archives)

10. WOOD'S FIRST CAMP AT KAMBULA

Wood's first camp at Kambula which covered an enormous area of approximately 50 acres. It was completely entrenched and accommodated within its defences all the troops, their tent lines, the wagons, horses, oxen and cattle. However, there were three exceptions; the Transvaal Rangers, the Border Horse and the Kaffrarian Rifles who had lately arrived at Kambula and were probably advised to remain outside due to insanitary conditions within. A few days after this contemporary sketch was drawn by twenty-two-year-old Colour Sergeant McAllen of the 90th LI the camp was moved to the actual battle site a quarter of a mile to the west where McAllen was mortally wounded. (Natal Archives)

were obliged to go even further afield for supplies. A certain amount of coal had been found locally and those soldiers who had been miners in civilian life could earn an extra shilling a day if they volunteered to turn out and dig. But such dirty work was unpopular and there were few takers. The wood-gathering fatigues were only slightly less onerous. Every day an infantry company, escorted by a mounted unit, was required to march six miles out to the mountains and there scale the steep kloofs in which many trees flourished. The cut timber was then carried or thrown down the slopes and finally manhandled a quarter of a mile to where the wagons waited. Finally there was the long trudge back to camp. The boulders and foliage of the kloofs provided excellent cover for idle men to hide away and snooze, so to ensure the officers kept constant vigilance against such malingering, all were forbidden to sit down for a moment. Any officer so caught was to be reported directly to Wood as neglecting his duty!

Wood was a popular commander with officers and men alike, and was much concerned with the welfare of his troops. He endeavoured to relieve the hardship and monotony of the common soldier's existence with sports and competitions. Tug-of-war was one of the favourites and although the team of the 90th LI had beaten all comers wherever they had been stationed (including teams from the Royal Navy and Marines) they had been pulled off their feet by Piet Uys's burghers. Foot races were organised at an entry fee of one shilling, whereas to compete in any of the equestrian races, over distances of up to a mile, cost five shillings – all entrance fees being given away as prize money. The native auxiliaries were not forgotten, with spear-throwing competitions being provided: the British infantry joined in with gusto if little skill! Exclusive to the officers were the games of tennis and polo (of sorts) – Wood himself keeping fit by playing one or other every day. The purchase of hard liquor by the rank and file was strictly forbidden – alcohol being the usual cause of most crimes and offences. The wagons of traders bringing goods for sale were searched for alcohol and any peddler caught breaking the rules could expect immediate retribution, such as the confiscation of his goods or even a flogging.

By 1879 flogging had been abolished in the Royal Navy but was still permitted in the British army – to its lasting shame – on active service. It was liberally applied as a punishment during the Zulu War – most victims being frightened youngsters of the newly arrived regiments from England. Chelmsford encouraged flogging as a punishment for 'funky soldiers'. Among the seasoned regulars, such as Wood's regiments of the 13th and 90th LI, flogging was rarely administered; when it was, the crime was generally gross insubordination or, worse still, striking a senior officer, the culprit invariably being roaring drunk at the time – hence the strict control of intoxicating liquor. During March there had been a spate of serious drunkenness among the troops at Utrecht, Wood's supply depot. The local civilian authority reported to Wood: '... a great deal of drunkenness has been going on in the town ... to the great annoyance of the inhabitants and danger of the town, and scares caused by drunken soldiers firing their rifles at night.'

To Wood, flogging would have been a loathsome business; however, there is one incident of it being applied at Kambula, it being recorded in a smug, light-hearted vein by a colonial officer who was exempt from such punishment: 'The men were edified by the sight of a punishment parade, two regulars were flogged; this gave them food for most wholesome reflection.' Yet, the reaction of a young soldier, when writing home after watching a similar gruesome parade, was full of apprehension: 'I am very sorry to state we have had to see a very terrible sight,' he wrote. Flogging was finally abolished two years after the Zulu War.

The two British infantry regiments were the backbone of Wood's defences. The outcome of the anticipated battle would much depend upon their discipline, courage and ability. Both were 'old' regiments – that is to say the men were not 'boy soldiers', puny and ill-trained youngsters, whom the War Office had recently recruited and sent out to Zululand. Most were hardened bearded men; tough, resourceful and used to living rough. Both were regiments of ancient origins and fine traditions – the 13th had a history going back 200 years and the 90th had been a regiment since 1794 – and both had fought for the Empire from Egypt to Afghanistan and from Martinique to China. More recently they had fought in the Crimean War and the Indian Mutiny and a number of veterans of those campaigns still served amongst the officers and men.

Wood had every confidence in his infantry and they had confidence in themselves. There is little doubt that Wood and all his troops hoped their camp would be attacked head-on by the Zulu army and anticipated the outcome with cheerful expectation.

The day of 29 March 1879 dawned in thick mist. Wood had visited his sentries on two occasions during the night even though he was satisfied that so large a body of men as the Zulu army could not have been deployed in darkness. His great fear was that of the enemy laying siege to the camp and he was anxious that his supply of fuel should suffice for several days. Despite the enemy being close by, somewhere to the south-east, he nevertheless decided to send out wood-gathering fatigues to the hills west of Kambula, though taking the precaution to have two young subalterns, with ponies saddled, ready to gallop off and recall the work parties at a moment's notice.

Before the mist lifted, scouts were dispatched to find the enemy. Despite having been in the saddle almost continuously for days on end and despite the awful events of the previous day, Raaff, with twenty-four men of the Transvaal Rangers, carried out a reconnaissance to the south-east while one patrol of the FLH rode south and another headed north-east. Raaff's scouting took him seven miles to the southern edge of the Zunguin range; at 10.00 am the mist cleared and he saw, 500 feet below, the whole of the Zulu army spread out among their cooking fires, still busy with breakfast.[1] Raaff immediately sent a messenger back to Wood, deciding to stay to watch the enemy and its subsequent direction of march. He would not have long to wait.

Raaff was observing the Zulu army at the zenith of its power. It had vanquished an invasion of its homeland by the most powerful nation on earth and still held part of the defeated army under siege at Eshowe. It had inflicted a further disaster on the enemy at the Intombi River, and yesterday a local clan regiment, with little more than moral assistance from the main army, had outwitted, outmanoeuvred and finally routed a force of more than 600 horsemen (an arm of the invaders which hitherto had been considered invincible), killing nigh on a quarter of them in the process. The horsemen had come from 'Somtseu's Impi', which was thought to be the most dangerous of the British columns – it had certainly been the most successful with its continuous raiding and pillaging and its triumphant feat of stealing Hamu and his clan. But if its mounted men could be so easily defeated, its foot soldiers, trifling in number compared to the Zulu host, would soon be strewn, mutilated and bloody, amongst the debris of their camp. A surge of elation swelled up in every warrior at the thought of repeating the carnage and triumph of Isandlwana, for these were the regiments that had carried out that day's work and, in order to leave the enemy in no doubt as to who they were, would shout, 'We are the Boys from Isandlwana!' as they raced toward the Kambula laagers.

They were a formidable force indeed; in physique, courage and numbers they were without equal in Africa. The men of the younger regiments, with few exceptions, had the physical perfection of trained athletes, and could give their counterparts of the British infantry at least 3 inches in height and probably 20 pounds in brawn.

There were eleven regiments from Ulundi, totalling approximately 21,000 warriors, all in their prime of life.[2] The average age was thirty-three, with the 1500 men of the Tulwana Regiment, at forty-five, being the oldest. All regiments had been originally raised by Mpande, father of Cetshwayo, with the exception of the largest and youngest regiment, the Nkobamakosi, 6000 strong and averaging twenty-four years of age; this was the most eager and ferocious unit and would prove to be the most difficult to restrain.

Each regiment was divided into two wings with an overall commanding officer supported by two or three subordinates. The wings were further divided into companies of fifty men including three officers. Every regiment had its own barracks or home kraal, and was distinguished by its regimental headdress and shield colouring. Today the army would carry little in the way of finery or decoration. It would fight virtually naked and each man would carry into battle a gun, ammunition, shield, a couple of throwing spears and – the weapon most favoured above all others – the short-handled, heavy-bladed, stabbing spear which in shape more resembled a Roman sword.

The overall commander of this army was the ageing, but fierce Tshingwayo, accompanied by Cetshwayo's premier minister, Mnyamana, who was there as the embodiment of the king. (Like Hamu, he had not been in favour of war and in council had voted for the surrender of Sihayo's sons to the British.) After Cetshwayo these two were the most important men in the realm. Both had great powers of oratory. Mnyamana had the look of a statesman; tall, slim and with a grey pointed beard. Tshingwayo, shorter and tougher but just as grey, had commanded the Zulu army at Isandlwana.

Zulu courage by this stage of the war had become almost legendary and there were few adversaries upon whom the British lavished more admiration. 'They came on with the ferocity of tigers, never halting, never wavering ... no soldiers in the world could be more daring,' declared one British officer. 'Nature and patriotism makes the subjects of Cetshwayo formidable enemies,' was the opinion of *The Cape Argus*. And at this moment the Zulu army was at its most formidable, for apart from the thousands of firearms of various types that it possessed at the commencement of the war, it now had in addition almost as many breach-loading Martini Henrys, and as much ammunition as Wood could muster for his entire column.

Before leaving its bivouac, the Zulu army had gathered in a great circle around Mnyamana, who announced with eloquence that it was their king's strict instructions that whilst his soldiers must fight, and in doing so 'burn like a fire', the army was not to attack an entrenched position, but to draw the enemy out of its laager by taking or killing its oxen and cattle. If that failed, then the army was to lure the British from cover by skirting past Kambula and falling upon Utrecht, Luneburg and the surrounding farming community. At all events, the enemy must be coerced into the open. However, to restrain a Zulu regiment, inflamed by its commander's oratory on the one hand and the taunts of a jeering foe on the other, would be as difficult as restraining a stampeding herd of royal cattle – as Mnyamana would find, to the cost of the Zulu nation.

The army was ready and at 11.00 am began to march. It was nine miles to Kambula; there was plenty of time and the commanders set an easy pace. Raaff, still concealed in the hills 500 feet above, waited a few moments to confirm the direction of the enemy and then set off at a gallop. Nearing camp, he met Blaine and his scouts of the FLH, who had been fruitlessly seeking the Zulu army further to the west, and together they sped on to Kambula.

At once the subalterns were sent riding helter-skelter to call in the wood-gathering parties, and one can imagine the haste and apprehension with which those laden wagons were trundled back to camp. However, Wood had timed it well and they were in no danger. Furthermore, the troops would not fight on an empty stomach. A hot dinner was served to every man and consumed by all in a leisurely manner. The finishing struts were bolted to the palisade; the men began to stand by; the oxen and cattle were herded in: water and rations were strategically placed within the laagers and hundreds of artillery shells, some shrapnel, some common and some case-shot, with five- and nine-second fuses, were set about the guns. Perhaps most importantly, dozens of Martini Henry ammunition boxes were opened and distributed within the laagers; and the mounted men, their horses saddled and bridled, readied themselves to sally forth. The Zulu army would find Kambula a very different place to Isandlwana.

The white bell tents of Wood's column, perched high on their ridge, could be seen for miles around reflecting the glare of the early autumn sunlight: an alien encampment on the African veld. It came into view of the advancing warriors; in comparison with the long line of tents at Isandlwana, which they had all seen, this camp, with a front of only 400 yards, looked puny and vulnerable.

If the warriors had been able to vanquish the Isandlwana soldiers in little more than an hour, this camp of 'Somtseu's Impi' could surely be crushed and looted with ease. The young men especially became eager to close with the enemy. But

Mnyamana and Tshingwayo would not have it. The Red Soldiers must either be drawn into the open or the camp bypassed.

Three miles away at Kambula, every eye watched with mounting apprehension the black mass of the Zulu army which had been advancing in five separate columns but had now halted. Speculation was rife among the officers and wagers were made that there would be no attack that day. Most were of the opinion that Kambula would be outflanked or put under siege, while the majority of the Zulu regiments rampaged into Natal and the Transvaal. 'They will never be such fools as to run their heads against this wall; one lot will attack our depot at Baltes Spruit and the others will go on to Luneburg and Utrecht,' was the opinion expressed by many.

For almost an hour the British watched while the distant army seemed to have rooted itself to the veld. Within its ranks the young warriors harangued their commanders, demanding the opportunity to redden their spears and 'eat' the British camp with its riches of rifles and cattle. It will never be known exactly what happened but eventually the young men had their way. At about 12.30 pm the Zulu army began to deploy, commencing its distant encirclement of the camp. The left horn, containing such prime regiments as the Umcityu, the Umbonambi and the Nokenke, all made up of twenty-eight- to thirty-year-old warriors, began wheeling in a wide sweep westward, while the youngest, the 6000-strong Nkobamakosi Regiment, started a brisk march to the north; the main body, which would form the centre of the attack, remained stationary while its horns got into position.

The British, watching these manoeuvres, now became convinced that the Zulu attack would be initiated by its left horn which was the closer of the two. However, there was extreme rivalry between the Umcityu of the left and the Nkobamakosi Regiment of the right, it having been a point of contention between the two since January as to which had been the first into the British camp at Isandlwana. The warriors of both regiments seemed to have made up their minds that there would be no question as to who would be the first into Kambula.

At one o'clock, as the Zulu army rapidly deployed along a front of six miles or more, Wood finally gave the order to strike the tents. Three long blasts on the bugle and barely a minute later every tent in the camp had been collapsed flat upon the ground. To the advancing warriors, still one and a half miles distant, it appeared an inexplicable feat of magic; one moment the camp was there and then it was gone! The explanation was obvious: the Red Soldiers were escaping. The warriors surged forward, fearful that the British would evade them.

Wood studied the black ranks that were rapidly surrounding his camp, and decided that the ring of warriors must be broken before they arrived *en masse* at his barricades. One horn or the other must be induced into a premature attack before the rest of the army was in position. Buller was summoned and ordered to ride out and incite the Zulu right horn. It was a fortunate choice, for the young men of the Nkobamakosi would need little provocation.

The orderly bugler sounded 'Stand To Your Horses' and a wagon in a corner of the laager was removed. Buller, having selected men from the Frontier Light Horse, The Natal Native Horse and the Mounted Infantry, rode out to taunt the Nkobamakosi who were now little more than a mile away.

The cavalry force advanced at a fast trot and at 300 yards distance swung into line across the enemy front, dismounted and, at Buller's command, fired a volley straight into the massed ranks. The effect was frightening. With an enraged shout of 'Usutu!' the Nkobamakosi charged forward to clutch and spear the horse soldiers who, only yesterday, had fled before the abaQulusi, a 'farmer's regiment'.

There was little discipline in Buller's withdrawal; with the enemy racing forward, yelling 'Don't run away Johnnie! We want to speak to you!' there was no time for parade ground commands. It was a matter of mount up and ride for your life. But in many cases that was easier said than done. The ill-trained horses, having had a volley fired close to their ears, and with a wall of screeching humanity descending, were in no state to stand calmly by and wait for their riders to mount. They were anxious to bolt back to the horse lines with or without a passenger. Young Mossop, still mourning the loss of 'Warrior', had been issued 'Old Bones' – a horse of giraffe-like proportions in comparison to his dead pony. He had asked his corporal how someone as small as himself was supposed to mount an animal of this size and was told to 'climb up its tail, kid, it's tame enough!' However, like every other horse in the line, 'Old Bones' prepared to bolt; there was only one way to get aboard and that was by a flying leap – which, try as he might, Mossop was unable to achieve. Still clutching the double bridle for dear life, he was dragged along at full tilt, his feet hardly touching the ground.

Colonel Russell, no doubt anxious to make a showing after his sorry performance of the previous day, had joined the sortie and found himself in a similar predicament to Mossop. As he attempted to remount after the volley, his horse had gone frantic with fear, swinging wildly around on its reins, giving its struggling rider no opportunity to clamber up. Russell faced imminent death. He was saved initially by the action of Troop Sergeant-Major Learda, a Basuto of the NNH, who gallantly rallied a few of his men and, with the Nkobamakosi only yards away, surrounded Russell. Then Captain Edward Browne of the MI rode in and held the restive horse, allowing Russell to mount. Russell was doubly fortunate in that the MI and the NNH, sharing a line of tents, had formed a bond of friendship without which the latter unit would not have regarded him as 'one of their own'. Now astride his horse, however, the unhappy Russell was unable to find his stirrups or gather his reins before the terrified animal bolted right across the front of the oncoming warriors. Once again Browne went to the rescue and together he and Russell galloped back to the camp.

Mossop and a number of other dismounted men were similarly saved by brave comrades, Mossop's rescue being a particularly close call. The headlong flight of 'Old Bones' had taken him into some marshy ground below the redoubt which

11. THE NEW CAMP AT KAMBULA

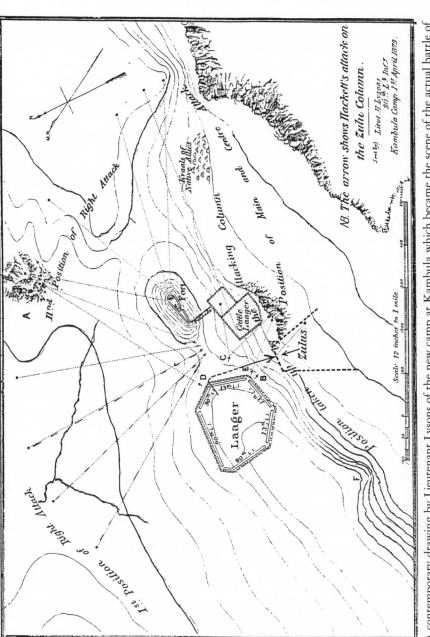

NB. The arrow shows Hackett's attack on the Zulu Column.

Sent by] Lieut. H. Lysons,
90th L.y. Inf.ty
Kambula Camp 1st April 1879.

A contemporary drawing by Lieutenant Lysons of the new camp at Kambula which became the scene of the actual battle of Kambula on 29 March. The area covered by this camp was a mere 10 acres and its defences consisted mainly of laagered wagons, the tent lines and a cattle laager remaining outside the main defences. The sketch was executed two days after the Zulu attack and shows the course of the battle. (Natal Archives) had dramatically slowed his progress. A rider just behind got thoroughly stuck in the soft going and was dragged from his horse and swiftly put to death – the sounds of his killing being all too audible to Mossop. The boy was about to suffer a similar fate when Captain Oldham of the FLH rode up and grabbed the horse's bridle just long enough for Mossop to half scramble aboard and reach the camp.

As the last of the horsemen cantered into the laager, it was again secured. At their own request, the men of the NNH, with their officer, Lieutenant Cochrane, remained outside where they continued to harass and skirmish with the enemy for the duration of the battle.

Before the retreating colonials reached the camp, the guns of the Royal Artillery had already commenced firing over their heads into the packed ranks of the advancing regiments. The range markers were clearly visible to the gunners and as the enemy approached, the muzzles of the 7-pounders were lowered time after time to the appropriate distance. At ultimate range the gunners had opened up with common shell then, as the enemy raced closer, they changed to shrapnel and finally case-shot which, in effect, resembled a giant shotgun cartridge full of 2-ounce lead balls each about the size of a grape. The carnage was appalling: as one soldier of the 13th was to describe: 'A more horrible sight than the effects of shell fire, I never saw. Bodies lying cut in halves, heads taken off....' Nevertheless, the Zulus came on. Schermbrucker, that veteran of the African frontier, was moved by the warriors' bravery: 'They came on without fear ... their courage was beyond praise. No European army could come on more steadily or charge more gallantly.'

Although their valour took them through shot and shell, they faltered against the volley fire of the British infantry. With their sights set to the exact range, the 90th LI were ordered to fire as the tide of warriors reached the distant markers. After the first crushing volley that smashed the leading ranks, the infantry changed to independent fire with each man blazing away as fast as he could pull the trigger. Within a space of five minutes, the splendid companies of the Nkobamakosi had been broken. It had been a magnificent charge but more admired by the British than the mature warriors of the veteran Zulu regiments; one forty-five-year-old of the Tulwana commented, 'They acted like fools.'

The remnants of the Nkobamakosi, alone and defeated – for the left horn still had a long way to advance – retired to a large rocky outcrop 400 yards north of the camp. Here they commenced an ineffectual fire at the main laager which was immediately returned by the British infantry. The four guns on the ridge, in sections of twos, under the command of Lieutenants Bigge and Slade, who courageously stood in the open, also began pounding the Nkobamakosi position.

The time was now 2.15 pm; the advance of the right horn had lasted little more than thirty minutes. The feint of the horsemen in luring it into a premature attack could not have been more successful. All attention in the redoubt was turned to the south-west where several regiments were advancing rapidly: the Umbonambi

(uMbonambi), Nokenke (uNokhenke) and the Umcityu, the great rivals of the Nkobamakosi, all warriors in their prime of thirty years and younger.

Mnyamana, the king's minister, had long since taken up a position beyond the range of rifle and artillery fire, as was the accepted custom for men of such high rank. Such privilege would also have applied to Tshingwayo, the general, but rather than isolate himself from his troops and watch their progress from afar, he had advanced with the centre of the army establishing his command post only 700 yards east of Wood's redoubt.

At 3.00 pm the left wing, with a great rattling of shields and war cries, raced toward the little ravine below the redoubt. As they came on they were received with heavy volley fire from the 13th LI manning the south face of the laager, and then pounded with shrapnel and case-shot from all six guns, which ripped the warriors and their pathetic shields to pieces as though both were made of paper. Lieutenant Nicholson, commanding the two guns in the redoubt, stood fearlessly exposed, directing his battery until shot through the body and mortally wounded.

Those warriors who succeeded in running the gauntlet of fire hugged the safety of the ravine where they began to mass in ever-increasing numbers, mad with fury at their loss and the impotency of their attack. The dead ground less than 100 yards from the cattle laager was now providing a rallying place for the Zulu army. The lip of the ravine under which they hid had been a dumping ground for horse dung which, induced by rain and the African sun, had produced a small crop of mealies (Indian corn). This growth now gave cover to forty Zulu marksmen who scrambled up amongst the stalks and leaves. Two other groups of marksmen, armed with captured Martini Henrys, occupied some deserted huts of Wood's Irregulars to the east, and the debris of the British rubbish dump to the west. There were now Zulu riflemen at 400 yards on either side of the camp, plus those in the mealies. The cattle kraal was the closest target, and against all claims of incompetent Zulu marksmanship, two-thirds of the infantry defending the cattle laager were driven to abandon their position for the protection of the redoubt – the remaining one-third of the garrison sheltering among the rear wagons, but not for long.

The British retreat filled the warriors with new heart. They advanced from the ravine and across the intervening 100 yards, having to contend only with the fire from one face of the main laager. As they pushed their way through the chained but undefended wagons, the remaining men of the 13th hurriedly departed, sprinting for the redoubt. Not all reached it in safety, four were killed and seven wounded, including one man who fell headlong in front of the advancing warriors. He was saved by three officers from the redoubt, Captain Maude, young Lysons and Lieutenant Smith, who dashed forward to rescue him, Smith being wounded in the process. Private W. Grosvenor also displayed great gallantry in remaining behind to assist his wounded sergeant, but both men were overrun and assegaaied. The men in the main laager were also suffering casualties, among them Gardner, that survivor of desperate situations, who was shot through the thigh while standing to take aim.

With the cattle kraal now in their possession, more and more warriors were crossing from the ravine to loot the wagons and consume any uneaten food from the 13th's cooking pots. Even at this crucial moment in the battle they could not restrain themselves from driving off some of the cattle.

The situation for the British had become critical. Unless the cattle kraal was retaken immediately it could harbour 5000 warriors not fifty yards from the redoubt walls. A mass charge over so short a distance would be difficult to restrain. Without hesitation, Wood ordered two companies of the 90th to fix bayonets and retake the kraal. A wagon was detached from the north-east corner of the main laager and the men of the 90th, under the command of Major Robert Hackett, swung through the gap, marching as though on parade. Captain Woodgate of Wood's staff led the way, sword held aloft, 'marching as leisurely and unconcernedly as if he was pacing a piece of ground for cricket wickets,' as *The Natal Mercury* reported. On command the sortie formed line and at the double charged the enemy with the bayonet, throwing the Zulu back into the ravine. The 90th halted, formed up along the lip of the drop and opened fire into the massing warriors below. However, the 90th themselves were then caught in a withering crossfire from marksmen holding the abandoned huts to the east and the rubbish dump to the west. Completely exposed, the infantry were soon taking casualties at an alarming rate. Wood, watching from the redoubt, could see their position was untenable and, in alarm, ordered their recall, but not before Hackett received an appalling wound, the bullet passing right through his head, completely blinding him.[3] Another officer, a young man of great promise, Lieutenant Arthur Bright, also fell mortally wounded.

The British counter-attack had succeeded, the cattle kraal had been retaken, and Wood himself had lent a hand by shooting four warriors in quick succession with a Swinburne-Henry carbine at 195 yards. The enemy had been dispersed from the immediate area of the redoubt – but the cost had been high: forty-four men of the 90th had either been killed or wounded. It was crucial that the Zulu snipers be destroyed. The gunners in the redoubt gave the abandoned huts their full attention and with shell and shrapnel reduced them to ruins. The marksmen in the rubbish heap were more difficult to dislodge as the main laager stood between it and the guns. The position, however, was cut to pieces and flattened by sustained volley fire, and the British were not bothered again by snipers from either side. At about this time, the Umcityu regiment began to congregate in the dead ground west of the ravine, for a direct attack on the main laager. Once again a wagon was manhandled aside, and on this occasion a company of the 13th charged out to engage the enemy with the bayonet, only to be thrown back through the gap with the Zulu after them, and more swarming out from cover.

Fortunately for the British, the entry in the barricade was immediately below the guns of both the redoubt and the ridge – the latter now being within a spear throw of the leading warriors. At point-blank range, the gunners, loading and firing with practised skill, shredded the Zulu ranks with case-shot. The Umcityu fell back only to rally once more as all around the perimeter of the British defences, the courageous warriors charged again and again. 'There was one continuous roar from cannon, rifles and the voices of men on both sides shouting. The smoke blotted out all view,' Mossop was to recall. Then the Nkobamakosi, who had suffered such terrible loss in the first charge three hours earlier, came out of their rocky gallery, where they had kept up a continuous fire all day, and ran once more at the camp, intent on overwhelming the redoubt. 'Still they came on with the ferocity of a tiger, never halting, never wavering . . . no soldiers in the world could have been more daring than were the Zulus that day,' wrote the correspondent of *The Scotsman*. It was true, but to wasted purpose. Had they laid siege to the camp, keeping up their skilful sniping, and had they obeyed the orders of their king, the battle might well have been another Zulu victory. Perhaps they were too brave and confident, the victory of the previous day being responsible for engendering reckless courage and the belief that they were invincible.

The afternoon was drawing to a close. In the distance the shadow of the Skurweberg range lengthened across the plain, yet still they fought, and with one last gesture of resolve, a large body of warriors assembled in the ravine, readying themselves for a final assault against the main laager. Before the attack could gain impetus, however, two companies of the 13th LI, led by Captains Thurlow and Waddy, accompanied by Raaff and some of the colonials, doubled to the edge of the ravine and fired down at almost point-blank range into the milling regiments.

The Zulu army began to withdraw. It was as though every warrior had individually decided at that moment to retire. The time was 5.30 pm and since the attack had begun four hours earlier, the British had expended 138,000 rounds of Martini Henry ammunition and 1077 miscellaneous shells.

A pent-up cheer of victory echoed from the British camp. The Zulu had at last been beaten – and they were not going to get away with it that easily. Yesterday the British had been routed: now it would be the enemy's turn.

The bugle sounded, the wagons were unchained and the men mounted up; beneath them their horses, well fed and rested, felt fresh and responsive. As they swarmed out of the laager, an awful eagerness to pursue and kill seemed to grip the horsemen like a madness.

The infantry cheered and cheered and the riders responded with wild yells. 'Remember yesterday!' was their war cry. 'Remember Hlobane! Remember Isandlwana!' The Zulu had shown them no mercy; he would expect none and get none. They rode in three columns, the NNH joining in from the west from where they had harried the Nkobamakosi throughout the day.

The 600 horsemen chased after the jogging warriors who made no attempt to group or rally. The gap closed and to a shout of triumph the slaughter began. The

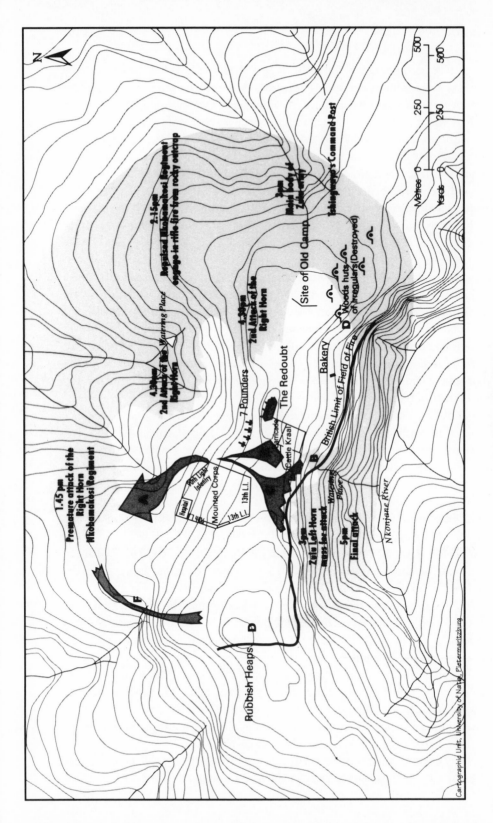

12. **BATTLE OF KAMBULA**

(Caption on facing page)

colonials, not equipped as cavalry, were unable to wreak execution in the traditional manner with sabre and lance; although a few officers, who considered
themselves fortunate, carried swords, the rest had to make do with their carbines
which became too difficult to load in the fury of the chase. So, using their guns as
clubs, they smashed the Zulu heads with the ease of a polo player striking a ball –
and when that did not satisfy, they snatched assegais from the dead and 'gave
point' to the living like a Hussar with a sabre, 'stabbing them right and left with
fearful revenge,' as Schermbrucker put it.

They were all there, all the survivors of Hlobane, and it was their joy to pursue
the enemy towards Zunguin Nek, back over the very ground from which they had
themselves been chased at the same hour the day before; and it was their particular
delight to see the abaQulusi, only lately arrived at the battle, bolting with the rest.

Buller, their leader, set the standard for ferocity, '. . . like a tiger drunk with
blood,' as one officer was to recall. 'The cavalry followed them up for about eight
miles, killing everyone they could lay their hands on. It was a most awful sight,'
wrote the correspondent of *The Natal Mercury*; while a young officer of the NNH,
writing home, told his family, 'We killed a fearful lot in the retreat, shooting them
down at fifteen yards, and having a good many hand to hand struggles. The Zulus
were quite knocked up and some laid down and got into holes and hiding places. I
should not like to count how many I killed, and every man did the same.' An
officer of Wood's Irregulars reported:

> Towards the end of the pursuit, they were so tired and exhausted that they couldn't
> move out of a walk, some scarcely looked round and seemed to wish to die without

Caption to Map 12 (on facing page): The battle of Kambula. Wood's No. 4 Column
under attack by the main Zulu army. This was the conclusive battle of the Anglo-
Zulu war. Although the Zulu were not finally defeated until the battle of Ulundi
several months later, Cetshwayo's warriors never really recovered from the catastrophic rout inflicted upon them by the colonial horsemen.

Key:
A. 1.30 pm   Mounted units sally forth and provoke Zulu right horn into
             premature attack.
   5.30 pm   Buller leads mounted units in rout of the Zulu army.
B. 3.00 pm   Zulu left horn attacks out of ravine and captures the cattle laager.
C. 3.00 pm   90th LI counter-attack and drive Zulu back into ravine but in turn are
             driven by Zulu sniper fire from the rubbish heap and the huts at 'D'.
D. 3.00 pm   Zulu snipers.
E. 3.30 pm
   and
   5.15 pm   13th LI counter-attacks.
F.   Natal Native Horse skirmishing throughout the battle.

seeing the shot fired. Some turned around and walked to meet their death without offering resistance, some threw themselves down on their faces and waited for their dispatch by assegai or bullet, some got into antbear holes, reeds, or long grass and tried to evade detection, but very few succeeded in this. It was indeed a slaughter.

Yes, it was a slaughter from which the Zulu army would never quite recover. It would fight one more pitched battle against the British three months hence at Ulundi, but not with resolve nor in the belief that it could win. Unknowingly, the British army bought its victories of Kambula and Ulundi with the price of its defeat at Hlobane. However, the great debt that it owed the colonial horsemen for its success was never to be acknowledged.

At about 6.30 pm, with the coming of dusk, a thick mist descended over the plains and hills surrounding the Zunguin range, rendering further pursuit impossible. The next morning James Francis, a colonial officer, walked around the camp and within a radius of 800 yards counted 800 Zulu dead. He did not know it but among them were two sons of Mnyamana. Further out, and along the line of pursuit, it is likely that another 1500 perished. A pit, 200 feet long and 10 feet deep, was dug to accommodate the dead. The British casualties, killed and wounded, were 83.

Let Commandant Schermbrucker, who the previous year had buried Sandile, the paramount chief of the Xhosa, have the last word. He wrote what could have been the Zulu army's epitaph: 'They succumbed to superior weapons and the murderous fire of big guns, but they died like brave men and good soldiers in defence of their chief and country; we buried the Zulu dead with full military honours.'

1. The town of Vryheid now occupies the position of the Zulu army's bivouac area.
2. The number given for the Zulu army and its regiments are approximate, and are as compiled by H. B. Finney in 1878 at the request of Lord Chelmsford.
3. Wood was convinced the wound was mortal; however, Hackett lived to a ripe old age.

8
AFTERMATH

The British victory at Kambula, great as it was, did not cause peace bells to ring throughout the Disputed Territories. Although the Zulu army dispersed, the warriors refusing to reassemble at Ulundi, the abaQulusi, quite naturally, returned to Hlobane and Mbelini reoccupied his mountain stronghold. The warriors of the Disputed Territory would be the last to admit defeat and would offer open resistance for some time after the battle of Ulundi. It is not surprising, then, that within a few days local raiding recommenced with one of the biggest forays, an impi of 400 warriors, attacking the farm of the late Piet Uys, where thirty cattle and 1500 sheep were driven off.

The burghers had returned to duty and although Uys's son, Piet Uys junior, had been elected leader, he stood down in favour of Adrian Rudolph who was appointed commandant. A number of Hamu's warriors also returned. Those who had not deserted were rewarded with a pound each.

On 4 April a burgher patrol was shot at from Hlobane. After an exchange of fire, Uys junior began to parley with the Zulu leader, calling upon him to surrender. In reply the warrior shouted that he did not require the white man's protection and that he and his men were ready to fight as soon as the soldiers came out from their Kambula laager. A volley of Zulu shots ended the discussion.

Lord Chelmsford, accompanied by the newly arrived and highly inquisitive young Prince Imperial,[1] descended on Kambula five days after the battle. The prince had been at Woolwich with Lieutenants Slade and Bigge, of the Royal Artillery, and much enjoyed a reunion with them. Chelmsford and his entourage were later taken to the Zunguin range where Buller pointed out the details of distant Hlobane. The party did not linger as it was also subjected to distant rifle fire.

It was not long before Mbelini was again raiding around Luneburg, but the wily warrior's luck was about to run out and he would shortly die at the hand of the most unlikely assailant, seventeen-year-old Heinrich Filter. Since Filter's father was described as 'a severe specimen of the Lutheran pastor of the sixteenth-century type, equally prepared to lead his flock spiritually to heaven and bodily against the Zulu', perhaps it was not so surprising that Heinrich, who had escaped from Hlobane only a week earlier, should be the one to rid the area of the man responsible for so much terror. On 5 April, Mbelini swooped on Luneburg, robbing a homestead of a number of horses. The raiders were spotted by a small British patrol led by a Major Prior of the 4th King's Own Regiment, which included Heinrich as interpreter. The patrol opened fire, killing one man and wounding another. Heinrich, however, recognised the leader of the raiders as Mbelini and set off in pursuit, inflicting a gunshot wound from which the warrior bled to death. Heinrich was deservedly a hero – a status which sadly he did not enjoy for long. Some days later he saw another gang stealing his own family horses; with a few of his native workers he set off after them. He had a favourite well-trained horse by the name of 'Garibaldi', but as it was out grazing he saddled the first nag that came to hand, which was unfortunately green and unschooled. Soon he and his men were led into a trap, being surrounded by many warriors hiding in the long grass. Heinrich's untrained horse let him down and, being soon dismounted, he was placed upon an anthill where he sat, head in hands, while the raiders discussed his fate. They were all local Zulus and Heinrich was known to many and well liked by some; he came close to being released, but among them was Mbelini's brother who insisted on Heinrich's death as royal blood had been spilt. With no more ado Heinrich was speared to death. Some stones and a rusty iron stake still mark the spot where he fell.

For many months there had been a price on Mbelini's head, dead or alive, of £600. Clearly Heinrich was entitled to this bounty, but the German account of the incident relates that neither he nor his family received it. 'So much for English honour!' the narrator spitefully concluded.

Raiders continued to operate from Mbelini's stronghold long after the battle of Ulundi, in fact until the caves were destroyed with dynamite by men of the 4th King's Own Regiment on 8 September 1879. But Mbelini was to have the last laugh, as it were, for the two British NCOs who laid the dynamite charges, Sergeant Major Smith and Corporal Pomfret, accidentally blew themselves to pieces together with the caves.

On 18 May, another teenage volunteer was to die a violent death under rather strange circumstances. Commandant Schermbrucker had been promoted to command the whole of the Border District, with his headquarters in the vicinity of the abandoned Potter's store site. He must have been bursting with pride for he now had imperial troops, the King's Own Regiment, under his direct command. Schermbrucker had ridden over to Luneburg accompanied by his young orderly and interpreter, Danen Larsen, and, together with a Captain Moore of the King's Own, set out on a patrol. They had not gone far when, riding through long grass, they were surrounded by Zulu. Schermbrucker's horse was shot, and it is plain from two separate accounts that he commandeered Larsen's mount, ordering the lad to get up behind. However, the restive horse would not permit the boy to seat himself and to quote a report in *The Graphic* some weeks later, 'The horse refused the double load, and presently it was decided that Larsen should seek safety on foot.' Not surprisingly the account continued, 'The poor fellow, however, never returned to camp.'

A German manuscript, published sixty years later in 1938, tells a far more dramatic story: 'Schermbrucker was on a most unreliable horse and Larsen said, "Herr Commandant Schermbrucker, you will never get through the Zulu lines. You cannot die: You must not die! If the Zulu kill me it doesn't matter so much."' At this point the narrative relates that the commandant's horse was shot and Larsen offered him his own, which Schermbrucker reluctantly accepted. Larsen then attempted to escape on foot but was surrounded and speared to death near the Intombi River. 'The young hero had given his life for Commandant Schermbrucker and the Germans of Luneburg,' the account concluded. *The Graphic* report adds a little more detail. After Larsen had tried to escape on foot, at a time when the Zulus were 'within a hundred and fifty yards', Moore's horse was also shot and killed. Schermbrucker then urged Moore to mount up behind and they 'adjusted themselves to the double riding'. By noon the horse, which 'proved equal to the occasion', had its two riders safely back in Luneburg. That evening Schermbrucker, with an escort, set out to search for Larsen, 'but in vain, and it was afterwards ascertained that he had been shot,' ended *The Graphic*. Before nightfall there was a tremendous rainstorm which caused the Intombi to burst its banks. The reed and river rubbish left behind by the subsiding flood covered Larsen's body, which was not found for many months. He was eventually buried where he was slain and his lonely grave covered by a pile of rocks.

* * *

Four days after the battle of Kambula Lord Chelmsford defeated a Zulu army of approximately 11,000 warriors at the battle of Gingindlovu, and the following day relieved Colonel Pearson and his besieged garrison at Eshowe.

Apart from the death of the Prince Imperial on 1 June, there were no shattering events until the final battle of the war on 4 July 1879. The Zulu army, gallantly charging for the last time against modern weapons, including Gatling guns, was defeated and routed at Ulundi.

To finalise Britain's victory over the Zulu nation, Cetshwayo's capture was essential. For over two months after the battle of Ulundi, British mounted patrols scoured the remote valleys and forests of Zululand, but Cetshwayo's subjects remained ever loyal and refused to betray the whereabouts of their king. Eventually, Major Marter, leading a patrol of the 1st Dragoon Guards, captured Cetshwayo, who was thereafter imprisoned in Cape Town Castle. Three years later he was sent to England, accompanied by Henrique Shepstone, where he was a great favourite with the London crowds. He was granted an audience with Queen Victoria, had lunch with her at Osborne (which was by all accounts a great success) and was presented with an enormous silver beer tankard capable of holding a right royal draught or two. In keeping with its proportions, it had three silver handles. The tankard was subsequently lost. In 1937 it was found buried in a stream and bartered for a blanket and a cow to a local trader. It can now be viewed at the Ondini Cultural Museum.

In 1883, Cetshwayo was at last allowed to return to Zululand which had, during his absence, been dissected by Wolseley, using the principle of 'Divide and Rule', into thirteen little kingdoms – Hamu being awarded one of them. The findings of the Boundary Commission had been ignored by Wolseley; the lands of the Disputed Territory had been given to the Transvaal, whilst other large areas of Zululand were to be handed over to white settlement. Within a year of returning, Cetshwayo was dead – having possibly died of poisoning. The disastrous effects of Wolseley's policy led to civil war among the Zulu and almost to the destruction of the Zulu nation.

To return briefly to the battle of Isandlwana, it is said that when messengers arrived at Ondini to inform Cetshwayo that the British army had been found, the king retired and seated himself on his Inkatha which, reputedly, held a mystic strength capable of projecting his personality into the battle and unifying his warriors. The Inkatha, an heirloom handed down in the Zulu royal family since the reign of Shaka, comprised many things: the body dirt of Cetshwayo and that of his ancestors, soiled straw from the floor of the royal house, vomit, animal teeth and hair, the whole being shaped into a coil and stuffed into a python skin. On this Cetshwayo sat for hours anticipating the progress of the battle. If he moved he was harangued by the women lest he broke the magic spell and endangered their menfolk fighting far away. When news of the victory at Isandlwana arrived by fast runners, Cetshwayo arose from his vigil, and this precipitate action, while the battle still raged at Rorke's Drift, was the cause of the Zulu repulse – or so the Zulu women maintained, blaming Cetshwayo for the defeat. The British are reported to have destroyed Cetshwayo's Inkatha; however, almost a hundred years later it could be said to have reappeared, phoenix-like, as a political party, aimed at unifying the Zulu people under the leadership of Chief Mangosuthu Buthelezi, himself a direct descendant of Shaka and Cetshwayo. Later, Inkatha was transformed into the Inkatha Freedom Party (IFP), whose membership is open to all. In South Africa's first democratic elections, held during April 1994, the IFP won the provincial election of KwaZulu-Natal and Chief Buthelezi was appointed Minister of Home Affairs in the first South African Government of National Unity. The prospects for the Zulu people have not looked better since 1879.

*   *   *

By the end of June 1879 both Chelmsford and Frere had been superseded in Natal by Sir Garnet Wolseley. He had arrived in Durban six days before the battle of Ulundi and had fruitlessly endeavoured to overtake Chelmsford and assume command; He also gave precise orders that Zulu forces were not to be engaged unless fired upon. Chelmsford, nevertheless, managed to keep one step ahead and achieve the victory he so desperately desired. Believing his reputation restored, he refused to serve under Wolseley.

In January, after the defeat at Isandlwana, it will be recalled that Chelmsford had written to Wood saying, 'I wish I saw my way with honour out of this beastly country and had you as my travelling companion.' His wish now came true: he would not only have Wood as his companion but also Buller, Crealock, Grenfell and a number of other prominent officers (including young Lysons), who would all go home together leaving Cape Town aboard RMS *German*.

Wood and Buller had been members of the 'Wolseley Ring',[2] indicating Wolseley's high opinion of both men. However, Chelmsford had written that they were 'pretty well used up and must go home'. They in turn confided in Wolseley that they considered Chelmsford not fit to be a corporal and that 'nothing would induce them to serve under him again'!

Chelmsford, Wood and Buller all saw out the century. Chelmsford, ever a favourite of Queen Victoria's, was eventually promoted to the rank of a full general, given the appointment of Governor of the Tower of London, and also that of Gold Stick. He aged well but never again received an active command (for which he was probably grateful) and died whilst playing billiards at his London club in 1905.

Wood had many years of soldiering still ahead of him and again saw active service in both Southern Africa and Egypt. He rose to the highest rank of all, that of field marshal, and despite his sickly constitution and his almost hypochondriacal obsession with his various ailments, continued riding to hounds well into old age. Like Chelmsford, he was also appointed Governor of the Tower of London when the position became vacant. As late as the First World War he was still up and about improving the lot of wounded soldiers. He died in 1919 at the age of eighty-one.

Buller also had a long military career. His great chance for glory came with the Anglo-Boer War. In 1899 he was back in South Africa, this time as commander-in-chief. On arrival he took personal command of a British army of 25,000 men, which was to relieve the siege of Ladysmith. Within two months of landing he had been defeated by the Boers in the disastrous battles of Colenso and Spioenkop, and was superseded as commander-in-chief by Lord Roberts. He did retain command of the Natal army and although he succeeded in relieving Ladysmith a few weeks later, it was the end of his career. He left the service for his Devonshire acres in 1901.

* * *

A number of British officers at the time of the Zulu War joined the army through circumstance – the circumstance of being poor. In those days the gentry did not go into commerce or trade so there was little prospect of improving one's financial lot: not that the army presented much in the way of golden opportunity but it was better than nothing. There was also the chance of glory: and if one was particularly lucky there could be the possibility of both glory and cash.

Chelmsford was by no means a wealthy man and had not married into money;

the daughter of an Indian army general would not have brought much in the way of a dowry. Perhaps one of Wolseley's kindest thoughts when he superseded Chelmsford was that he wished 'to build for him a bridge of gold to retire by', no doubt hoping that, when the time came, someone would do something similar for him as he also came from an impoverished family. Although the Wolseleys could trace their military background to before the Norman Conquest, his widowed mother did not have sufficient funds to send him to school; so she taught him herself at home. Nor did she have £400 to buy his entrance into a regiment. Instead she sought a 'commission without purchase' from the Duke of Wellington, for it was only the commander-in-chief who could lavish such a bounty. She eventually obtained the commission for her son but only after persistent nagging for five years.

Wood also came from a genteel but far from wealthy background. His father, Sir John Wood, who had been a clergyman, died leaving his wife to bring up nine children. Wood frequently requested a rich aunt for money and when she died he caused a public scandal by contesting her will, as she had left all her wealth to his sister. Buller, the son of a Devonshire squire, was probably better off than Chelmsford, Wolseley and Wood all put together.

Impoverished warriors therefore hoped the army would provide promotion which brought with it extra pay; they also hoped for active service and the prospect of loot – as in the instance of cattle raiding during the Zulu War. The most sought-after prize was a special pension or a lump sum grant from a grateful government as a reward for some great deed.

It is difficult now to understand the Victorian concept of glory in war – the First World War put paid to all that. It is evident from Mrs Campbell and Barton's sister that even the women of Victorian military men understood the glory of a soldier's death – and the tangible signs of glory were, as a rule, medals and decorations. Lieutenant Colonel Philip Anstruther,[3] 94th Regiment, newly arrived in Zululand, perceived the quest for glory when he remarked on the attitude of Chelmsford's top commanders: 'The jealousy that there is amongst them is absurd. They all have different ideas and all their ideas point to their own glory . . . Wood is the greatest nuisance.'

As early as 28 January, six days after the battle of Isandlwana, Chelmsford was concerned that the War Office had not given Wood sufficient recognition for his services in the recent Ninth Frontier War: 'I was horrified when I heard that there was talk of giving you a CMG (Companion of the Order of St Michael and St George). I have written before to the Duke and I wrote again when I heard it, to say that the least reward you were entitled to was a KCMG.' The latter decoration (Knight Commander of the Order of St Michael and St George) was four degrees of honour higher than a CMG and second only to the Order of the Garter – obviously Chelmsford had got his honours confused! Nevertheless, Wood accepted his disdained CMG and on arrival in England was elevated in one giant stride three steps up the knightly ladder, being invested a KCB (Knight Commander of the Order of the Bath). Queen Victoria also wasted no time in inviting Chelmsford to Balmoral where he was created a Knight Grand Cross of the Order of the Bath. No doubt both men were reasonably well satisfied.

The real glory awards, however, were the VC (Victoria Cross) and, to a lesser degree, the DCM (Silver Medal for Distinguished Service) – decorations awarded only for the greatest valour – although bravery was not always enough to secure attention and acclaim. Quite often a man had to have a sponsor with the right connections to push his case.

The award of the VC did not mean much to the ordinary soldiers, although they were acclaimed as heroes. Nor, it seems, did the award enhance their military careers: of the six other ranks who won the decoration for the defence of Rorke's Drift, only two continued serving in the army and of these only one received further promotion. Of the four that returned to civilian life, one became a cloakroom attendant, another a messenger, while the other two either ended up in the workhouse or committed suicide later in life.

Dealing only with the three battles fought solely by Wood's column, Intombi, Hlobane and Kambula, there were a total of six VCs and seven DCMs awarded. The single VC to Sergeant Booth for his bravery at Intombi is straightforward enough – there seemed to be no one else deserving of mention. Nevertheless it took a year for the award to be gazetted, almost as though it were an afterthought on the part of Booth's commanding officer.

The disastrous assault on Hlobane received the richest haul of decorations, no less than four VCs and the same number of DCMs. (Many sources have an additional VC being won at Hlobane, that of Lieutenant Edward Browne, but this is incorrect: if fact he won the honour the following day at Kambula.) There was undoubtedly a tendency for defeated commanders to draw attention away from their disasters by shining a spotlight on deeds of valour. Sonia Clarke remarks in her book *Zululand at War 1879*: 'It appears that the military authorities desperately sought to find some deeds of gallantry connected with Isandlwana to reward.' Such was not the case with Hlobane; there was no need to seek as there were gallant deeds aplenty – but unfortunately there was partiality aplenty as well.[4]

Wood, as the column commander, was the final arbiter as to who would be recommended for a gallantry award, with various senior officers bringing acts of bravery to his attention. After Hlobane his immediate thought was to decorate Buller with the VC. Chelmsford acknowledged Wood's recommendation, writing 'I was delighted that you were able to nominate Buller for the Victoria Cross. There is no doubt that he has earned it many times over.' Buller's courage was legendary, and he risked his life on at least three separate occasions on 28 March rescuing horseless troopers at the bottom of Devil's Pass. Yet there were men equally gallant and successful in saving dismounted comrades who received no award and, perhaps more to the point, were, unlike Buller, in no way responsible for the disaster! Adjutant Brecher, Lieutenant Blaine, Corporal Vinnicombe, Trooper Hewitt and an unnamed Trooper of the NNH[5] all rescued men under the same perilous conditions but received no recognition – except for Vinnicombe, who received a DCM. Knox-Leet, who had taken up behind him Lieutenant Metcalfe-Smith, was initially overlooked in both Buller's and Wood's lists of 'mentions'. However, Metcalfe-Smith was quick to acknowledge that he owed his life to Knox-Leet, writing a detailed report to that effect, dated 31 March, which was given over to the press.

Buller and Knox-Leet therefore account for two of the VCs, and almost three years was to elapse before Wood recommended the award of an additional two, those to Lieutenant Lysons and Private Fowler, but only after continuous pressure from Lysons's father, General Sir Daniel Lysons KCB, who was Quartermaster-General at the War Office and as such in frequent contact with the Commander-in-Chief, the Duke of Cambridge. Wood really came under pressure from the Lysons family as soon as the provisions of the VC warrant changed to include acts of bravery performed in the course of duty. On 25 July 1881, he felt beholden to write to General Sir Alfred Hastings Horsford, Military Secretary to the Commander-in-Chief, HRH The Duke of Cambridge: 'Please read the accompanying letter from Sir Daniel Lysons about his son . . . Sir Daniel and Lady Lysons have, on different occasions, addressed me on the subject of Mr Lysons's gallant conduct and lately Lady Lysons informed me verbally, that HRH had said that Mr Lysons ought to have been recommended for the Victoria Cross.' Wood went on to explain to Horsford that he had not made the recommendation previously because of the provisions of the warrant, but now felt he would like to do so. However, Wood had a problem: if he was going to recommend Lysons, he would also have to recommend Private Fowler who was with him at the time – and how about the brave Walkinshaw who had run the gauntlet of fire for Mrs Campbell's prayer book? A late request for three VCs was out of the question, so he recommended Walkinshaw for the next best thing, a DCM. The awards were confirmed in April of 1882, almost three years to the day after the battle.

The recipients of the remaining DCMs were Private J. Power, of the Mounted Infantry, for a combination of gallant actions during the Ninth Frontier War and at Devil's Pass, and Trooper Robert Browne of the Frontier Light Horse.

The gallantry awards for Hlobane were therefore distributed within a small and favoured circle smiled upon either by Wood or Buller; Trooper Browne was Buller's orderly and Corporal Vinnicombe was favoured because of his Devonshire connections. The DCM to Power was the only Hlobane decoration that was awarded outside the favoured circle.

In analysing the distribution of the above decorations, there is no intention to detract from the brave deeds performed, but there is intent to draw attention to the fact that out of a force that comprised more than ninety percent colonial and native troops, all the VCs and half the DCMs were pinned on the breasts of imperials despite the recommendations contained in Buller's original report. It was the custom for commanders to conclude their battle reports by drawing to the notice of the general commanding those men who had excelled in courage or service: 'But for the exertions of a few our retreat would have been a rout,' wrote Buller. 'Especially distinguishing themselves in the retreat I wish to mention Commandant Raaff, Transvaal Rangers, Captain Gardner, my Staff Officer, both of whom were also conspicuous in the assault in the morning, Major Leet, Captain D'Arcy although himself dismounted rallied the men saving the lives of many footmen, Lieutenants Blaine, Smith, Wilson, Lorraine White, Brecher....' Buller continued to name a further eight NCOs and men of the Frontier Light Horse, yet out of the total of seventeen men mentioned, of whom fifteen were colonials, the only colonial who received recognition was Vinnicombe whose name had come last on Buller's list! In December 1879, Raaff was appointed CMG 'for services rendered in the South African War'. However, a year or so later, when it came to distributing 36,000 South African General Service Medals (a medal issued to all who served in the various campaigns in Southern Africa between 1877 and 1879) Raaff's name and that of his second-in-command, Captain J.G. Jullian, were deleted from the roll with the notation, 'No medal should be prepared financial transactions unsatisfactory'. In view of over 13,000 medals being issued to colonials, and this being the only instance of such a deletion, it is a most extraordinary and defamatory accusation – especially so as Raaff had done as much, if not more, than any other colonial in the British forces, hence his CMG. Who could have written such a remark? The application forms for the medal were required to be completed and returned to the assistant-adjutant-general, Colonial Forces, who happened to be none other than Captain W.F.D. Cochrane who had commanded the NNH at Hlobane under Russell! Could the deletion have been the result of an old enmity between Cochrane and Raaff going back to Hlobane? A puzzle that remains to be solved.

The decorations for Kambula are not contentious, although there is an element of mystery concerning the one Victoria Cross. Of the three DCMs, those to Sergeant Quigley and Private Page are straightforward awards for gallantry. The remaining DCM to Troop Sergeant Major Learda of the NNH (the first black soldier ever to receive the decoration) is coupled with the award of the only VC to Lieutenant Edward Browne, commanding the MI. Learda's citation reads in part: '... at Kambula, when Lieutenant Colonel Russell was dismounted and unable to mount through the restlessness of his horse he [Learda] rallied a few men within a few yards of the Zulus who were moving on to the attack in large numbers thus enabling Captain E.S. Browne, commanding the Mounted Infantry, to save Lieutenant Colonel Russell's life'. The slight mystery concerning the incident is that most authorities have Browne winning his VC the previous day for saving 'a man's life' – Russell is never mentioned by name. Further drama is added to this award by Browne offering to resign rather than serve under Russell again and submitting to Wood a 'straightforward letter' to that effect early in April. It was just what Wood wanted – the last nail for Russell's coffin! Chelmsford could protect his friend no longer and Russell made his way to the remount depot at Pietermaritzburg.

Russell, however, also laid claim to rescuing a wounded man during the race back to the Kambula laager. Let the letter of gratitude from 'J.W.P.', which was published in *The Natal Mercury* three weeks after the battle, speak for itself, even allowing for the fact that the writer did perhaps lay it on a bit thick:

> Colonel Russell, Dear Sir, – Allow me to express my humblefulness of heartfelt gratitude, for your noble and gallant conduct in the preservation of my life at the sad risk of your own noble self, from the hands of black savages and unmerciful foes. Dear Sir, I only wish I had it in my power to show you the feelings of my grateful heart, all that I can offer you, noble Sir, is my prayer. May God protect you and shield you in all the dangers of war, and may He watch over you and prosper you in all undertakings, may God in His gracious power prosper you in health and wealth in this world, and at last take you to a heaven of everlasting rest, where there are no troubles of war or sorrow, is the prayer of your humble and grateful servant J.W.P.

It was Sir Garnett Wolseley's lot, as General Commanding, to present a number of Zulu War decorations. Wolseley was unquestionably one of the bravest men ever to serve in the British army yet he never had the luck to be decorated for gallantry and it clearly irritated him to decorate others. He confided to his diary:

> I gave away the VC to Captain D'Arcy today on parade. I don't think he was a good case for this citation as he did not succeed in saving the life of the man he dismounted to assist.... I presented Major Chard RE with his VC – a more uninteresting or stupid looking fellow I never saw. Bromhead who was second in command of the post, is a very stupid looking fellow also....

Glory, it would seem, had two faces!

* * *

The battle sites mentioned in this book remain by and large as they were at the time of the Zulu War. Isandlwana, being the most famous, has a scattering of monuments, a small museum with a curator, and has recently been fenced. One can still roam and pace the battlefield among the cairns of whitewashed rocks, and gaze toward the blue hump of Isipezi Hill ten miles away, with the plain below that was once covered by 25,000 advancing Zulu warriors.

Meyer's Drift, at the Intombi River, at one time such an important crossing between Luneburg and Derby, is a crossing no more; Derby has disappeared from the maps and farmlands have long since obliterated the road. A monument to the men of the 80th stands above the river, and the mountain strongholds of Mbelini and Manyanyoba are given over to grazing cattle. But, in essence, little has changed except for Mbelini's caves where the evidence of their destruction by dynamite is still apparent.

Nor has the battlefield of Kambula changed to any great degree. The position of Wood's redoubt is easily ascertained; the little ravine, much shallower than depicted in all the battle illustrations of the day, is still there. Wattle trees have been planted at some distance from the ridge, but fortunately they neither encroach nor restrict the magnificent views – in fact the plantations can, with a little imagination, enhance the scene; half close your eyes and the trees are transformed into the advancing Zulu army – most of them are in about the right position for such mental fiction.

The battleground of Hlobane has in part altered beyond recognition – but in part not changed at all. The coal that the men of the 13th and 90th Light Infantry once dug for was discovered to be available in large quantities. By 1908 a full mining operation with railway lines, a preparation plant for the process of coking coal, offices, housing, roads, water towers, and all the other structures that make up the awful visual pollution of a coal mine, were there. All this development has taken place around the base of Hlobane, over the ground where Lysons rode with his message to Russell, and where the Zulu army chased Weatherley and Barton back up Intyentika Nek. Yet there is a paradox: the mining that has despoiled the base of Hlobane has preserved the plateau and Devil's Pass exactly as they were in 1879! The only intrusion has been the construction of two wireless masts; but if one forgets their purpose and uses them as landmarks – and landmarks are often necessary on that high barren moor when the mist is coming down – then they do not intrude and nothing has changed.

On the lower slopes, if you know where to look, the weather-beaten cross that marks the grave of Campbell and Lloyd is not difficult to find. In 1993, accompanied by Fred Duke, a local 'fundi' (expert) on Hlobane, Paul Naish and I set out to find the snipers' cave which was charged by Lysons and Fowler after Campbell had been shot. Consulting the sketch which Lieutenant Slade RA drew for Lady Wood in 1880, and using the distances mentioned by Wood in his autobiography as our guides, we were soon fighting our way through thick undergrowth which had grown up over the years due to the absence of cattle. Much to our surprise, however, we eventually stumbled on the stone cattle kraal where Wood had sheltered his horses from the abaQulusi marksmen. Just above the kraal was a jumble of great boulders and slabs of rock, much collapsed upon each other over the last 113 years, and no longer offering an entrance high enough for a standing man. We could have crawled through and perhaps found a way into the mountain – but although the labyrinth no longer harboured Zulu snipers, it could well have been the cosy habitat of the odd puff adder, spitting cobra or other nasties! Unlike Lysons and Fowler, we lacked the courage to enter, deciding to call again another day. The area near the Campbell and Lloyd grave had recently been swept by fire

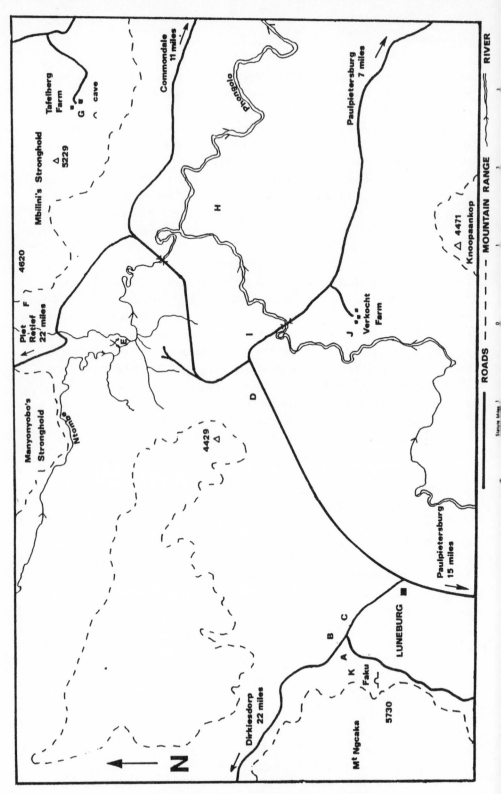

13. LUNEBURG DISTRICT TODAY

(Caption on facing page)

and the Tambookie grass, which during the season grows to 10 feet in height, had been reduced to blackened stubble. A number of stone mounds were visible, clearly graves, and likely those of Weatherley's first casualties.

Not long after the battle two burial parties visited Hlobane; the first, led by Wood on 20 May 1879, consisted of Raaff's Transvaal Rangers and the NNH. They gathered together a number of bones and corpses, some recognisable by their clothes and other bits of identification. Charlie Potter's remains were confirmed by a cartridge found in the waistcoat pocket, as only he and Combrink, one of the burghers, had guns of the same calibre. The bodies of Potter and twenty-four-year-old Lieutenant Cecil Williams were buried in the same grave, with Wood reading the burial service – presumably from Mrs Campbell's bible. Another burial party visited the mountain in September and reported that the remains of Barton and Weatherley had been found and put to rest. This report was false, no doubt made to pacify grieving relatives. Barton's body was not buried until 1880, after it had been found by Trooper Robert Browne DCM, who had been led to the spot by the Zulu who had slain Barton. It is doubtful if Weatherley's remains, and those of the Border Horse and FLH who were killed on Intyentika Nek, were ever found as the Zulus threw the bodies into the valley below.

Apart from Campbell and Lloyd's weather-beaten cross, there are no other marked graves or memorials on Hlobane with the exception of a concrete plaque marking the spot where Piet Uys was killed. The plaque was restored in 1993 and a memorial service was held at the bottom of Devil's Pass. To accommodate the occasion, the mine management generously cut a track for four-wheel-drive vehicles up the mountain to the bottom of the pass. Without constant maintenance, it is doubtful if this impromptu track will survive the first severe rains.

* * *

Caption to Map 13 (on facing page): Luneburg District today indicating historical events and places during the Anglo-Zulu War, 1879.

Key:
A   Position of Fort Clery
B   Heinrich Filter's former homestead
C   Graveyard where Capt. Moriarty, Civil Surgeon Cobbin, Heinrich Filter and others were buried
D   Memorial to Heinrich Filter and Schermbrucker's Danish groom, Larsen
E   Scene of the Intombi River disaster 12 March 1879
F   Former wagon track to Derby 28 miles distant
G   Intombi caves blown up on 8 September 1879
H   Van Staden's Farm 1879
I   Position of Col. Sgt Booth's stand
J   The place where Heinrich Filter met his death on 8 June 1879
K   Faku's former military kraal 1878

In July 1879, the colonial mounted units which had performed such sterling service for Chelmsford's army were, for the sake of economy, quickly given the axe. The sounds of the last imperial volleys had hardly ceased to echo around the Ulundi hills, when the FLH was dismounted – in spite of Chelmsford's advising Wolseley that the 17th Lancers, after their spectacular charge at Ulundi, would be a liability in any further bush fighting. The men, horseless, were marched to Utrecht, paid out and the regiment disbanded – never to be raised again. The same fate lay in store for the rest of the mounted force, although the odd unit was resurrected at various times for brief service: for instance, Baker's Horse took part in a couple of minor uprisings, the Natal Native Horse saw service again as a scouting force during the whole of the Anglo-Boer War and were present at the siege of Ladysmith, and Raaff's Rangers saw service in the Transvaal later in 1879. But all the units that rode with Wood have now passed into history, their names and deeds long since forgotten.

1. Prince Louis Napoleon, the only son of Emperor Napoleon III and the Empress Eugénie, born 1856. After the defeat of France at the conclusion of the Franco-Prussian War, the empress and her young son were exiled to England. In 1872 Prince Louis entered Woolwich as an officer cadet in the Royal Artillery. After graduation several of his friends were posted to South Africa. When news of the Zulu War reached England, Louis became desperate to follow his comrades and experience active service. After much pleading he was allowed to join Lord Chelmsford in Zululand as a junior staff officer. A few weeks after taking up his appointment he was killed in a Zulu ambush, much to the consternation of Lord Chelmsford and the British Government.
2. Officers especially selected by Wolseley for campaign service.
3. Mortally wounded at Bronkhorstspruit 20 December 1881.
4. In 1879 the award conditions of the original warrant of 1856 were still applicable in respect of the VC whereby the decoration could not be awarded for an 'Act of Duty' no matter how brave, nor could it be awarded posthumously. The warrant was revised in 1881 to include acts performed in the course of duty and at the turn of the century provision was made for posthumous awards.
5. Schermbrucker gave the trooper a reward of five pounds as the rescued man was of the Kaffrarian Rifles.

BIBLIOGRAPHY
UNPUBLISHED SOURCES AND PRIVATE INFORMATION

Brickhill, James. Manuscript. Killie Campbell Library, Durban.
Cope, N.L.G. *The Defection of Hamu*. Killie Campbell Library, Durban.
The Sir Evelyn Wood Papers. Killie Campbell Library, Durban.
The Sir Evelyn Wood Papers. Natal Archives, Pietermaritzburg.
Symons, Frederick. Manuscript. Killie Campbell Library, Durban.

NEWSPAPERS AND PERIODICALS
SOUTH AFRICA

The Bloemfontein and Free State Gazette
The Cape Argus
The Farmer's Weekly News
The Friend
The Natal Mercury
The Natal Witness
The Port Elizabeth and Eastern Province Standard
The South African Catholic Magazine 1893
The Times of Natal
The Transvaal Argus

UNITED KINGDOM

The Graphic
The Illustrated London News
The Journal of the Anglo-Zulu War Research Society
The London Gazette
The London Times
The Scotsman
The Times Weekly Edition
The Victorian Military Society – Soldiers of the Queen

Published Sources

Abbot, P.E. *Recipients of the Distinguished Conduct Medal, 1885–1909.* London, 1975.

Abbott, P.E. and Tamplin, J.M.A. *British Gallantry Awards.* London, 1971.

Ashe, Major, and Wyatt-Edgell, E.V. *The Story of the Zulu Campaign.* London, 1880.

Bancroft, James W. *The Zulu War VCs.* Liverpool, 1992.

Barthorp, Michael. *The Zulu War; A Pictorial History.* Poole, 1980.

Bennett, Ian H.W. *Eyewitness in Zululand.* London, 1989.

Binns, C.T. *The Last Zulu King – The Life and Death of Cetshwayo.* London, 1963.

—— *The Warrior People.* London, 1975.

Bulpin, T.V. *Discovering South Africa.* South Africa, 1970.

Clarke, Sonia. *Zululand at War 1879.* Johannesburg, 1984.

—— *Invasion of Zululand.* Johannesburg, 1979.

Clements, W.H. *The Glamour and Tragedy of the Zulu War.* London, 1936.

Coupland, Reginald. *Zulu Battle Piece – Isandhlwana.* London, 1948.

Creagh, Sir Garrett O'Moore and Humphries, E.M. *The V.C. & D.S.O.* London, 1924.

Creswick, Louis. *South Africa and The Transvaal War.* London, 1903.

Crook, M.J. *The Evolution of the Victoria Cross.* Tunbridge Wells, 1975.

Droogleever, R.W.F. *The Road to Isandhlwana; Colonel Anthony Durnford in Natal and Zululand, 1873–1879.* London, 1992.

Durnford, Edward. *A Soldier's Life and Work in South Africa 1872 to 1879.* A Memoir of the Late Colonel A.W. Durnford, Royal Engineers. London, 1882.

Edgerton, Robert B. *Like Lions They Fought.* New York and London, 1988.

Elliott, W.J. *The Victoria Cross in Zululand and South Africa and How It Was Won.* London, 1882.

Emery, Frank. *Marching Over Africa.* London, 1986.

—— *The Red Soldier.* London, 1977.

Featherstone, Donald. *Victorian and Colonial Warfare.* London, 1992.

Filter, H. and Bourquin, S. *Paulina Dlamini.* Pietermaritzburg, 1986.

Forbes, Archibald. *Barracks, Bivouacs and Battles.* London, 1892.

Forsyth, D.R. *Medal Roll, The Colonials, South African General Service Medal.* Johannesburg, 1978

Furneaux. *The Zulu War: Isandhlwana and Rorke's Drift.* London, 1963.

Fynney, F.B. *The Zulu Army.* Pietermaritzburg, 1878.

Gon, Philip. *The Road to Isandlwana.* Johannesburg, 1979.

Gordon, Ruth. *The Place of the Elephant.* Pietermaritzburg, 1981.

Guy, Jeff. *The Destruction of the Zulu Kingdom.* Johannesburg, 1979.

Hamilton-Browne, G.A. *A Lost Legionary in South Africa.* London, 1912.

Harford, Col. Henry. *Zulu War Journal.* Pietermaritzburg, 1878.

Hattersley, Alan F. *Carbineer; The History of the Royal Natal Carbineers.* Aldershot, 1950.

Holme, Norman. *The Silver Wreath.* London, 1979.

Holt, H.P. *The Mounted Police of Natal.* London, 1913.

Knight, Ian. *Brave Men's Blood.* London, 1990.

—— *Zulu.* London, 1992.

—— *Nothing Remains But to Fight.* London, 1993.

—— (ed) *By The Orders of the Great White Queen*. London, 1992.

Krige, Eileen Jensen. *The Social System of the Zulus*. Pietermaritzburg, 1957.

Laband, J.P. and Thompson, P.S. with Sheila Henderson. *The Buffalo Border Guard, 1879*. Durban, 1983.

—— *Field Guide to the War in Zululand*. Pietermaritzburg, 1979.

—— *Kingdom and Colony at War*. South Africa, 1990.

Laband, John and Mathews, Jeff. *Isandlwana*. Pietermaritzburg, 1991.

Lugg, H.C. *Historic Natal and Zululand*. Pietermaritzburg, 1949.

McKay, James. *Reminiscences of the Last Kaffir War*. Cape Town, 1970.

MacKinnon, J.P. and Shadbolt, Sydney. *The South African Campaign, 1879*. London, 1880. Reprinted London, 1995.

Milton, John. *The Edges of War*. Cape Town, 1983.

Mitford, Bertram. *Through the Zulu Country*. London, 1883. Reprinted London, 1988.

Moodie, Duncan Campbell Francis. *The History of the Battles and Adventures of the British, the Boers and the Zulus, etc., in Southern Africa from the Time of the Pharaoh Necho to 1880*. Cape Town, 1888.

Morris, Donald R. *The Washing of the Spears*. London, 1966.

Nash, M.D. *The Settler Handbook*. Cape Town, 1989.

Norris-Newman, Charles L. *In Zululand with the British Throughout the War of 1879*. London, 1880. Reprinted London, 1988.

Ritter, E.A. *Shaka Zulu; The Rise of the Zulu Empire*. London, 1957. Reprinted London, 1990.

Roberts, Brian. *The Zulu Kings*. London, 1974.

Rothwell, John Sutton. See War Office.

Samuelson, R.C.A. *Long, Long Ago*. Durban, 1929.

Smith Dorrien, Horace. *Memories of Forty-Eight Years' Service*. London, 1925.

Tomasson, W.H. *With the Irregulars in the Transvaal and Zululand*. London, 1881.

Tylden, G. *The Armed Forces of South Africa 1659–1954*. Johannesburg, 1954.

Vijn, Cornelius (translated and edited with notes by J.W. Colenso, Bishop of Natal) *Cetshwayo's Dutchman*. London, 1880. Reprinted London, 1988.

Von Kehrhahan, J. *Das Filter-Larsen Denkmal*. South Africa, 1938.

War Office. *Narrative of the Field Operations Connected with the Zulu War of 1879* (Compiled by J.S. Rothwell). London, 1881. Reprinted London, 1907 and 1989.

Webb, C. de B. and Wright, J.B. *A Zulu King Speaks*. Pietermaritzburg, 1978.

Wilkins, Philip A. *The History of the Victoria Cross*. London, 1904.

Wolseley, Sir Garnet. *South African Journal 1879–80*. Cape Town, 1973.

Wood, Evelyn. *From Midshipman to Field Marshal*. London, 1906.

—— *Winnowed Memories*. London, 1918.

Wright, John B. *Bushmen Raiders of the Drakensberg 1840–1870*. Pietermaritzburg, 1971.

Wright, John and Manson, Andrew. *The Hlubi Chiefdom*. South Africa, 1983.

Young, John. *They Fell Like Stones; Battles and Casualties of the Zulu War, 1879*. London, 1991.

INDEX